Tom Jeffords

TOM JEFFORDS

Friend of Cochise

DOUG HOCKING

TWODOT®

GUILFORD, CONNECTICUT
HELENA, MONTANA

A · TWODOT® · BOOK

An imprint of Rowman & Littlefield

Distributed by NATIONAL BOOK NETWORK
800-462-6420

British Library Cataloguing in Publication Information available

Library of Congress Cataloging-in-Publication Data available

ISBN 978-1-4930-2637-1 (paperback)
ISBN 978-1-4930-2638-8 (e-book)

∞™ The paper used in this publication meets the minimum requirements of American National Standard for Information Sciences—Permanence of Paper for Printed Library Materials, ANSI/NISO Z39.48-1992.

Printed in the United States of America

To my wife, Debbie, who loves everything I write, and to my dad, William John Hocking, who served as a model for understanding all strong men.

To Carol Markstrom, whose fascination with the Tom Jeffords legend piqued my interest.

And to Van Fowers, whose wonderful personification of Jeffords led me to seek out his source material and learn there had never been a biography.

Contents

Acknowledgments

NOBODY COMPLETES A PROJECT LIKE THIS ALONE. I'M ESPECIALLY thankful to four scholars who set out before me to write a biography of Tom Jeffords. They never finished the work but left a blazed trail in the form of notes and collected papers including material from National Archives and Records Administration (NARA). They were Robert Forbes, John Bret Harte, William De Stefano, and C. L. Sonnichsen. Caitlin Lampman and Laura Hoff were always helpful at the Arizona Historical Society Library and Archive, as was Larry Ludwig with material stored at Fort Bowie. Debra Chatham, Sierra Vista Library, ordered up articles and books that were hard to find and came from all over the country. Walter Lewis, Maritime History of the Great Lakes, saved me a trip to Ohio by sharing his knowledge of the lakes and shipping. Special thanks goes out to Doreen Crowe, curator at the Arizona Historical Society. She managed to turn up everything in the collection that had ever passed through Tom Jeffords's hands, especially the Brown Ranch guestbook with Tom's signature. Christine Rhodes, Cochise County Recorder, was my guide through the Cochise County Records, where the earliest records are in a confused state. Kevin Pyles, Cochise Country Archivist, was also helpful with his knowledge of financial records. Kellen Cutsforth of the Denver Library and Denver Corral of the Westerners saved me a trip to Colorado by looking into records of Tom Jeffords's time there. Stephen Gregory, Fort Huachuca Museum, showed interest and spent time in digging out photos and information about Tom Jeffords as sutler.

No one knows the Butterfield Overland Mail better than Gerald T. Ahnert, and he was helpful in confirming Tom Jeffords's role in the Overland Mail. Gene and Rosanna Baker, Bisbee Corral of the Westerners, helped with encouragement, and Gene was always there when I wanted to visit one or another of the sites associated with Jeffords. Pat Ross, Pinal County Recorder, dug into records of Tom's holdings at the Owl Heads. Rick Collins, Tumacacori, New Mexico, pointed me toward Fred Veil, Sharlot Hall Museum, who provided me with information on an ancestor who'd dined with Cochise. Rick also sent me an important carefully compiled and lengthy list of primary source statements and facts about the Bascom Affair. There are many others who have been helpful and encouraging in this effort. Because of them, I am very confident in the historical accuracy of the account of Cochise's interaction with Lieutenant Bascom. Patricia Hewitt, Fray Angelico Chavez History Library, was helpful in digging out material on Tom's time in New Mexico. Charles Wommack, University of Arizona Special Collections, helped in locating material from the University of Arizona. Stuart Rosebrook, *True West* magazine, has always been a friend providing encouragement and assistance. Kathy Klump, Sulphur Springs Valley Historical Society, has been helpful with all manner of assistance and information about the death of Cochise.

Introduction

*Riding by the side of the commanding officer was a tall, slender
citizen with a long flowing beard of reddish hue, his face shaded
by the broad brim of a drab slouch hat, but with a pleasant face
lighted up with a pair of bright, piercing eyes of light blue. I looked
at this man with considerable curiosity, for this was Jeffords, the
man who was to take us to Cochise, if any man could.*[1]

THIS WAS HOW CAPTAIN JOSEPH SLADEN, AIDE-DE-CAMP TO GEN-
eral[2] O. O. Howard, described Thomas Jefferson Jeffords at their first
meeting. The Apache called him *Tyzaalton*, Red Beard, and respected
him. Their chief, Cochise, called him brother and friend.[3]

It fell to me to write a biography of Thomas Jefferson Jeffords
because no one had ever completed one, unless you count Ben Traywick's eighteen-page pamphlet.[4] Historians relied on Elliott Arnold's
1947 novel *Blood Brother* as the best available source.[5] Besides, I
thought everyone knew of Tom Jeffords. Today I get blank stares. I
grew up with Tom Jeffords and Cochise every week on TV in *Broken
Arrow*. Jimmy Stewart played Tom to Jeff Chandler's Cochise in the
1950 *Broken Arrow*, still a classic. Tom Jeffords had the courage to
ride alone into Cochise's Stronghold to make the peace and end the
Apache Wars.

Digging into the record I soon found that Tom didn't leave
behind a journal or body of letters to tell us what he was thinking
or feeling. The letters that have come down to us from Tom Jeffords

are not in his hand. Clerks, partners, friends, and lawyers wrote them for him. His signature doesn't match the body of any document. We come to know Tom Jeffords through his friends. Ranked among them are mayors, merchants, and businessmen, the wealthy and powerful men of early Arizona, the Arizona Pioneers who arrived before 1870. Closest and most important of all his friends was a man who was also the most unlikely of comrades, a hostile Apache chief, Cochise. Among these founders and leaders were men who were also scoundrels. Fred Hughes served in the legislature, as Pima County clerk, and as president of the Pioneers Society. He absconded with money meant for the Pioneers but was forgiven. Zebina Streeter looked up to Tom as an older brother, but chose to ride with Geronimo, perhaps avenging wrongs done to Tom. Nickolas Rogers ran a stage station and "saloon" for the soldiers of Fort Bowie. Tom's friend and occasional partner, he paid with his life when he sold whiskey to the wrong Apache. As a frontiersman, Tom Jeffords had high regard for his personal code of honor, but low respect for formal rules. Smuggling seemed natural to him, though whether he engaged in this activity is unclear. His enemies said he did and we learn about him from them as well. They opposed his efforts to treat the Apache as men and to provide them with schooling. They distrusted him for this unorthodox approach and claimed he sided against his government and country. Nothing was ever further from the truth. We see Tom Jeffords not from what he said about himself but from the shadow that he cast, a more honest picture.

Jeffords was a man with many friends who was always welcome. When the occasion called for it, he liked a drink. The military and government officials saw him as a crude frontiersman, but his peers respected and trusted him, placing him at the head of companies and projects and putting him forward for political office. He said little about himself. We hear his statements as garbled as a children's game of telephone. These pronouncements contradict each other. He was misunderstood and his statements misinterpreted. We also see in this his sense of humor. He'd let a tenderfoot who misunderstood believe what he wanted to believe, undoubtedly enjoying the green-horn's confusion.

I found the tracks of a number of historians who had gone before me and left notes and collected documents. None of them succeeded in producing a biography, though some left interesting published articles. I applaud their work and have incorporated much of it. They blazed the trail and made the way easier.

At a similar impasse, I found myself with many inferences drawn from knowledge of time and place and person, but unable to find a document to prove each point. If I explain why I believe something to be so and lay out the argument in my text, it will become ponderous and hard to read, thoroughly academic and of little interest to the public who deserve to know Tom Jeffords as a real man. I'll tell the story as it should be told and leave the explanations to the endnotes. Read a few of them so you can decide why I've taken this path and decide for yourself if I'm an honest broker of the past. I hope you'll find the notes interesting.

As an historian I believe that only one thing happened and that, even though we may only know what it was imperfectly, it is the his-torian's duty to come as close to truth as possible. How this or that class of person may have felt about it and may feel about it today is interesting, but doesn't make it what happened. Sometimes these per-ceptions are key to why things happened as they did and why players chose one path over another. In the final analysis, perception is not history. Historian John L. Kessell tells us:

> *The historian has but few tools, so he must use them well. First off let us ignore the postmodernists' claim that none of us can possibly know objectively what actually happened, only objectively what is said to have happened. As historians, that is our business to say what happened, to pursue historical truth as objectively as possible. Historians Jacques Barzun and Henry F. Graff suggest in* The

Modern Researcher *(1992) that practitioners of the craft apply six rules: accuracy, orderliness, logic, honesty, self-awareness, and imagination (I might add calmness). Evidence gathered in this way one bit reinforcing or challenging another, provides us with the probability upon which to base our "truth," that is, the probability that something actually happened pretty much the way we say it did.*[6]

Please measure me by these standards to see if I have done my job. I'll be working from a handful of statements from Tom Jeffords and the statements of others that say they are repeating something Jeffords said. The first of these often leave blanks, while the second require interpretation. For instance, Tom Jeffords wrote:

Dear Sir:

I hereby acknowledge your invitation to attend a meeting of the "Arizona Pioneers." I am in full accord with the object of the meeting. I presume I may be regarded as a pioneer. I came to the territory first in 1860. In 1862, when I saw Tucson, the population did not exceed one hundred, outside of the California column of soldiers. It was at this time that I first met Hiram Stevens, W.S. Ouray and Wheat. Tucson was a very small place then. The Apache was in full possession of the country from the Rio Grande to Tucson. In those days, the Pioneers had about all they could do to save their hair, but they were men of determination, and came to stay, and the present general prosperity of the territory shows plainly that they were men of foresight, as well as of industry and enterprise. I regret my inability to be with you in person, but I assure you my best wishes are for the complete success of the association.

Very Truly Yours,
T.J. Jeffords
Tombstone, Jan. 30, 1884[7]

If he came to Arizona in 1860, why didn't he see Tucson? Why does he write as if he first saw the town in 1862? Since Tucson was almost the only town in 1860, it was hard to miss. All of the trails except one ran through Tucson. Tom must have taken the other. The record shows that he was going from gold rush to gold rush. There was no gold in Tucson. Many of the statements attributed to Jeffords come to us through various filters. Tom was prone to letting tenderfeet pull their own legs. If that was what they'd heard and believed, he wasn't going to disabuse them. His one and only interview with Professor Robert Forbes ended abruptly. Jeffords excused himself and didn't come back. This didn't stop Forbes from referring to himself in later years as "friend of Tom Jeffords." Here is an excerpt from that interview, important because Forbes told us that this is what Tom said:

In the early 1860s he had a contract for the carrying of mail between Tucson and a point east, through dangerous Apache country. The delivery was by riders on horseback whom he paid liberally, but he rarely settled with them because they were killed en route by the Apaches. He stated that he lost twenty men in this way and that he, himself, had the scars of Indian arrows on his body.

The situation became so bad that he determined upon a most dangerous contact with Cochise to make arrangements for the passage of his riders with mail through Indian territory. Alone, he rode into Cochise's camp in the Dragoon Mountain Stronghold and, dismounting and laying aside his weapons, made his way to Cochise's wickiup where the astonished chief asked him if he expected to return. Jeffords, speaking the language, stated that he came to talk with a brave and honorable man about his riders passing through Apache territory. . . .

Cochise died in 1874, with Jeffords nearby. He was buried in open ground out in front of the Stronghold. His Apaches rode their horses over the area until the grave was completely obscured, only Jeffords knowing its exact location. Asking, with promise of secrecy,

*for information, I was refused by Jeffords who said, "It would soon
be a bone here and a bone there," and the secret died with him. . . .
My dinner with Jeffords ended rather abruptly as though he was
tired of the curiosity of a tenderfoot and my refusing refreshments.*[8]

Part of this statement is Forbes letting his imagination run away
with him. Part can be reconciled to history. Tom did not become
superintendent of the stage line from Tucson until after 1867. Tom
Jeffords may have driven a stage on the Butterfield Road, albeit the
stage was a buckboard, and it was the Butterfield Road, not the Overland Mail stage line that Congress ordered moved in 1861 to the California Trail through South Pass. Apache arrows may have wounded
him, but we have record of Apache attacking only one stage and Tom
was not the driver. Apaches rarely molested his pony riders. Their
horses were fast and they didn't carry anything the Apache wanted.
The job still required courage more for the threat of what might hap-
pen to a man alone than for that which did occur. Tom Jeffords kept
the secret of Cochise's grave.

From such material I'll try to tell an honest tale.

Elliott Arnold's 1949 historical novel, *Blood Brother*, was well
received by the critics. It is a wonderful, powerful, exciting novel.
The literary world saw it as history. According to the *Library Journal*:
"[Elliott Arnold] has translated matter-of-fact historical incidents
into thrilling episodes. . ." The *New York Sun* went even further. "[*Blood
Brother*] is authentic history, presented, however, with fictional vivid-
ness." *The Chicago Tribune* called the novel "superb history . . . excellent biography. It takes place with the major works on the American
Indian." Apparently literary critics have as hard a time distinguishing
a novel from history and biography as the public does distinguishing
movies from reality. Cochise called Tom brother. Arnold invented the
mystical blood brother ceremony to show how close the tie was, but
the ritual was his invention, a literary device. In 1950, Jimmy Stewart

played Tom in *Broken Arrow* and took an Apache bride to show his close relations with the Indians. In reality, such a bond would have caused Indian agent Jeffords no end of problems. Elliott Arnold's work is a marvelous novel, part history, part solid ethnography, and part pure fantasy. His history was good for the times, but modern scholarship has shown it to be mostly legend.

Recently, another scholar has written about the Bascom Affair. You'll find his conclusion at variance with mine. He describes himself as a cultural historian and has shown the important place of legendary history in our culture. He eschewed many of the primary accounts, relying instead on accounts that came later from men who were not present to witness the events they were writing about. Because they told a simpler story in accord with our cultural perceptions, and because of the lack of historical tools available to us today, these accounts became the basis of our cultural history for the next century. I've gone back to the primary sources, which tell a more complex story that blames a generation rather than an individual.

I've found the primary accounts of men I can verify were at Apache Pass with Lieutenant George Bascom in January and February of 1861 in substantial agreement with each other differing only in minor details. These square with Bascom's own reports. The account of Sergeant Dan Robinson is especially illuminating and complete. I have rejected the accounts of Charles Poston, Reuben Bernard, and Sergeant Hubert Oberly. None of them were there. Their accounts do not agree with each other or any of the other accounts. Oberly's version enraged Surgeon Bernard Irwin, who was there. Each contains preposterous elements and shows a lack of understanding of the actual situation at Apache Pass. It is unfortunate that Bernard's and Poston's accounts were picked up by early historians. The accounts were available when other material was not. Without them, a very different picture of George Bascom emerges, one of a diligent young officer trying hard to do his duty.

I've tried to be an honest broker of history. I won't tell of Apache wives, mystical blood brother ceremonies, or shooting a pistol out of Will Harden's (John Wesley Hardin?) hand. Even without the fancy stage dressing and legendary nonsense, the story is still compelling. It is the story of a strong man doing what he thought right.

CHAPTER 1

Growing Up

EBER ROCKWOOD JEFFORDS TRUDGED WESTWARD THROUGH THE dark forest.[1] The road was muddy, stirred up by the big wagons passing over it. The broad-leaf forest dripped. Eber, on his first trip away from his birthplace in Massachusetts, knew he would probably never see his family again. He didn't have a trade and the family farm was too small to divide again. He would have to go west to find the newly opened lands. Chautauqua seemed the ticket as pioneers had opened the hardwood forests to farms a few years before. Land, Eber thought, would still be free or at least cheap for those with the courage to settle it. It sounded like paradise, the farthest west of New York's counties on the shores of Lake Erie. There was a new canal being built and it would open soon, in 1825 the newspapers said. He held the long pole that was his whip for guiding the two yoke of oxen that pulled the heavy wagon.[2]

As he pulled his moccasined feet from the muck below him, he scanned the trees looking for Indians and highwaymen. His flint-lock rifle stood ready, near at hand on the wagon. Open farmland broached the muddy road and there were little towns growing pretty as any in New England. But there were still mysterious forests where Indians might lurk. There had been major battles with the Mohawk, Seneca, Onondaga, and Cayuga during the Revolutionary War, and the Indians were still here in the forests. Eber looked at the wagon.

Would he give his life protecting another man's property? He supposed he would. That's what the owner had hired him to do—drive the oxen and defend the cargo. There were noises in the forest and his hair stood on end. He'd heard terrible stories of what Indians did to their captives.

The axle screamed like a dying woman, begging for grease. At the noon halt he'd make sure it got some. Meanwhile, there were streams to cross and hills to climb. The oxen would have to be hitched and unhitched, linked together to make the hard pull up grades. Eber was glad he had a well-trained team. Who would have thought dumb cows could learn so much and answer verbal commands? Who would have thought they could become so powerful? Two big steers were his wheelers, the strong ones who pulled the load. His leaders were a bull and a cow; and she still gave milk! A useful animal.

Yoking up had gone easily in the morning. His oxen stood still the right distance apart as he placed the oxbow yoke on their shoulders and then inserted the bent-hardwood U-shaped bows that came up from below the animals' necks and pinned each in place. He chained the oxbows to the wagon tongue allowing the animals to pull with their shoulders. Recently, Eber had heard about a mule train returned from Santa Fe, a far and mysterious land, to Missouri bringing fabulous wealth and strange stories. One had to do with the yoking of oxen. The Mexicans yoked the beast by its horns, forcing it to draw the load with its neck instead of its shoulders, reducing what it could pull. According to the story, the Mexican wagons had wheels of solid wood. They weren't prepared to pull any kind of load.[3]

As a young man of twenty, Eber liked the other stories coming from Mexico. The women smoked in front of men and not from pipes. They rolled tobacco into a tube of cornhusk. Their skirts came high, exposing their legs to view, and their blouses were cut low, exposing their bosoms. He had heard that men and women bathed together in the river. This was too exciting to be true for a young man who had scarcely seen more than a young lady's neck or ankle.[4] Before William

Becknell's successful mule train expedition, everyone who had tried to trade in Santa Fe had been arrested and their goods confiscated by the Spanish. But now Mexico had won her independence and had a different attitude toward trade. It gave hope to a young man.

One day as they crossed the breast of a hill, Eber looked down on a body of water that stretched as far as the eye could see. The young man had heard of Lake Erie. It was a lake as big as the ocean. He hadn't really believed it and couldn't wait to sample its water to see if it was fresh. From the hilltop Eber could see the billowed, white sails floating above ships like those he had known on the seafront in Massachusetts.

On reaching the lake, the wagon's owner paid Eber off for his service. Money was scarce. Banks printed and coined their own, and it was difficult to keep up with how much one bank's currency was worth against that of another. What really mattered was how much it was worth in goods. Young Jeffords took his pay in kind, a rifle and a few tools he could carry. His real pay had been his passage west. The owner of the wagon had provided food the whole way, and Eber couldn't have afforded that on his own. He travelled southwest along the lakeshore to the farthest corner of New York, looking for free land.

He didn't find it. What he found was a land of stumps where pioneers had cleared the hardwood forest to make way for farms. The frontier had been open too long, and all the free land was in the possession of the farmers who had come first. He decided he'd go to work and save money to buy a farm. Land wasn't free but it was cheap. He worked as a hired hand helping a more wealthy man pull stumps, cut down trees, and build rail fences to keep out the numerous deer. There were few towns, and these were small but built on a New England pattern around a common or green with a community church at one end.

Eber did not have strong feelings about religious doctrine, though he believed firmly in God. He was aware that when pilgrims settled New England two centuries before, two kinds of people had come.

There were the Puritan pastors, theologians, and religious teachers. The other half of the people on the *Mayflower* had been members of the Church of England, and they had been artisans and farmers on whom the Puritans desperately depended for sustenance. Towns weren't big enough for more than one church so the two religions, opposed to each other in England, had to share one building and one service. It was unwise to talk doctrine in such circumstances. They needed each other and didn't need to alienate one another. Decades later their religious rivalry would result in witch trials. Churches were not Puritan or Church of England. They became community churches and their members left behind the rigid rules of the Puritans and the high pomp and regal ceremony of the Church of England. Instead they adopted a simpler, blander service. Jeffords knew his family's roots were Church of England, but he accepted the bland religion of the community church. One had to attend church. It was expected and it was a way to meet girls.

Labor on frontier farms was back breaking. Eber and his master would dig around the stumps of trees and then cut the roots they could reach with an axe. Finally, they would hitch up a yoke of oxen and have them pull until the stump came free. Stumps could be stubborn. As they worked they watched the forest for Indians. There probably were no hostiles, but fear of the unknown dies hard. There were those among them who remembered times when Indian attacks on isolated farms came frequently. Daniel Boone was only a year or two in his grave somewhere out west in Missouri.

The community looked forward to the day when the Erie Canal would open. Then there would be commerce from Chicago across the lakes and over the canal to Albany, then down the Hudson River to New York City and from there to anywhere in the world. For now, commerce was limited. Men grew wheat and rye to make into whiskey. In bulk and weight, whiskey was cheap to transport, cheaper than grain or beer. Congress had set heavy taxes on whiskey, and men of the frontier had revolted in the past for the tax was ruinous. In these distant parts, shipping costs cut into everything. If Buffalo grew into a city, if trade were established with Chicago, if the canal opened, produce could be shipped more cheaply and men might begin to know wealth. For now, they were subsistence farmers. They grew things for their own table and had few options for selling surplus.

Monotony was broken by church and by dances. It seemed like everyone knew how to play a musical instrument of some kind, even if it was only a Jew's harp. Those who played well were treasured and idealized. The girls seemed to flock to them. Musicians reminded Eber of the story of the grasshopper and the ant. He felt like an ant, until one evening he danced with Almira Wood. To him she seemed beautiful. She was only fifteen. Her parents had been among the first to settle Chautauqua.

They were old frontier stock, their history lost. They went west, cleared a patch of land, and farmed a bit. They hunted for meat and fur and used the pelts as their currency. When neighbors got too close or game too scarce, they moved west again. They were of the same sort of long hunters as Daniel Boone, people who followed and moved with the frontier. The frontier had extended south of New York through Ohio, Indiana, and Illinois to Missouri, going around Chautauqua, leaving the woods without a frontier near at hand. The frontier was far away, so they stayed.[5]

Eber and Almira married on October 5, 1824, when she was sixteen and Eber twenty-one years old. Good news came two years later when daughter Susan was born in 1826. In 1828, James, who would become a sea captain, followed Susan, and Eunice joined her siblings in 1830. Thomas Jefferson Jeffords was born January 1, 1832. There was other good news. On October 26, 1825, the long-awaited Erie Canal opened its locks for business. Construction had begun in 1817.

The canal offered a new life for Eber. He could give up being a farmhand and working for his room and board and the hope, perhaps, that the farmer might remember him in his will. Now there was commerce. There was a place to sell things. Ships came to Buffalo at the mouth of the canal and Buffalo grew. More than that, the asheries opened and there were jobs.

The asheries burned the hardwood trees and entered the ash into commerce. The most valuable product was pearl ash, which the asheries shipped to New York City and London for use in making glass and ceramics. Factories used other forms of ash to make soap and saleratus, baking soda. The jobs paid real salaries, and a man might feed his growing family and still put a little aside to buy a farm.

Tom spent his first seven years in Chautauqua County attending school for the first time. The county was proud of its civic institutions: schools, churches, government. Chautauqua historians make much of being a station on the Underground Railroad that spirited escaping slaves into Canada. Its historians have less to say about the economy, treating it as something there in the background of no particular importance. They detail for us the growth of their institutions. Tom learned tolerance for other races.

The children grew in a loving family[6] and soon they were off to school. By the time Tom was seven, there were four children in school. Eber had to pay for his children's schooling. This stretched Eber's meager resources. He wasn't getting any closer to purchasing his farm. He needed to make a change, and in 1839, he decided to move the family to a lakeport, Ashtabula in Ohio, only a little over forty miles from Chautauqua County.

Along the way, the family passed through Erie, Pennsylvania, which was connected by river and canal to Pittsburg at the head of the Ohio River. Riverboats were beginning to ply the waterway, taking goods down to New Orleans and bringing the merchandise of New England and the world back up to Pittsburg, where merchants forwarded it to Buffalo and Chicago. Ashtabula, too, saw its share of lake trade and sailing ships. Eber settled in near the docks and went to work. Soon his sons were working as well. They'd had some schooling, but there wasn't enough money for all of the children to continue on indefinitely. The family needed their economic assistance. Prepared for the ways of the lake, four of them would go to sea and three would rise to be lake captains, two in their early twenties.[7]

Getting started again in Ashtabula was difficult for the growing family. Martha had been born in 1834, Cornelia in 1837, and Eber Jackson Jeffords in 1839. Eber had seven children when the family arrived at the port and four of them were school-aged already. The family's arrival in Ashtabula coincides with Tom's first break in schooling while he was just learning cursive. The family worked hard and the children grew to adulthood healthy and sound. It took years to save enough, but shortly before 1850, Eber finally purchased his farm near Morgan in Ashtabula County. By then his elder sons were at sea.

His sons, experiencing the difficulty Eber endured saving up for his farm, learned that they should make their fortune first and then marry. Follow the dream but find your fortune before you take a wife. Four of them would never marry. Tom pursued a golden dream all his life and never took a bride. Younger brother John, a man of violent temper, followed Tom west and often worked for him. Other brothers led a life on the lakes.

Ashtabula was in the Western Reserve. The King of England had granted this land to Connecticut long ago even though it was separated from that colony by parts of New York and Pennsylvania. Connecticut clung to its claim even after the War of Independence. Its northern and southern boundaries extended westward to the Mississippi River, creating a 120-mile-wide band of Yankee land in Pennsylvania and modern Ohio, Indiana, and Illinois. After the American Revolution, the new state ceded its claims everywhere except Ohio in exchange for the Federal government assuming its war debt. The lands in Ohio became the Western Reserve and the state released them to developers who began to sell parcels. The government administered the Western Reserve, and the lands south of it as far as the Ohio River, as the Northwest Territories. Connecticut Yankees flocked to Ashtabula after 1796, creating a society remarkably like the New England villages of Connecticut. The Western

Reserve sprouted Yankee villages built in New England style and peopled by New Englanders. This was another area proud of its Underground Railroad stations. The Presbyterians came with a doctrine close to Puritan, and Church of England came as well, and, of course, the community church. Methodists, made ubiquitous on the frontier by their circuit-riding preachers, were late to arrive.

Tom's family probably belonged to a community church. The stiff-necked Yankees had tolerance for the black slaves making their way north, but they knew themselves as God's chosen people, a cut above anyone else, people who knew what was right and proper. Tolerance is one thing; it doesn't mean you want to marry a social inferior. This might have made it difficult for Tom to look seriously at Mexican damsels as spousal material. While he was open to other cultures, he may have found it difficult to accept the differences in a spouse. In Tucson, he paid court to a few Yankee women. In later life, we don't find Tom Jeffords much inclined to attend church, nor do we find him rejecting religion. The frontier where Tom lived seldom provided a handy church. We do note that he grew up with a strong sense of what was right and proper, of fair play, honesty, and loyalty to friends. He always acted as if he was responsible to something beyond himself, to friends, to country, and perhaps to God.

Webster Jeffords, born in 1853, inherited the farm after his brothers had gone on to other pursuits. Brothers Edward and Locke, born in 1843 and 1848, were also farmers, and may have inherited part of Eber's farm after pursuing other employment. Locke went to sea first, as did his elder brothers. That the eldest and second son and subsequent sons went to sea is an indication that they weren't waiting around for their share of the farm and that their father didn't need them at home as he might have on a large farm. Sister Cordelia married a sea captain, and this is another indication of strong links to life on the waves.

Neither Eber nor his sons left much mark on Chautauqua or Ashtabula. Historians don't mention them amongst the hundreds of prominent citizens deserving of a brief biographical sketch. Although most of the family remained in Ashtabula throughout their lives, they made little impact. The only member of the family mentioned is the son of Cordelia Jeffords Blair, and from that sketch we learn a few details about Eber.[8] The family lived in the port of Ashtabula for a long time after they moved to Ohio. Saving his money, by 1850 Eber was able to purchase a farm in the country near Morgan. By then James and Tom were grown and serving as sailors on the lakes, James as captain of a ship. Eber stayed on his farm until he and son Eber Jackson Jeffords joined the Union Army at the start of the Civil War. Both served in Battery E of the 1st Ohio Light Artillery. Brothers John and Henry also joined the army. John served in Company D, of the 3rd Ohio Cavalry, and Henry in Company C of the 60th Ohio Infantry. Eber passed away in 1862 while in active service and the army buried him at Nashville, Tennessee. Tom went west before the war.

Eber thought of himself as a middle-class farmer. The middle class has always been protective of its status, anxious to preserve its good name and careful to appear dependable. Eber only fell on hard times when trying to get back into farming. He wasn't a laborer of no consequence who passed from job to job with few cares for the morrow. Such men drank and cared little for how others viewed them; there was always another job. Life on the docks threw Eber and his sons together with men from all of the northern European cultures, with lower-class people and even with half-Indian French Canadians. This life taught Tom acceptance and tolerance of others even as he maintained his own personal discipline and standards. He was capable, in a way few are, of making friends with those of other cultures.

CHAPTER 2

Lake Sailor

THE DOCKS OF ASHTABULA WERE BLAND WITHOUT THE TANG OF salt in the air, without the white crust of salt on pilings, without the strong scent of ocean on the breeze. To a boy standing on the shore, the docks were boring, a place of hard labor and little excitement. But he could gaze out across the endless waves and dream. There must be adventure out there. The lakefront abounded in stories of ships lost and missing. Missing ships—what had become of them? They just disappeared. Shipwrecks were commonplace. Storms, ice, freak waves, and winds took them down. There were narrow passages between lakes full of snares, snags, and shoals. Sailing must be an exciting life. It was certainly better than manhandling cargo on the shore.

Tom Jeffords grew up on the lakefront, and stories persist that he had commanded a ship. If so, he must have left home very young. Tom was twenty years old in 1852 and was in Denver, far from the lakes, by 1859. Four of Tom's brothers sailed the lakes and without doubt one, James Jeffords, was a captain while still young. A newspaper article lists a Captain Jeffords on the bark *John Sweeney* in 1856. If this was Tom, and not his brother James, he would have been only twenty-four.

On October 13, 1851, the brig *Chicago* under Captain Napier went down with loss of first mate, second mate, and a seaman. Captain Jeffords of the schooner *Home* rescued the captain and balance of his crew.[1] This is the earliest reference to a Captain Jeffords of Ashtabula.

Tom would have been nineteen, so this must have been his brother, James. The brig *Caroline A. Bemis* sprang a leak on August 27, 1852, en route to Sandusky; her cargo of wheat and flour became water-logged, and so she swelled, burst her seams, and went down. She was under the command of Captain Jeffords.[2] Capsizing or sinking due to a wet cargo was quite common on the lakes. On September 6, 1854, the docks launched the schooner *Robert Bruce*. A new ship, she had a new skipper. Captain Jeffords commanded her.[3] Tom would have been twenty-two. In 1855, Captain James Jeffords of Ashtabula narrowly missed going down with his ship, the propeller *Charter Oak*. That fall he was the listed commander, and initially the press reported him as lost and drowned, but he was at home with an attack of "fever and ague." About noon, people on shore saw a trunk floating on the water near where the wreck went down. Inside was a miniature, two inches square, which the newspaper kept, awaiting a claimant.[4]

GOOD TIME.—The bark J. SWEENEY, Capt. Jeffords, left Chicago on Friday of last week, and made the run to St. Clair Flats in 69 hours and 45 minutes, where in consequence of the collision she grounded. This is but little short of the CANADA's famous time and from what we know of Capt. Jeffords we believe he would have equaled the CANADA's trip but for the accident referred to.

Buffalo Daily Republic
Saturday, July 5, 1856[5]

The commander of the *J. Sweeney* is the most likely candidate for being Thomas J. Jeffords. He would have been twenty-four. Before 1859, Tom left the lakes forever. He may have left disgraced since in racing he had caused a collision and might have found himself "on the beach." This was probably not the case, as setting new records for fast runs was common practice. He may have seen one too many shipwrecks and left this line of work. This seems unlikely, as in later life Tom took risks that suggested great courage. More probably he found the life boring and unprofitable as he was working as an employee of ship owners. He may have thought going west for gold held better prospects. He would pursue gold for the rest of his life.

On the ocean the wind is in your face, bringing the tang and smells of saltwater. In seaports the smell of fish is always nearby, brought by mounds of clam and oyster shells and fish being processed—dried, salted, and canned. Ashtabula in the 1840s, when Tom Jeffords was young, smelled something like this. The fish smell was there but not the tang. The town smelled of the products coming through, and in the nineteenth century many of these were much more crude and aromatic than would suit us today. Ship builders required pitch and tar to caulk ships' hulls and protect cordage. There would have been a strong aroma of hemp, as that was the plant from which the rope walks made cordage. Lumber was a principal commodity in lake trade and it smelled of pine forest and resin. The ships stank of damp and moldy things that had settled to the bilges but, perhaps in fresh water on short runs, not as much as saltwater craft on long voyages.

On the lakes, ships would slide along to the gentle *shush* of water passing underneath. Square sails on the foremast pulled the ship along while triangular sails aft tilted the decks to one side, allowing the craft to sail closer to the wind's eye. That advantage could kill a ship especially in the narrow channels around harbors and between lakes where the wind could shift suddenly. Because the lake ships were nearly flat bottomed with no great, deep keel to provide resistance, a sudden shift in wind would capsize a ship, as witness the accounts of Captain Jeffords's ship coming to the rescue.

Another danger came from cargo, which could shift if not properly stowed. Cargo was often flammable. Even grain was a risk. If the hull leaked and the grain became wet, it would swell and tear a ship apart from the inside. Flour, too, was an explosive risk as the dust it brought aboard was combustible. The crews were small, three or four deck hands, just enough to hoist the sails. In danger, there were few hands to respond.

Ships of the Great Lakes didn't make long voyages. They made short runs from port to port. After the run, the small crew departed, leaving the captain to recruit anew. He'd need another officer to stand watch, three or four deckhands, and a cook, often a woman. The cook was important. Without a good one the captain would never find deckhands. Lake ships smelled of the cooking of fresh food and bread, not the hard meals of long voyages on salt water. Descriptions of sailing on the lakes from the Canadian side compare it to the hard life of sailors in the Royal Navy. Perhaps it was so, but on the American side, sailors recorded conditions as much better.

The small crew huddled together and ate at the captain's table. Although their time together was short, officers and crew would have been much closer than on blue-water ships where the quarterdeck kept far aloof from foremast jacks. Relations would have to build quickly. Officers had to earn respect quickly and keep it in order to enforce discipline even as the ship left port for the first time. On the lakes, the close quarters of the small ships threw officer and deckhand together. Officers were guarded in front of the sailors; they couldn't unwind in public, or they'd never be successfully obeyed. At the same time, they had to be on companionable terms with the deckhands. Meals at the captain's table would have been horribly uncomfortable if they'd tried to keep Royal Navy rules for dinner in the captain's cabin: Don't speak until the captain speaks to you; use the proper fork. Dinnertime, when sailors could relax, needed to be polite and easy. Men needed to feel they could speak freely even as officers maintained much of their reserve. Officers needed to exude courage and calm and never lose their tempers. Such a man would make an impression on people he met.

Tom Jeffords rose to command before he was twenty-five. He gave orders to men much older than he was, so he had to maintain his reserve, appear wise, and, most important, earn respect rather than demand it. The boy skipper lacked the natural respect that comes with age. He would have needed to earn respect across cultural barriers with crews of Dutch, German, English, French-Canadian, and Swedish sailors. This ability served him well in later years, earning swift respect from Apaches who called themselves *Indeh*, the people, implying that everyone else wasn't quite human and deserved little or no respect.

The Great Lakes offered the terror of sudden sinking against a backdrop of familiar peoples—Americans or at least Northern Europeans—familiar lands, fresh water, and fresh food. The lakes lacked the charm of exotic ports and peoples, of colorful parrots and strange goods. Lacking as well was the terror of long, violent storms, of being becalmed on a salt sea—water, water everywhere but not a drop to drink. To an active, intelligent young man in search of wealth, captaining a ship on the lake must have felt a bit like driving a semi-truck. He'd have seen the same ports, the same cargos, and the same people in a land as bland as the water. Adventure and fortune lay farther west where there were Indians, mountains, and, in California, gold, gold that could be picked up off the ground. In 1858, the adventure drew closer with news of gold at Pike's Peak and Cherry Creek.

James Jeffords was first mate of the schooner *Adriatic* under Captain J. B. Hall with a cargo of lumber and staves bound from Ashtabula to Boston on September 8, 1859.[6] The route would have taken James through canals to the St. Lawrence River and finally out into the salt sea and south to Boston. There was commerce not just through the Erie Canal from New York City and the Hudson River to Buffalo by canal boat; ships also sailed out into the salt sea linking Chicago to the world.

In 1849, the Corps of Topographical Engineers finally completed the first comprehensive chart of Lake Erie. Captain William G. Williams, operating out of Buffalo with four topographical engineers, was responsible for much of the work, which involved more than six thousand miles of shoreline. The surveyors had to determine longitude and latitude; measure the discharge of rivers into the lakes; survey rivers, narrows, and shoals; develop charts and maps; and mark points of danger. Other lakes and the hazardous narrows and channels between them came later. Uncharted lakes posed significant navigation hazards. It seems no wonder that capsizing and grounding were commonplace. Their work made the lakes safer for shipping.

The corps had only a few dozen officers. Unlike other army corps, it had no enlisted men. The officers hired civilians to assist them with the work whenever Congress approved the money to make hiring possible. The Topographical Engineers had a whole continent to survey, together with its rivers, coasts, and harbors.

Each body of water had its own challenges and types of boats and sailors. We picture nineteenth-century sailors voyaging off to exotic ports bringing home parrots and shrunken heads or perhaps some porcelain or a bejeweled dagger. Ship owners allowed sailors to carry a few pounds for personal trade as part of their compensation, and many took advantage of this. They returned home with strange stories of the customs and ladies of distant lands. Suffering on long voyages was unfathomable. Becalmed, they would suffer from thirst, perhaps catching a few drops of rainwater off a sail, or the crew might be driven to madness drinking seawater. When there was water it was stored in huge casks and scuttlebutts. It was slimy and it stank and crawled about on its own. If the water was bad, the food was worse. The sailors ate hardtack full of weevils and salt-horse (preserved beef) green about the edges. They kept what greens they could but when those ran out, they drank precious drops of lime juice. Without it they suffered scurvy. Teeth fell out. Old wounds opened and men went mad. The life of a sailor was hard and dangerous.

It took many men to handle a square-rigged ship. They had to know the ropes—that is, which one to pull on, and when, to get a certain effect. They scrambled one hundred feet aloft to make and furl sails in weather fair and foul. The captain and his officers lived apart from their men, the foremast jacks, who lived in the forecastle forward of the first mast. The two might have been different species for the distance they kept from each other. But it was necessary. The captain was supreme, like nothing so much as a god pacing his quarterdeck. The crew obeyed his orders instantly. On a long voyage with fair winds the boredom could be crushing. The foremast jacks sang and danced. They carved scrimshaw and made things of macramé, fancy knots, to while away the time. The reward for their endurance was legendary ports of call and years away from home.

For the lake sailor, life was very different. He visited ports of call no more exotic than Chicago and met people no more interesting than Canadians. It's true that in some ports the customs and languages of France, Holland, Germany, and Sweden were preserved, but these were a pale reflection of the native countries across the salt sea. The lake sailor didn't make long voyages. He engaged in runs lasting no more than a few days or weeks at best. He was always close to land and ate fresh food prepared by a good cook. If food became scarce, there was always a port nearby. He ate fresh bread (soft tack), vegetables, and fresh meat. Nor did he worry about being becalmed and dying of thirst. Lake sailors tell the story of an old salt, fresh from the ocean sea, who was horrified to find the water butts nearly empty. "We'll die of thirst," he cried. "Throw a pail over the side," his comrades replied.

The lake sailor didn't have to worry about climbing aloft in a freezing winter storm. Winter ice closed the lakes from November through March and the sailor warmed himself by his home fires or found a job in another trade, perhaps as a lumberjack. He seldom went aloft in any event. He controlled his ropes from the deck and it only took two or three hands to manage them. Lake ships were schooners and barks, the two being similar in many respects. They were rigged fore and aft with triangular sails; the bark had square-rigged sails on its foremast. To run a ship took only as much crew as was needed to raise the sail. The sails then took very little setting or attending.

Schooners and barks could sail very close to the wind's eye, that is to say, toward the direction from which the wind was coming. Square-rigged ships do best with the wind at their backs, but can adjust their sails to the side so that the leading edge of the sail points closer to the wind. Air moving over the belly of the sail must go farther than air moving behind and creates a vacuum that pulls the ship toward it. This is the same principle by which an airplane flies. The wind also blows the ship in the direction of the belly of the sail, so the ship slides to the side as the wind pulls it forward. A deep keel prevents the sideward movement and redirects motion toward the bow. Square-rigged ships can only adjust their sails so far and no farther, and so are not weatherly, unable to sail close to the wind's eye. Fore-and-aft-rigged ships have sails that are constantly set so that the wind draws them to itself. Lake boats, unfortunately, were shallow draft so they could sail the rivers between lakes and skim over port entrance bars. Some were equipped with dagger boards that the crew could raise and lower, providing additional resistance against sideways motion. The ships were vulnerable to crosswinds, and a sudden change in wind direction without the resistance of a deep keel could put a ship on its beam ends or side. Such mishaps were common.

The crew of a schooner might consist of two officers (captain and mate), a cook, and as few as two foremast jacks. With such small crews everyone dined at the captain's table. The skipper could not afford to be as distant or as god-like as his ocean-going counterpart. He had to find a way to be affable and available to his hands while retaining discipline and expecting his orders to be obeyed instantly on deck. Such a captain had to be close to the working class while keeping himself above them. If he offended the crew, the opportunity to desert was available in days at the next port of call. His behavior must be sober, proper, and formal. The men must see their captain as a leader but also as friendly.

These are lessons Tom Jeffords learned well. Some writers have accused him of being a loner. It was true that Tom was comfortable on his own, but the writers base the loner accusation on his later life at Owl Head Buttes. The place was not nearly as lonely then as now. It was closer to Tucson. Today the roads run in a great circle around the buttes. When Tom lived there, the road ran directly toward town and there were small towns, now gone, in between. He had neighbors and, more important, many close friends in Tucson. He was a man comfortable with workers and management alike.

On the lakes, captains and crews parted company and from their ships almost as often as they made runs. It was a benefit to the owners that they could pay off the crew as soon as they came to port and not pay them while they waited for dock space to be unloaded. Deck hands preferred taking their pay, their newfound wealth, to squander in the dives ashore, rather than lying about the decks with naught to do. If the captain and ship had a good reputation, finding a new crew wasn't too difficult. The lakeshore had plenty of men who had spent their pay.

The official registries of ships and captains are spotty at best. Many more ships appear in the newspapers than are reported in registries. A Buffalo, New York, newspaper reported the following:

> *Launch—A schooner of 330 tons burthen, called the ROBERT BRUCE was launched yesterday morning from the shipyard of Mr. Leavaya, on the Creek. She was built for E.K. Bruce, of this city, and sold by him to Capt. Dennock and others, for $15,000. She will be commanded by Capt. Jeffords.*[7]

Unfortunately, as was usual, the newspaper did not provide the Christian name of the captain. We are left to wonder if he is James or Thomas. Disasters also appeared with regularity in the papers and with equal regularity lack first names, as in this piece:

> *The Brig. CHICAGO, Capt. Napier, which cleared on Saturday for Chicago in ballast, was capsized about 4 o'clock yesterday morning*

by a sudden squall, about 90 miles from this port and nearly in the middle of the lake, and we regret to hear that John Fullock, 1st. Mate, W.L. Reed, 2nd Mate and John Carver seaman were lost. The Schooner HOME, Capt. Jeffords, bound for this port, fell in with the wreck about 10 o'clock and took off Capt. Napier and the balance of the crew and brought them to port. Capt. Napier informs us that when taken off himself and the men were exhausted, and could have held out, but a short time longer. The first mate belonged to Cleveland, where he had a young wife, having been married but a short time. The 2nd. Mate resided at Chicago, and he also leaves a young wife, have been married but a few months. Young Carver was a single man and belonged at Chicago. The vessel was owned by Tom Dyer of Chicago, and was insured for $6,000 equally in the Buffalo Mutual and North Western of Oswego.[8]

In the loss of the propeller *Charter Oak*, the papers mentioned Captain James Jeffords, of Ashtabula, Ohio, by his name and place of origin.[9] Captain James Jeffords provided these additional particulars:

THE CHARTER OAK—From Capt. James Jeffords, of this ill-fated vessel, we have the following additional particulars, with the list of those who perished on her. She landed at Fairport on Saturday afternoon at 4 o'clock, for the purpose of putting the captain ashore, who was very sick. She left Fairport about 7 P.M., with a full cargo of staves, &c. The weather then very clear, with the promise of a fair night. This was the last time he saw her. The following are the names of the lost.

George A. C. Wood, Buffalo, Captain.
Wm. Stillman, 1st engineer, parents live near Ogdenburg—no family.
Stephen Smithers, 2nd engineer, Buffalo, left a wife and 2 children. They have gone up in search of the body.

Daniel McIntosh, wheelsman, has a sister in Buffalo.
——Reinhardt, deck hand, residence unknown.
John Inkster, from Trenton, deck hand.
Adolphus Anderson, mulatto cook, from Cincinnati, and two
other deck hands, names unknown.[10]

This one report displays many of the aspects of Great Lakes sailing. The crews were small and shifted boats often. Jeffords didn't know the names of two deck hands, suggesting they'd come aboard as he departed. They carried cargos of wheat and flour, staves and lumber. Captain James Jeffords certainly wasted no time in finding another ship. On September 19, 1855, he was in command of the brig *Globe* then at Chicago rescuing the crew of the brig *Tuscarora*.[11]

In 1856, there are records of a Captain Jeffords commanding the bark *J. Sweeney*.[12] No first name is given. However, Richard Wright, of Bowling Green State University, wrote in April 1976, "In checking customs records for the Buffalo Creek (N.Y.) District, we find that Captain Jeffords is listed as master of the bark *John Sweeney* (Permanent enrollment #163, issued July 10, 1856)."[13] His letter refers to Thomas J. Jeffords.[14]

In 1859, Tom Jeffords worked his way west, building a road from Leavenworth, Kansas, to Denver. Those who knew him said that between 1856 and 1859 he worked on the Mississippi and Missouri as the captain of a paddlewheel steamboat. It seems unlikely. There are only three years missing between earning his captaincy and arriving in Denver. He must have spent some time enjoying his newfound authority as a captain. His family says he spent some time in southern Ohio working at different jobs, finding none of them satisfactory.[15] He wanted to make his fortune so he could marry well and avoid his father's poverty.

Men went west for many reasons. Bankruptcy, perhaps caused by a shipwreck, is possible, but there is no record of such a wreck. A broken love affair might send a man seeking solace far from his former paramour, but this doesn't seem in character. Lake sailing was a lot like long-haul trucking. Captains traversed the same routes over and over again while a man spent a great deal of time away from home. One didn't get rich quickly working for others; the ship owner took the lion's share. Despite the sudden challenge of capsizing or the slow agony of having a soaked cargo of grain pull your ship down, the lake didn't offer much that was new or exciting. A man might seek a new challenge pitting himself against the frontier and seeking to make his fortune in gold.

Riverboats, those great gingerbreaded floating hotels, would have been a challenge. They were completely different from lake schooners. They ran on huge, dangerous steam engines with an engineer and a black gang (black because they were covered in soot) to care for them. Stories of fires and exploding boilers abounded. They were floating hotels with crews of stewards, cooks, and housekeepers to care for guests. There were gamblers and thieves there to fleece the unwary farmer or plantation owner returning home with proceeds from the sale of cotton or produce. Others carried money to stock mercantile shelves in New Orleans or St. Louis.[16] Poor travelers slept on deck amidst the cargo. The boats were also freighters with crews of deck hands moving merchandise on and off at every stop and bringing aboard firewood to stoke the boilers. There would have been a lot for Tom Jeffords to learn before he could captain such a ship. Moreover, on the river the pilot was king.

On vessels plying the seas and lakes, a pilot was a man who came aboard to guide the ship past shoals and headlands as it entered a harbor. The pilot lived in his harbor and specialized in that one place. On the river, shoals and snags were everywhere and changed with the weather. A pilot was the most important member of a crew. The steamboat was always in shoal water and needed a pilot constantly. Out of work, pilots sailed as guests on the great steamboats, keeping their eyes on the river's moods and changes to be ready for the next job.[17] They stayed aloft in the pilothouse, keeping themselves current on the condition of and changes in the river. They learned to read the water in the dark by ripples and reflections. They were its acolytes, sensing the river's moods.

A man or boy apprenticed to a pilot and stood watches learning about the more than two thousand miles of Mississippi River. Moving to the Missouri or Ohio and even the Colorado would have required a new education. Spring flood would bring down new snags, submerged, waterlogged trees. Channels shifted and changed constantly. A storm could remove a bend and shorten or lengthen the river by miles. Weston, Missouri, once a river port abandoned by its mistress, is now a mile inland. It took years for a man to learn before he was ready for the challenge. The pay was excellent, and having risen to the sublime position of pilot, a man did not easily walk away. The river was a challenge.

If Tom Jeffords left home in his late teens to sail the inland highway that was the Mississippi River, he might have risen to be a captain in his mid-twenties in 1857 or 1858. The complex society of the riverboat would have been an education in gaining and maintaining respect in command and in learning to deal with people from many backgrounds. The river seems unlikely, but might have been his home for a while.

From his time on lake schooners, Tom learned to get along with and even like others at close quarters despite their differences in outlook, culture, and hygiene. The schooner was small, the crew small. The officer had to be able to command at all times, but at the same time he had to be available in friendship to his crewmates. It is a difficult task, one that the modern armor officer, tanker, learns. He commands his platoon, company, or squadron, but is always especially close to the other three men of his tank crew. He has to do this without offending the rest of the unit. He is close, but not too close, friend but not quite equal. The situation calls on him to show admirable behavior at all times. Living so close to others, he has to be accepting of their differences and foibles. When Tom Jeffords met Cochise he was prepared to see a friend despite differences of culture and skin color.

A lake captain might thirst for something more adventurous, something at which he might make his fortune quickly and return home to find a handsome bride. Too young to be a Forty-niner, Tom got word of the Pike's Peak Gold Rush and headed west as a Fifty-niner.[18] He spent most of the rest of his life prospecting for gold, successful, but never quite rich.

A Call to the Mines

By Flop

Hurra for Pike's Peak! Hurra for Pike's Peak!
A rich El Dorado has lately been found,
Far, far to the Westward, and near Cherry Creek;
Where gold in abundance is scattered around.
Ah! hurra for Pike's Peak!
Hurra for Pike's Peak! Hurra for Pike's Peak!
There's gold in the Mount'n, there's gold in the vale,
There's plenty for all who are willing to seek
Believe me; believe me—'tis no idle tale.
Come, hurra for Pike's Peak!

CHAPTER 3

Going West

THOMAS FARISH, ARIZONA STATE HISTORIAN, IN THE TEENS OF THE twentieth century, interviewed Tom, and from him come recollections of Tom's journey west and his first years as a prospector:

> *Captain Thomas Jonathan[1] Jeffords was born in Chautauqua County, New York, in 1832. He laid out the road from Leavenworth, Kansas, to Denver, in 1858. In the fall of 1859 he came to Taos, New Mexico, and wintered in Taos. The following spring he went into the San Juan mountains to prospect and mine. In 1862 he carried dispatches from Fort[2] Thorn[3] to General Carleton at Tucson. At that time, he was on the payroll of the United States Government as a scout, and piloted the advance companies of the California Column into New Mexico, to old Fort Thorn near the Rio Grande near Las Cruces. He is said to have taken part in the battle of Val Verde and the other engagements which resulted in the expulsion of the Confederates from New Mexico.[4]*

Thomas Jefferson Jeffords, bored with lake sailing and looking for a faster way to make money, spent the rest of his life searching for gold, prospecting and mining. Prospecting and mining are two very different activities. The prospector seeks surface indications of a ledge or load or, in very different circumstances, of sand where a river might have dropped the heaviest particles it was carrying, gold dust; these latter are called placers. The miner, on the other hand, apart from the underground laborer who is also called a miner, is a gambler and a man of means who invests in operations developing a prospect hole into a producing mine. Jeffords at times was both. He set out for Denver to search for a placer in the sands of Cherry Creek. To get there he worked his way building the road from Leavenworth on the Missouri River to Denver.

Lake navigation taught Jeffords many of the skills he would use surveying the road. Each day Tom checked his chronometer. When it showed noon, he held up his sextant to the sky and, peering through its sight, he twisted a knob to bring the reflected sun down to the horizon. He turned to its side and read the angle, then wrote it in his book. With a few calculations he would determine the longitude and latitude of the spring he was looking at. A Gunter's chain stretched between two points as many times as necessary by Tom and an assistant gave distance, sixty-six feet to the chain, eighty chains to the mile. They measured direction with a magnetic compass or a vernier, an instrument that measured horizontal angles. They calculated height with a simple level. The most important part of road building in 1859 was laying out the road. The road builders considered distance, direction, and elevation in laying out the most efficient road. It would stretch from waterhole to waterhole and run alongside rivers, close enough to get water but not so close that constant washes and creeks would pose a problem for wagons. The builders rarely made cuts to level the road. When necessary they leveled the road with the new Fresno scraper drawn by horses or mules. There wasn't much more to it. The companies paying for the road didn't need it flat. They only needed it flat enough for wagons and stagecoaches. Besides, it was a dirt road and during rains traffic would chew up the surface.[5]

One sunny day, Tom crested a hill, and there before him he saw the Rocky Mountains, shimmering purple in the distance, the Shining Mountains, the Big Stoneys. Each day they grew a little taller and came a little closer. The plains weren't flat. They dipped and rolled and often hid the mountains from view. Here and there stony outcrops made small cliffs overlooking little creeks. The land was dryer than Tom had seen before. The tall grass gave way to short grass, the home of buffalo and prairie dogs.

The towns of these rodents were interesting. They could stretch for miles. Each den looked like an anthill, with dirt thrown up around the edge and a large hole in the middle. As Tom approached, lookouts among the dogs—he thought them as more like squirrels—would bark and the others would scramble. They'd come together for a meeting, split up, and dive down their holes, only to reappear moments later. Jeffords soon observed that they didn't live alone. Large rattlesnakes also emerged from the dens and disappeared into them as well. Tom was startled when a small owl suddenly flew up out of a burrow. Apparently owls lived with the prairie dogs as well.

His camp of surveyors was small. There was no need for a large party. The Indians were mostly peaceful, though some were inclined to steal horses and equipment. The surveyors shot buffalo and antelope for camp meat and used buffalo chips[6] to make their cook fires, and it seemed to add additional savor to their meat. There was little firewood—only what grew along the creeks, and that did not burn well. They soon learned that they could not keep fresh meat in camp. One night glowing, red eyes, just beyond the circle of firelight, surrounded them. The gray wolves howled so close Tom felt he could reach out and touch them. Perhaps he could have. They came into camp to steal meat and would even take boots and leather tack.[7]

Tom Jeffords came to Denver in 1858 and found the settlement a few miles from the base of the mountains where rushing mountain streams slowed to meander across the plains. He saw a collection of tents and mud houses called adobes. There were a few log cabins. Those who wanted log homes brought the logs from the mountains and few wanted to waste the time when they could have been moiling for gold.[8] A few newcomers figured out that there were other ways to make money. Prospectors and moilers needed supplies, so some set up stores. Men needed entertainment, and soon there were tents labeled as saloons, dance halls, and gambling palaces. Some would find work as lawyers grubbing money from overlapping mining claims and grubstaking agreements.[9] Others would seek government jobs handling mail or the law, while still others sought political office. Tom ran for office but didn't stay in the area very long.[10]

He soon joined on as a junior partner to a mining claim. Tom needed to learn this new trade. He had money after being paid off on road building, and so had the means to buy into a claim and to buy supplies, but he lacked the skills needed.[11]

A large part of the rush localized around Cherry Creek. Pike's Peakers set out for Pike's Peak or Bust. The newspapers called them Fifty-niners, for the peak year of the rush. Kansas (it wasn't Colorado as yet) offered many opportunities on many creeks for men like Tom, but he arrived late and found the best spots taken. This was a rush for placer gold, the heavy particles left behind in river sands where the rushing mountain torrent slows to become the creeping, meandering river of the plains.

Gold does not tarnish. It does not easily bond chemically. Nature superheats minerals before driving them up through cracks in the earth toward the surface. They rise on steam, sulfur, and chloride. Other minerals bond chemically along the way, but gold stays pure and as the mass cools, it settles out and with quartz forms a thin sheet along the boundary with country stone. Other minerals solidify at different temperatures and end up in different sections of the mountain. A single mine will produce many kinds of minerals. Gold is the first that men seek after, and silver next. The prospector can take enough gold and silver in his saddle bags to make him rich. That can't be said of minerals like lead and copper. Those will wait for men building roads, railroads, or river transportation to haul great quantities of metal.

Tom learned to select likely spots along rivers and streams where nature had deposited the heavy gold. He also learned to look for fossil, that is, abandoned, river beds, which might still hold rich deposits. Black sand, iron, was an indicator that heavy gold was also present. There was prime country from Cherry Creek, soon to become Denver, down to Pike's Peak, seventy miles to the south, soon to be called Colorado Springs. The streams of the Rockies dropped their load of wealth at the foot of the mountains. A man with a shovel and a pan might swirl sand and water until the lighter sand went over the edge and gold was left behind.

There was little law in the west. Each camp made its own rules, but based on experience in California, the rules tended to be very similar and more conducive to placer mining than load mining. A man could claim fifteen hundred feet along a stream and three hundred feet on each side, depending on the rules of the camp, since the Federal government failed to legislate the law until the General Mining Act of 1872. Camp rules generally allowed prospectors one claim in each mining district, and they had to do at least one hundred dollars' worth of work each year in improvements to keep it. After 1872, a prospector could make as many claims as he could afford to do assessment work. Prospectors paid a few dollars to file and in five years, if they kept up the assessment work, they might file for a patent, that is, private property and full ownership. The prospector had to provide a legal description of his property and stake its corners. Unfortunately, the government hadn't surveyed the land as yet. Private surveyors would find ample work around bustling camps. However, prospectors provided the roughest descriptions imaginable of their claims. Legal descriptions might say "halfway between here and there, approximately 15 miles from there." There was much confusion over boundaries and over abandonment. Claims accidentally overlapped, causing battles, legal and otherwise. When the overlapping was deliberate it was considered claim jumping. If the prospector didn't keep up his assessment work, or if someone accused him of not keeping it up, a new prospector might stake the ground. This too caused fights.

Tom's partners showed him how to build a sluice, which does the job of the pan but more efficiently. A long box was built, which was lined with ridges every foot or so. The miner forced water to run along its length. He then shoveled in dirt and sand at the top and as the water flowed it carried away the lighter elements while heavy gold fell out at the ridges. The miners cleaned out the ridges and poured in mercury. Gold and silver form an amalgam with mercury. As the amalgam forms, it effectively separates the gold and silver from the remaining sand and gravel. They heated the amalgam in a retort, the mercury recovered for reuse and the gold and silver left behind as sponge-gold, looking like a sponge where the mercury had boiled out of pockets in the amalgam.

Tom Jeffords soon found that he'd come to western Kansas, soon to be Colorado, after the best placer claims along the streams had been taken. He stayed a while in Denver, long enough to appear on the Great Roll of voters, but soon headed south. He showed up on the voter rolls in Taos County, New Mexico Territory, in 1859. Taos County then included southern Colorado's San Luis Valley and ran west to the Colorado River, places that are today part of Utah and Arizona. In 1859, Tom wintered in Taos.

In the spring, he set off across the San Juan Mountains following a new gold rush. It took him along the Old Spanish Trail to the San Juan River on the western slope beyond the Great Divide.[12] Prospectors explored the area around Pagosa Springs, now in Colorado. They also pushed out as far west as the Mancos River between modern Farmington, New Mexico, and Durango, Colorado.[13] The area was remote, on the west slope of the San Juan Mountains, inhabited only by Ute, Jicarilla Apache, and Navajo. The rush was short lived. Men would return to these areas in later years when there were roads and railroads, and mine in places like Durango, Silverton, and Creede. But in 1860, there were too many Indians, too many mountains, and too few roads.

The Old Spanish Trail ran through this country from Abiquiu, New Mexico, north along the Chama River and then northwest to the San Juan River. There were many branches to this trail. It was a route for pack trains meant for mules, not wagons. Although called old, the trail was younger than the Santa Fe Trail founded in 1821. The Old Spanish Trail brought mules from California to trade for manufactured goods with Yankees from Missouri. Its traces are faint.

By his own account, in 1860, Tom Jeffords first came to Arizona: "I presume I may be regarded as a pioneer. I came to the territory first in 1860. In 1862, when I saw Tucson, the population did not exceed one hundred, outside of the California column of soldiers."[14] Arizona was still western New Mexico until 1863. In 1860, there was a gold rush to the Colorado River at a place called Gila City, a few miles up the Gila from the Colorado and Fort Yuma in California. Prospectors discovered placers. Jeffords joined a group of men headed west over Kearney's Route, a pack trail along the Gila River.[15] The rush was short lived.

There wasn't enough water to work placers. Dry washing for gold was the order of the day. Men found that they could toss a shovel load of sand on a blanket. Four men would pull on the corners, tossing the load high in the air. The wind blew away lighter material. If the miners repeated this process enough times, the wind left behind the heavy gold. A team of four could make five or six dollars after a day of backbreaking toil. This did not appeal to most Americans, who left the diggings to Sonorans and headed east to yet another gold rush at Pinos Altos near the headwaters of the Gila, a few miles north of modern Silver City, New Mexico. Fort Craig was nearby, and that is where Tom showed up during the Civil War.

Tom Jeffords learned a new kind of mining at Pinos Altos. There were small mountain placers there, but much of the gold came from lodes underground. The earth heats minerals in its depths until they rise up through cracks in the country stone, surrounding rock without minerals—limestone, quartzite, and granite. In a molten state, minerals combine with water, sulfur, chlorine, and other elements and rise, slowly cooling so that gold settles out in one place, often with quartz, forming a thin sheet or flecks along its interface with the country stone, while other minerals, cooling at different rates, settle out in other places in the rock. Tom learned to search for ledges where nature exposed the mineral-rich deposits at the surface. He searched for "color." Where the country stone tends toward beige, mineral deposits are brilliant blues, turquoise, reds, yellows, black, and gold. He looked for places where several springs occurred in a line along a hill, a sign that there was a discontinuity in the earth that might signal a place where minerals had pushed to the surface.

Because it does not bond with other elements, gold is the easiest mineral to process. Silver is not far behind, so they are the first minerals sought. Copper, in comparison, requires expensive processing and smelting. Tunneling for minerals is expensive. Men hammer star-drills into the rock until they create a honeycomb. They then load the holes with explosives, shattering the rock. Processing is even more expensive, requiring stamp mills, concentrators, and smelters where men heat ore until molten to burn off impurities. Because the miners sought gold, a simpler course was open at Pinos Altos.

Instead of expensive stamp mills, costly to purchase and heavy to transport, they built *arrastras* to pulverize quartz and stone. The miners constructed a circular floor of flat stones with a stone wall and a center pivot. A long arm ran from the pivot to a draft animal, which they induced to walk around the arrastra in a circle. They hung heavy stones from the pivot arm in contact with the floor. Ore, quartz laced with gold, was placed on the floor and the stones broke it into powder as they passed over it. Miners collected the powder and mixed it with mercury, which amalgamates with gold and silver. Heated in a retort, the mercury evaporated and was recovered for future use, leaving behind sponge gold.

The ore came from underground. Tom learned to use a drill and hammer to chisel a small hole deep into the rock face. He learned to single jack, one man working both hammer and drill, and double jack, where one held the drill while the other worked the eight-pound hammer. At day's end, they packed the holes they had drilled with explosive black powder, carefully, with brass tools that wouldn't spark on the rock, and then set and lit fuses. Chunks of rock broke away from the face and were mucked into ore cars to be carried to the arrastras. The work was hard and dangerous. The mines were small. So much labor was involved that passages were limited to the minimum size needed to follow and work an ore vein. Mines twisted and turned and changed size like rat holes. Men worked by candlelight, burning as few as possible. Candles were expensive.

The mines needed timber for shoring to keep them from collapsing. The camps needed wood for the fires under retorts, as well as for cooking and heating. Pinos Altos (Spanish: tall pines) was located in pine forest and it prospered.

Tom didn't leave a record of what he did during the year 1861. We surmise that he prospected in New Mexico's Black Mountains. Each camp kept its own records locally. We don't know if Tom found a good claim or if he was able to start a mine. A prospect hole is a hole in the earth made by a prospector to open up a surface vein and prove its worth. It becomes a mine when money is invested to make improvements and ore, stone with enough mineral in it to cover the expense of extraction and still leave a profit, is taken out. Few prospect holes become mines. In Pinos Altos, there were few investors buying prospects. Prospectors did most of the mining, and so the mines remained small and the miners removed only the richest ore. Mining is an economic activity. Mines open and close as the price of minerals on the market rises and falls.

Pinos Altos was six miles north of the future Silver City and a thousand feet above it in the pines. It was only a dozen miles from the famed Santa Rita del Cobre mines, which miners, James Ohio Pattie among them, had been working since Spanish times. They were known simply as the Copper Mines. In the 1850s and '60s there was little production. Apache raids and the cost of extraction inhibited work on low-value copper. Later they would make men rich as new techniques made it possible to extract more mineral from the ore and improved transportation made shipping less expensive. Pinos Altos was in the heart of Mangas Coloradas's Gila Apache (Bedonkohe) domain, a branch of the Chiricahua. Tom Jeffords went from gold rush to gold rush, from the San Juan to the dry placers near the Colorado River and then to green mountain claims at Pinos Altos.

Freighting companies, like those of Estevan Ochoa, who would later partner with P. R. Tully and with Tom, and Mariano Samaniego, tied Pinos Altos to Tucson. Mills in Tucson provided flour unavailable from the Mexican communities along the Rio Grande. The freighters brought flour and supplies from steamboats plying the Colorado. In Tucson, Silver Lake on the Santa Cruz River was a millpond. Tom Jeffords nearly drowned there while swimming with friends in 1884.[16] Fort McLane, a satellite of the 7th Infantry headquartered at Fort Buchanan, was guardian to Pinos Altos and the Santa Rita Mines and received supplies from distant Fort Buchanan on Sonoita Creek, fifty miles southeast of Tucson.

There were small settlements on the Arizona side of the Colorado across from Fort Yuma in California. In 1860, Tubac was a small mining community south of Tucson, a small, dusty, dirty adobe town of a few hundred where there had once been Spanish and Mexican presidios, frontier forts. Going east from Tucson the next towns were Pinos Altos, and then Mesilla on the Rio Grande almost three hundred miles distant. In 1857, Congress decreed an overland mail route that ran along the Great Oxbow from St. Louis, through Arkansas and Texas, to Tucson and Fort Yuma, and then north to Los Angeles and San Francisco. The mail linked the nation together on a southern, all-weather route. In 1857, the Jackass Mail, the San Antonio and San Diego Mail, was born. In October 1858, it was replaced by Butterfield's Overland Mail, which carried the mail from St. Louis to San Francisco in twenty-three days of non-stop travel.

The mail was key and was subsidized by the government. Passengers were an afterthought. In the west, the Overland Mail used light, celerity wagons with canvas tops and sides. The Overland Mail Company built these wagons with a flat, board floor on which three seats were mounted. The first two faced front and back. The driver and conductor faced front and three passengers faced back, interlocking their knees with the passengers on the next front-facing seat. The final row faced front. Driver and passengers were all on the same level. The wagon was only forty-two inches wide, which meant that when three men sat side by side, those on the outer edge had a leg dangling outside the coach. The coach ran day and night, stopping for fifteen minutes to change mules and give those aboard time to visit the outhouse or eat a meal. At night, passengers folded down the middle seat so that they could lie side by side and on top of each other to sleep. Few managed and many arrived in a demented state from lack of rest. They traveled over rough roads, bounced from side to side and knocked about.

Stations, separated every fifteen to twenty-five miles, supported the stagecoaches with changes of mules and drivers and with food. In Apache country, Butterfield built ten of these stations of stone with walls ten feet high. The station keepers brought mules inside the stations at night to present less temptation to Indians. Other stations were made of adobe. Butterfield armed his men. He also made gifts of food and goods to Mangas Coloradas (Red Sleeves) and Cochise, his son-in-law. The Apache found the Butterfields useful. The company advised passengers to go armed. The Overland Mail did not carry specie, making their stagecoaches less of a target for thieves. Two to three men occupied each station: a station keeper, hostler, and a relief driver. Support from the dragoons at Fort Breckenridge or infantry at Fort Buchanan was often more than one hundred miles and many days away.

Before February of 1861, the Apache did not attack the stagecoaches, nor wound or kill any drivers. The Apache threatened some of the stations, especially the one at Apache Pass, but there were no major incidents. The peace was tense, broken by Apache livestock raids, but the Chiricahua and other Apache focused most of their raiding on Sonora and Chihuahua in Mexico. Dr. Steck was Indian agent and he brought wagonloads of gifts, called annuities, given to discourage raiding. On March 3, 1861, Congress shut down the southern mail route. This had nothing to do with the Apache. The Great Oxbow Route ran south into Arkansas and Texas, which had left the Union to join the Confederacy.

In August 1861, Lieutenant Colonel John Baylor invaded New Mexico at the head of the 2nd Texas Mounted Regiment and declared himself governor of Arizona. Confederate Arizona included the southern portions of New Mexico and Arizona with its capital at Mesilla on the Rio Grande. The Civil War had come to the west. Federal troops were pulled back to the Rio Grande to defend against the Texans, leaving Tucson, Pinos Altos, and Tubac exposed to Apache attacks. The Apache soon realized that with the troops gone, the Norte Americanos were vulnerable to raiding. In February 1861, an incident at Apache Pass marked the beginning, if not the cause, of more intense hostilities with the Chiricahua Apache.

Chapter 4

Apaches

"Cochise is about 6'2", strongly muscled, with mild, prominent features, a hooked nose, and looks to be a man that means what he says; age is just beginning to tell on him. He is now 50 years old."[1] On February 21, 1869, Brevet Major Frank Perry reported his meeting with the chief from near Cochise's Stronghold in the Dragoon Mountains. He was there to propose peace, but the Chiricahua didn't like the terms.

The sky islands of southern Arizona, New Mexico, and northern Sonora and Chihuahua, Mexico, are home to the Chiricahua Apache. Peaks rise to seven, eight, and nine thousand feet above grassy prairies riven by intermittent rivers that rise above ground where rocks impede their flow, only to sink below the sand again. The Chiricahua are mountain Indians, making their homes in the land between five and seven thousand feet of elevation, where streams flow from mountain canyons to disappear under the prairie. Their favored habitat is called the oak-pinyon zone and the Apache subsist on the nuts of both along with the fruit of banana yucca, the stalk of agave, and the berries of the manzanita, the little apple. There were deer and javelina, a relative of the pig, in the mountain forests. The Apache did not eat their brother the bear, nor did they eat fish, who were to them a kind of snake. There were no great buffalo herds for them follow and hunt. The horse was more important to them as food than as a mount or source of wealth.

Rainfall was from nine to twenty inches, coming mostly in the summer and highly variable from year to year and place to place. The availability of plant food and game varied with the rain. When rainfall was light the Apache raided their neighbors to supplement their diets, taking cattle, mules, horses, and corn along with captive slaves.

Ethnologists call the Apache nomadic hunter-gatherers, but this hardly begins to capture the reality of their lives. They are Athapascans, among the last Indians to arrive from Asia. They made their way south less than a thousand years ago. Traditional history says that they came to Arizona and southern New Mexico after 1540. In the past, scholars have claimed that Coronado did not encounter them as he went north in search of Seven Cities of Gold. More recently, archaeologists like Deni Seymour are saying he did encounter them and recorded the encounters. Modern readers simply did not recognize them as Apaches from the few hints given. Dr. Seymour has pushed back the date of their arrival to at least 1000 AD.[2] The Apache say they have been here forever. Since they have intermarried with other groups in the Southwest and adopted elements of their cultures, the Apache claim has validity.

They are not horse lords, and are as likely to eat as ride a horse. There are limits on this statement. It applies to the Western,[3] White Mountain (Coyotero),[4] and Chiricahua Apaches and to a lesser extent to the Jicarilla and Mescalero. These latter two are, along with the Kiowa and Lipan Apache, plains Indians and people of the horse. All Apaches speak variations of the same language, understanding each other well. Anglo-Americans and Hispanics identified the Wolves of the Southwest by where they found them—Gila, White Mountain (also known as Coyotero), Cibeque, Pinal, Jicarilla, Warm Springs (also known as Mimbres), Chiricahua—and by what they ate—Mescalero. The names hold little reality for Ndeh, the people, as they call themselves. Their political divisions were ephemeral, temporary, and customary. Hatreds arose between bands, as between the Jicarilla and the Kiowa Apache, their deadliest enemies and closest relatives, and lasted until they had long forgotten the cause of the division and their relationship. Of a band, at best we might say that they often intermarried, conducted ceremonies together, and joined each other in warfare. Alliances were temporary and personal. In 1880, Victorio's band consisted of Warm Springs (Chihenne) and other Chiricahuas, Mescaleros, and Lipans.[5] Tribe was not a political reality but an accident of language.

It was convenient for Europeans to define Apache tribes and sub-tribes. That way they could deal with one chief and expect a large number of Indians to follow his lead, and they could blame him and his people as a whole if individuals departed from agreements. The American government meted out punishment to members of the tribe whether or not they were personally guilty. If raiders attacked, scattered military units would be long in picking up the cold trail and had little hope of encountering the actual raiders. By naming them a tribe, the Army could attack any member or village and punish them instead of the actual raiders.

The Apache were matrilocal. That means that men typically went to live with their wife's family. This made sense. A woman, her mother, and sisters undertook many communal tasks. More important, the mother had something to give her daughter as inheritance, the places she gathered herbal foods. The tribe respected these traditional collecting places as a kind of real property. With plural marriage and high death rates, the rules became complex. A band formed around a senior woman, her husband, their unmarried children, and her married daughters. Others might join, aunts and cousins and the families of men who respected the chief male.

Absolute individuality, independence, and freedom of choice characterized the Apache. If a man did not like conditions in one village, he moved to another, taking his wife or wives with him.

White men supplied the political divisions of this warrior nation to keep track of the group with which the government was currently at war. Chiricahua raided with Mescalero and Coyotero. Jicarilla speak the same language as Kiowa Apache but are their sworn enemies. One division of Jicarilla, the Olleros, lived in the mountains. The other, the Llaneros, lived on the Llano Estacado, the Staked Plains, and hunted buffalo. These latter live in tepees while most Apache live in wickiups, brush shelters. All speak a mutually understandable language. Europeans named them for where they found them, hence Chiricahua for the Chiricahua Mountains and Gila for those who dwelt near the Gila River, also called Mimbres or Warm Springs for those near the springs. But Warm Springs, Gila, and Chiricahua are all Chiricahua spread along the west bank of the Rio Grande from Warm Springs, modern Truth or Consequences, and southward deep into Mexico and westward to the Dragoon Mountains. The Chiricahua subdivided themselves as Chihenne, Nednhi, Bedonkohe, and Chokonen.

The Chokonen dwelled in the Animas Valley, Peloncillo Mountains, Dragoon Mountains, and south into Mexico. South of them were the Nednhi, the band of Juh and Geronimo, and north and east were the Chihenne and Bedonkohe, Mangas Coloradas's people. A man married and went to live with his wife. So Geronimo, born near Warm Springs in the north, lived with the Nednhi in Mexico and Cochise of the Chokonen had a wife from the Bedonkohe. But Anglos and Mexicans had other names for them. The Bedonkohe were often called Gila or Mogollon, and the Chihenne called Warm Springs.

Every Apache was free to live and do as he saw fit. Only if he committed himself to a war party did he subordinate himself to others. There was no political organization above the rancheria, the small communities in which the Apache lived. A woman passed on her gathering spots for wild food to her daughter and this tied them together. There were good places to gather acorns, manzanita berries, walnuts, and mescal and they changed from year to year with changes in the weather. A woman would have many places to gather and some to farm. The farms were simple, often no more than a spot of ground that would get wet during the summer rains. The Apache sowed these moist areas with seed and left them until harvest. Some bands worked their fields more intensively. Colonel Hiram Hodge wrote in 1875 that Chiricahua were the only Apaches who did not plant fields. This may be true but seems unlikely. Mortality and infertility disrupted the pattern of mother-to-daughter inheritance and gathering sites, so women passed their inheritance between aunts and nieces. Newcomers to the band assumed vacant gathering spots. The women haggled over which spots belonged to whom. Peace depended on the wisdom of the senior man. Despite loss of inheritance, if a man became dissatisfied with conditions in his wife's village, they would pack up and move. No one could force them to stay. If a leader called men to war, it was a measure of trust and respect in the leader that anyone came. No one was required to come.

We don't really know much about Cochise. He might have been born around 1815, but Asa Daklugie says he was about seventy when he died in 1874, which would make him ten years older. An Army officer who met him in 1860 estimated his age at thirty, which would make him fifteen years younger, and this seems much too young. A leader of raids who might have been Cochise—transliteration of names and variations between Spanish, Apache, and English make for confusion—begins to appear about 1835, and a married man appears on Mexican rolls in 1842. Likewise we don't know the name of Cochise's father. He might have been Pisago Cabezon, Relles, or Juan Jose Campo, all chiefs of the Chokonen, who are believed to have been murdered during peace talks.[6] This should tell us with certainty that chieftainship among the Chiricahua was a matter of merit, not heredity, or we would be more certain of his parentage. Colonel Hiram Hodge, who visited with Cochise's sons in 1875, tells us that Mexicans murdered Cochise's father and elder brothers under flag of truce, placing the events as early as 1825 and 1828.[7] Edwin Sweeney, working from documentary sources, associated these events with the 1837 Johnson massacre and the 1846 James Kirker massacre, during which renegade scalp hunters operating in Mexico slew Chiricahua chiefs.[8] In one case, the people were fed mescal until they got drunk and passed out, and then they were slain in their sleep.

Cochise was careful about entering towns and forts and about coming in for parley. During the war years, we find him sleeping away from his rancheria. In 1871, when the Army brought Cochise's village into the Canada Alamosa Reservation, Cochise was away. In 1872, when Jeffords took General O. O. Howard to Cochise's stronghold high in the Dragoon Mountains, Cochise wasn't there. He was seven miles farther north in a rocky alcove with just a few of his men. The murder of his father and brothers, and the poisoning of his people in Mexico, left Cochise very wary of peace negotiations and of gifts of food and drink. Any hint of subterfuge or deception drew a violent reaction from him, a wary overreaction at times. He was so certain his enemies would slay him that he would not allow his enemies to take him under any circumstances. This violent response and subsequent unreasonableness took Lieutenant George Bascom by surprise in 1861. The chief was certain that the Americans or Mexicans would slay or sell into slavery anyone taken hostage.

There is little doubt that when Cochise died in 1874, he was living in what today is known as East Stronghold Canyon, which opens onto the Sulphur Springs Valley. Jeffords said that his people buried the chief in the Sulphur Springs Valley. When an Army patrol met Cochise in 1869, Captain Frank W. Perry[9] reported that the Apache came from a stronghold that opened to the west into the San Pedro Valley and the chief came through Middle March Pass to meet them on the eastern side of the Dragoon Mountains.[10] General Howard's aide, Captain Joseph A. Sladen, in 1872 reported going through the Middle March Pass and climbing up the western flank of the Dragoons to a high point with a narrow, rocky entrance, flowing stream, and thirty to forty acres of meadow.[11] This seems to describe a place known today as China Camp or China Meadow. High rocks guard a narrow entrance from which the San Pedro Valley is in plain view from Mexico to north of Tres Alamos. To the east, a short climb leads to the crest of the Dragoons, and the Sulphur Springs Valley is visible as far as Mexico in the south and Mount Graham in the north. The

Army could not approach without Cochise detecting the soldiers. The spot is impregnable. Winston Churchill wrote that if King Arthur wasn't historical, he should have been. If this eyrie wasn't Cochise's stronghold, it should have been.

When Americans first became aware of Cochise, he was living in Goodwin Canyon near Apache Pass, which was between the Chiricahua and Dos Cabezas Mountains. He seems to have been there continuously from 1858, when Butterfield established an Overland Mail stage station in Siphon Canyon, a mile and a half to the south, until February 1861, when Lieutenant George Bascom confronted him.[12] During this "friendly" period, Cochise's women sold firewood and hay to the Overland Mail Company, which made gifts of flour and trade goods to the Apaches. The walls of the station were made of rock ten feet high. Overland Mail station keepers brought livestock inside at night so as not to tempt the Indians. Butterfield armed his station personnel with Sharp's breech-loading rifles, the fastest-loading and most accurate weapons of their day. Attacking a stage would have been a bit like picking on a porcupine. There's nothing there you want to eat and you could get hurt. Only once did Cochise's people attack an Overland Mail stage in Chiricahua territory. It would be 1869 before they did it again.

During this period, as already noted, Arizona had two towns, Tubac and Tucson, both one hundred miles from Apache Pass. People in Arizona knew that Cochise was not friendly. He was prudent. The Americans had two forts, Buchanan and Breckinridge, where there were three companies of infantry, at least two of which had riding mules, and two of dragoon cavalry. It was safer to raid in Sonora and Chihuahua, Mexico, where there were fewer soldiers and the people were not so well armed. This did not keep Cochise's warriors from threatening to kill all the Butterfield personnel in 1859 and again in 1860, nor did it keep Cochise, when times were tough, from raiding the Anglo settlements for livestock. In 1860, Captain Richard Ewell went out to Apache Pass, forcing Cochise to return stolen livestock.

He swore that if he had to do it again, he would strike a blow.[13] Clearly, he was frustrated with Cochise's prevarication and hiding of stolen stock. Of course, Cochise lied to cover thefts. Faced with enemies, he had to defend his people and their much-needed supply of meat. The Apache weren't Plains Indians horse-stealing for glory. Apaches took horses and mules to eat. In 1860, Apaches raided the Overland Mail Stations at Dragoon Springs and Ewell's Station, making off with many mules.[14] While Cochise wasn't directly blamed, these raids were so deep in Chiricahua territory, it is hard to imagine them not having been done by Cochise's people. Cochise had to have been aware of the raids and aware that circumstantial evidence implicated his band.

In 1861, Cochise was drawing annuities from the United States for remaining at peace. That same year the Governor of Sonora offered him a better deal. Cochise had suffered several bad years. Game and vegetable foods were less abundant, making raiding and annuities more important. There were two principal wagon roads, with many subdivisions, across the continent. One ran through South Pass in Wyoming and led to Oregon and California. The other followed Cooke's Wagon Road or the Butterfield Trail. Today we call it the I-10 Corridor. It was an all-weather route that did not close with winter snows. It ran through Chiricahua country for three hundred miles from Mesilla on the Rio Grande to Tucson. The pressure was on. War was coming.

None of this is to imply that Cochise was anything but an exceedingly great chief, perhaps the greatest of all Chiricahua chiefs, and a man of his word. That he kept his word to friends and allies does not say that he didn't raid and steal from enemies and cover his tracks as well. If he made a bargain, he kept it, and what's more, his sons continued to keep his bargains after he was gone. In a society where no one had to listen to him, his people did. There were very few pitched battles in the Apache Wars. The Apaches were raiders, not an army. Cochise was able to mount an army numerous times.

Lieutenant Bascom believed himself surrounded by five hundred Apaches in February 1861. Cochise had called in the Bedonkohe of Mangas Coloradas and Francisco's Coyoteros, White Mountain Apaches. In August 1861, there was an attack on Tubac and on the Arizona Wagon Train at Cooke's Canyon involving large numbers of Apache. In July 1862, more than two hundred Apaches ambushed the lead companies of the California Column in the Battle of Apache Pass. In 1864, at Doubtful Canyon, a large body of Chiricahuas expertly ambushed Company I, 5th California Infantry.[15] Their use of terrain was brilliant. In October 1869, Cochise held off two companies of cavalry at the Battle of Turtle Mountain.[16] Apaches respected him and came when he called. He was a great warrior and a man of wisdom. Some authors have claimed that Cochise undertook eleven years of bloody warfare that cost his people heavily in lives because an arrogant young lieutenant called him a liar.[17] Cochise was not psychotic and did not engage in a lengthy war over a slight.

On March 3, 1861, the Civil War stripped away the Overland Mail. The Great Oxbow Route ran from St. Louis down into Texas across New Mexico and north to San Francisco. Too much of it was under Confederate control and Congress ordered the mail route moved north to the Oregon-California trail, closing the southern, all-weather route that ran through Chiricahua country. The lack of mail made it difficult for merchants and mines to operate in Arizona. Army officers departed to take positions at higher rank in state organizations both Confederate and Union, making it more difficult for the Army to patrol effectively. In July 1861, the Army ordered the four companies assigned to Arizona, two infantry and two of dragoon cavalry, east to the Rio Grande to defend against an invasion from Texas. In August, unprotected and without the Army and mines as consumers for produce and cattle, most of the settlers departed.

On January 27, 1861, Apache raiders stole a herd of cattle from Johnny Ward's ranch on Sonoita Creek, about three miles south of modern Patagonia. The raiders also took the young cowherd, a boy of ten or twelve, Johnny's stepson, Felix Ward. On January 28, Lieutenant George Bascom, Commander Company C, 7th Infantry, Fort Buchanan, was sent to find the trail and on the 29th took the field with fifty-four men of his company. Until 1868, the people of Arizona thought of Bascom as having done well in trying to retrieve the boy. Furthermore, in February 1862, Captain Bascom died a hero at the Battle of Valverde on the Rio Grande, repelling the invading Texans. The army named Fort Bascom in his honor. In 1860, people knew that Cochise was not friendly, that he was a raider. This changed when Captain Reuben Bernard returned to Arizona in 1868.[18]

Bernard had been First Sergeant of Company D, 1st Dragoons, assigned to Fort Breckinridge in 1861, although he was probably not in Arizona in January and February.[19] He was a ruthless self-promoter. In 1868, he found himself nearly the only person still around who had been in Arizona before the war. His commander turned to him for an explanation of the current situation, the Cochise War, and Bernard supplied it with a story that cast him as a hero and Bascom as a stubborn shave-tail ignorant of Apaches. In Bernard's version, Lieutenant Bascom led twelve dragoons of Co. G, 1st Dragoons, to Apache Pass where months after the kidnapping of the boy and, without cause, blamed Cochise for taking him. He tried and failed to take the chief captive but did take three adult males, two of Cochise's sons and his wife hostage. Cochise took James Wallace, an Overland Mail Employee, as his hostage and offered an exchange. Bascom refused because the boy was not part of the exchange. Sergeant Bernard pleaded with him to accept the exchange becoming so belligerent that the lieutenant had him court martialed. Wallace was slain and Bascom, over the sergeant's objection, hanged the three adult males.[20] Thus the story of the wise sergeant and the pig-headed lieutenant who started a war was born. The story presents the preposterous idea that Bascom, commander of an infantry company, was leading a platoon of dragoons from a post ninety miles away. It is well documented that

Bascom led his own company to Apache Pass and that by the time the hostages were hanged, 1st Lieutenant Isaiah Moore, commander of Co. G, 1st Dragoons, Bernard's own commanding officer, was in command and responsible for the hangings.[21] Charles Poston added to the legend in the 1880s. He'd been at Tubac when the events took place. His various versions claim: 1. The boy was taken in October 1860; 2. Johnny Ward, who arrived in Arizona in 1858, was the natural father of Felix Ward, which would have made the boy about eighteen months old in 1860; 3. Johnny Ward was disreputable and beat his son, who ran away to join the Indians; 4. Ward was too drunk to locate his missing stock; and 5. Without rhyme or reason, Bascom blamed Cochise, taken at random in the Whetstone Mountains.[22] Every bit of these stories conflicts with the newspaper accounts of January and February 1861, with the official military reports, and with the accounts of people who were with Lieutenant Bascom when he confronted Cochise.[23]

On January 28, Johnny Ward, returning from business in Sonora, discovered his herd and stepson missing and was told by neighbors that Apaches had taken them. He rushed to Fort Buchanan to inform Lieutenant Colonel Pitcairn Morrison, 7th Infantry, post commander. The colonel sent Bascom out to find the trail. That morning, he could not locate it. In the afternoon, he went out with Lieutenant Richard Lord, 1st Dragoons, on temporary court-martial duty at the fort. Together they found a trail that led east along the Babocomari River pointing toward Apache Pass where Cochise was living.

Experience taught the two lieutenants that Western Apache raiders, Pinals, Aravaipas and Coyoteros, returning from raids on the Santa Cruz River and into Sonora, would return home along Sonoita Creek and then follow Cienaga Creek to Redington Pass and the San Pedro River. Only Chiricahuas would go east. What they failed to recognize was that when, in October 1860, the Army reassigned two companies of dragoons from Fort Buchanan to Fort Breckinridge, at the mouth of Aravaipa Creek, near where the San Pedro emptied into the Gila, everything had changed. Cavalry patrols were interdicting returning raiders on the old routes. Everyone was now going east to the Sulphur Springs Valley and some were continuing on through Apache Pass to the San Simon on a circuitous route home. The evidence that would have indicted the Chiricahua before October 1860 had become equivocal. Bascom set out the next day with what he believed was clear evidence of the guilt of Cochise and his people.

On Sunday, February 3, Lieutenant Bascom arrived at Apache Pass and set up camp in Siphon Canyon, half a mile from the Overland Mail Station. Sergeant Dan Robinson and eleven men, returning from delivering supplies to Fort McLane, near modern Silver City, were already camped near the Apache Spring. Passing through Doubtful Canyon thirty miles east of Apache Pass, an officer, bound for the east from Fort Buchanan, alerted Robinson to possible danger. Cochise's people had behaved in a hostile manner when the officer had ventured through Apache Pass the day before. Lieutenant Bascom had not yet arrived. The addition of Robinson and his men brought Bascom's command to sixty-six men, of whom five were his own non-commissioned officers.[24] He twice sent messengers to nearby Goodwin Canyon asking Cochise to come in for a talk.

Cochise did not arrive until noon the next day. He came with his wife, two boys,[25] and three adult warriors, one of them his brother Coyuntura. They were offered lunch. Bascom, Johnny Ward as interpreter,[26] Cochise, and Coyuntura went into Bascom's tent for lunch. Bascom's sentries patrolled with fixed bayonets on otherwise empty weapons.[27] Bascom explained that he'd come for Felix Ward and Johnny Ward's cattle. Cochise said he didn't have them but thought he knew who did. If given ten days, he could go and get them. The lieutenant said that this was agreeable but that Cochise would have to remain as his guest and hostage against performance.

Enraged, Cochise leapt up and drew his knife, cutting his way out of the tent. Coyuntura tried the same at the rear entrance, but tripped over a guy-wire and was pinned to the ground by a sentry's bayonet.

Cochise fled up Overlook Ridge. Johnny Ward emerged and fired two shots after the fleeing chief.[28] Bascom had the wounded Coyuntura and two warriors as hostages. Cochise's wife and two sons were also guests of the Army.[29] Recognizing that he had a problem, the lieutenant moved his camp to the Overland Mail Station and fortified his position. Grain sacks went up on the walls to form a parapet. The soldiers pulled wagons in front of the gate and dug fighting positions under them. That night the soldiers saw signal fires on the peaks. Cochise was calling for help.

Cochise's response was extreme, as were the actions he took in following days. A reasonable man would have bargained for the release of the hostages despite any insult Bascom had given. His wife, son, nephew, and brother were in Bascom's hands. Those who place blame on Bascom for being unreasonable are hard pressed to explain Cochise's behavior. They rely on invented elements of culture or unwittingly brand Cochise psychotic. Cochise distrusted peace councils. He'd seen his father and brothers killed by Mexicans during such councils. In Chihuahua, officials had poisoned food during peace councils. Mexicans and American renegades had provided them with alcohol and massacred the Apache, as they lay drunk. In 1872, he refused a gift of food for fear it might be poisoned. Cochise was suspicious, with good reason, almost to paranoia. His response to Bascom was extreme but understandable. Bascom's attempt to take the chief hostage was not the wisest move he might have made, but it was at the time a common ploy.

One would suspect that an Apache chief, with his wife and sons, brother, and two warriors held hostage might behave in a reasonable and conciliatory manner. Cochise did not. Ed Sweeney wrote, "Perhaps he had already written them off, believing that his people would be killed regardless of his actions."[30] His father and elder brother had been slain during parley, thus in his experience Apaches in captivity were as good as dead. The chief did not know that in almost all cases the US Army merely restricted the mobility of hostages and seldom harmed them.

The next day, Cochise came in with Francisco, chief of the Coyotero, also known as White Mountain, Apache who lived about five days away, and two others. Lieutenant Bascom went out to meet him under flag of truce with Johnny Ward and sergeants Dan Robinson and William Smith. From this conversation, Sergeant Robinson understood that Bascom's orders were to find Cochise and through him to arrange return of the boy, holding Cochise as a hostage, if necessary.[31]

Robinson looked up to see Charles W. Culver, station keeper, Robert Walsh, hostler, and James F. Wallace, relief driver, all Overland Mail employees, emerge from the station. Two Apache women, possibly Mexican captives, were signaling to them from an arroyo fifty yards south of the station. Bascom ordered them back and they ignored him. Near the arroyo, warriors emerged and tackled Culver and Wallace. Culver broke away and he and Walsh ran for the station. Firing was general from both sides. Walsh ran into a bullet; a stray round wounded Culver. The meeting with Cochise broke up. Cochise violated the conditions of parley as surely as Bascom had the day before.

Some historians have argued that Bascom didn't use the right mix of diplomacy and saber rattling. If only he had done what Captain Richard S. Ewell had done on the several occasions when he had confronted Cochise, all would have been well. He should have known Cochise wasn't a liar. Ewell found the chief concealing stolen livestock and swore that if he had to go out again, he would strike a blow.[32] The difference in this case was that Cochise really didn't have the boy or the livestock, and not the degree of diplomacy employed. As a result of mistreatment of his people in Mexico, Cochise was also responding violently to what he saw as an underhanded violation of the truce of parley.

Cochise knew he didn't have the boy, and at this point he also knew that Francisco didn't have him. He knew that Coyoteros had been coming to Apache Pass with captives and stolen stock. It would have taken him about ten days to go to and return from Francisco's home in the White Mountains. If Francisco didn't have him, Cochise had a problem. This meant that Western Apaches, Pinals, Aravaipas, had the boy and he wasn't on friendly terms with them.

Cochise returned the next day with Wallace offering to trade the Overland employee and fourteen mules taken from Fort Buchanan for Bascom's hostages. Bascom said no, not without the boy. Bascom may have perceived minimum danger to Wallace, who had bragged of his friendly relations with the Chiricahuas. The lieutenant may also have thought that Wallace had put himself in harm's way. What's more, he knew he had no intention of harming his hostages. The Army took many Indian hostages before the Civil War and held them but usually did not harm them. Cochise and Bascom could not come to agreement.

The mail stages were due that night from east and west and Cochise knew the schedule. He laid a trap for the westbound coach at the lower end of the pass. The driver arrived four hours early and, finding the barricade unmanned, went around. Cochise and his warriors were at the other end of the pass attacking a wagon train. They killed six Mexicans, captured two more, and, tying them to wagon wheels, lit the wagons on fire. Cochise took Sam Whitfield, William Sanders, and Frank Brunner as additional hostages. Hostage Wallace prepared a note and the Apache left it in a tree near the station for the soldiers to find. After midnight, on February 7, the eastbound stage came in with nine on board. As it passed the spot where Cochise and his warriors had attacked the wagon train, the Apache opened fire, killing a lead mule and wounding the driver, Moses "King" Lyons. The passengers exited the stage and cut the mule free, and William Buckley, superintendent of the Overland Line from Tucson to Mesilla, drove the stage on to the Apache Pass Station.

On the morning of the 7th, there was snow on the ground. With the arrival of Mangas Coloradas and his warriors, Bascom now considered himself surrounded by five hundred Apaches. He had two wounded men, Culver and Lyons. His first sergeant, James Huber, delayed watering the stock until noon. He then selected fifteen reliable men including Sergeant Robinson. One would stand sentinel on Over-look Ridge. Robinson and four men would be in overwatch, weapons loaded and cocked, at Apache Spring. The others would bring out half of the herd to water. It was a sound plan, but Sergeant Robinson looked up from his position at the spring to see "King" Lyons riding amidst the stock, driving the entire herd before him. It was then that Apaches attacked from the south and Robinson was wounded.

At the station, Lieutenant Bascom saw the main body of Apaches waiting in the arroyo to his front. He believed their intent was to attack him in flank if he emerged from the station to go to the relief of the men at the spring. Lieutenant John Cooke, senior to Bascom, had arrived on the stage the night before. He was on his way east to resign his commission and join the Confederacy. Cooke placed himself under Bascom's command and with ten men went to the relief of the men at the spring. Lyons lost his life. The Army lost forty-two mules and the Overland Mail lost fourteen. That night three messengers left for Tucson and Fort Buchanan.

On the 8th, Company B, 8th Infantry, was marching north of the Dos Cabezas Mountains on its way to the Rio Grande. The unit had built Fort Breckinridge and was now on orders to defend against invaders from Texas. Their commander was unaware of Bascom's plight. His command was visible as a dust cloud from Apache Pass. Cochise, Francisco, and Mangas Coloradas saw the dust and recognized it as a military unit on the move. They suspected the Army was attempting to surround them. They had other problems as well. They had no commissary and had to rely on the food and water their men could carry. Cochise had tried to lure Bascom out and failed. He was not about to conduct a costly frontal assault on the station. This is probably when he killed his four hostages and departed. Neither Bascom nor his men saw the Apache again on subsequent days. They watered their stock in peace, still believing themselves surrounded.

That evening messengers arrived at Fort Buchanan and Assistant Surgeon Bernard John Dowling Irwin volunteered to lead the only twelve men available to Bascom's relief. Colonel Morrison sent word to the dragoons stationed at Fort Breckinridge. Irwin set out the next morning, and February 10, while crossing the Sulphur Springs Valley, he spied Coyotero raiders taking stock north. He ordered a pursuit and after six miles captured three of them and eleven steers. He arrived that night at Apache Pass to treat the wounded. Lieutenants Isaiah Moore and Richard Lord set out that day from Fort Breckinridge with seventy cavalrymen of D and G companies, 1st Dragoons. They arrived on the 14th and, expecting a fight with five hundred Apaches, rested for two days before mounting a reconnaissance-in-force with all of the dragoons and forty of Bascom's infantrymen. For two days they scoured the hills. Disturbing vultures, they discovered the bodies of four dead hostages.

On February 16, the mail stages departed. On the 17th, the Army burned Cochise's abandoned rancheria. At the pass, they stopped near the remains of the wagon train and held a council of officers. Irwin, Moore, and Lord were all senior to Bascom. Moore was in command. Sickened by the sight of the mutilated bodies of Cochise's hostages, Irwin, by his own admission, suggested that they hang the Apache hostages. Bascom objected. Irwin said that he had captured three and he would hang those. Bascom then agreed to hang his three as well. Moore could have stopped this. Instead, his men provided the ropes.

The bodies of the hostages hung there for many months, three Chiricahuas and three Coyoteros. Cochise and his people were at Doubtful Canyon in the Peloncillos, on what would become the New Mexico–Arizona border, and at Cooke's Canyon, northeast of the future Deming, New Mexico. They may not have seen the bodies of their kin or they may not have touched them out of dread of the dead. The Apache fear touching the dead and dispose of them in ways that seem almost disrespectful. Gifts for the dead—a favorite horse or dog, a favored rifle or saddle—are not so much so they'll have them in the afterlife, as a wish not to call back the spirit to his favorite things. For the same reason, the Apache do not speak the names of the dead.[33]

On March 3, 1861, Congress voted to move the mail route out of Confederate Texas and Arkansas. This left Tucson and Tubac without mail service. Mines and merchants, already in difficulty because of how remote their communities were, failed. In July 1861, the Army ordered Forts Buchanan and Breckinridge closed and their soldiers sent to guard against Confederate invasion on the Rio Grande. Within a month the communities that had supported the forts with produce and beef, along with the associated mines, closed up. The Sonoita Creek settlers moved to Tubac, which was soon, in the absence of the Army, attacked by Apaches. The settlers fled to Tucson, watching raiders burn the town behind them. The Arizona Wagon Train carrying many settlers left Tucson for the Rio Grande. At Cooke's Canyon, they were attacked by Cochise and Mangas Coloradas. A few people remained at Tucson and on the Colorado River. Arizona, lacking military protection, was otherwise abandoned.

Historians have made much of Cochise's eleven years of revenge for a lieutenant calling him a liar at Apache Pass in 1861. Cochise was not psychotic. His revenge came in two stages. In the first he killed whites who crossed his path. In the second, he fought to drive whites out of his territory and to keep them from returning. The first stage was over by August 1861, the second by 1869. The lesson he took from Lieutenant Bascom was that Americans calling for peace talks were little more to be trusted than Mexicans.

In April 1861, J. J. Giddings and four companions made a survey of Overland Mail equipment and stations with the intent of reopening the San Antonio and San Diego Mail for the Confederacy. They got as far as Doubtful Canyon before meeting Cochise. Giddings ended his life suspended upside down from a tree with a small fire under his head. A train of two wagons was attacked near Apache Pass. Teamsters Patrick Donaghue, Edward Donnelly, Paige, and O'Brien went missing in two incidents at Doubtful Canyon. Ochoa and Tully's wagons were attacked and so was the party of Grant Oury. In August, Tubac was attacked, though it's not clear that Cochise was involved.

On August 27, seven young men, many of them former Overland Mail employees escaping advancing Texans, stole a stage coach and headed west for California. They made it as far as Cooke's Canyon, where they were attacked by Cochise and Mangas Coloradas. The siege is said to have lasted three days and cost many Apache lives. All seven young men died.

In September 1861, Cochise and Mangas Coloradas attacked the Arizona Wagon Train at Cooke's Canyon. The Apache killed the people on the lead wagon. In the narrow canyon, the other wagons could neither turn nor bypass the leaders. Rather than slay them all, Cochise went after their livestock. The first stage of his revenge was over. Pinos Altos was attacked on September 27, 1861. The story is full of heroism and daring. Six women at Roy Bean's[34] store hauled out a small howitzer, loaded it with nails and buckshot, and fired it at the Indians. Many witnesses agreed that the blasts of the howitzer saved the day.[35] After that, a rally by the miners drove the Indians out of town. Cochise intended to drive out the Americans, who were no longer protected by the Army. He had progressed beyond exacting revenge and had stepped beyond raiding. He mustered large numbers of Apaches to attack the towns.

In February 1862, Captain Sherod Hunter, Company A, Arizona Rangers, CSA, took possession of Tucson for the Confederacy. On May 14, 1862, Hunter abandoned Tucson before the advancing California Column led by Colonel James H. Carleton. On May 5, Cochise awaited Hunter's stock drovers with 100 men in ambush near Dragoon Springs. As the party entered the narrow box canyon south of the abandoned Overland Mail Station to water their stock, Cochise sprang the trap. Accounts say four rangers died including Sergeant Sam Ford, Private Ricardo, and possibly two other privates, whose names are lost to history. The other rangers escaped, leaving behind twenty-five horses and thirty mules.[36]

On June 17, 1862, Colonel James H. Carleton ordered Major Edward E. Eyre, First Cavalry California Volunteers, to patrol the road between Tucson and Mesilla. With him Eyre had 140 men of Companies B and C. On June 25, they left Ewell's Station and arrived at Apache Pass. There Cochise met him with seventy-five warriors. Cochise came in to parley. Eyre insisted that he was a friend of the Apaches and only wanted to pass. He handed out tobacco and pemmican, which the Indians accepted. Eyre told them that a larger group of soldiers was coming commanded by a "great captain" (Carleton) who wished to make peace with the Apache and give them presents. According to Eyre, Cochise assured him that he would molest neither Eyre's men nor their animals. This agreement is known as the Pemmican Treaty.[37] It is possible that Tom Jeffords was a participant in this parley and this may have been his first meeting with Cochise. Jeffords tells us that he returned to the Rio Grande with the lead companies of the California Column. Captain Thomas Roberts and the lead companies of the California Column fought Cochise on July 15, in the Battle of Apache Pass. Major Eyre's companies were ahead of Roberts, and Jeffords doesn't mention the battle, which holds a special place in Chiricahua folklore.

Ewell's Station had a cistern that station keepers filled from a spring five miles to the north. The Overland Mail abandoned the station in 1861 and no one was filling the cistern. This meant that for CPT Thomas Roberts and the 126 men, twenty-two wagons, and two howitzers under his command, the last water before Apache Pass was at Dragoon Springs, forty miles behind them. They left Tucson on July 10, and on July 15, in temperatures over 110 degrees, arrived at Apache Pass. As they approached Apache Spring, the Chiricahuas ambushed the rear of the command and succeeded in temporarily capturing the howitzers. The infantry under Captain Roberts regrouped and attacked the Apaches. As Roberts approached the spring with twenty men, Cochise met the command with devastating fire from prepared positions among the rocks above. Captain Roberts brought up the howitzers and opened fire with explosive shells. Turning stone into shrapnel, the guns had a devastating effect on the Apache. Roberts realized the key to victory was seizing the high hill on his left. First Sergeant Albert Fountain with twenty men ascended the ridge. He ordered a bayonet charge and drove off the Chiricahua. The engagement lasted more than four hours before the thirsty men finally took the spring. Cochise said that he would have defeated Roberts if not for the "guns that banged twice." The ridge became the site of the first Fort Bowie, there to control the spring and patrol the pass.

In 1863, Congress divided Arizona from New Mexico along the 110th parallel and made the new mining town, Prescott, in central Arizona, its capital. Mountains stood between the town and Santa Fe. Communications ran through Ehrenberg on the Colorado River. Prescott linked Tucson to the outside world. During the Civil War, southern Arizona was dotted with new military posts—Camp Mason, Camp Wallen, Fort Bowie, and a post on the remains of Fort Breckinridge. There were very few civilians. The Army conducted operations against the Apache.

On May 3, 1864, Chiricahua Apaches[38] ambushed Company I, Fifth California Infantry, as they entered the descent into Doubtful Canyon from the east heading west toward Fort Bowie. Private Henry Dosher went missing, and was presumed dead, while in the initial moments the Apache wounded Sergeant Charles Tobias and Privates Chandler Abbott, Nelson Stone, and James R. Webb. Post returns for Fort Bowie claimed ten Apaches killed.[39] Survivors' accounts don't reflect a count of Apache dead, and it seems doubtful any were killed.[40] The site was wonderfully suited to an ambush. The road descends steeply to the canyon bottom. A ridge across the canyon, barely one hundred yards away, provided cover and concealment as well as a covered escape route. On the near side, there was a similar ridge. The company would have found it difficult to back out of the kill zone. Only the bravery of one officer saved the men. He calmly organized them to return disciplined fire against which the Apache could not stand. Although some men thought the fight had gone on for hours, the confrontation was over in minutes and the Apache disappeared into the mountains. This stands out as one of the last times Chiricahua Apaches deliberately engaged a large military force.

Even in guerrilla warfare, ultimately the guerrilla must engage and destroy the enemy military. Before 1861, Cochise raided for food and supplies, treating Mexicans, Native American farmers, and Americans as herds to be tended and from which to take sustenance. For a few months in that year, he sought revenge and murdered lone travelers. Throughout the Civil War, he fought to drive out the Americans and keep them from returning. After the war, he would return to smaller-scale raiding and murder but would never again deliberately seek large-scale engagements with the military. By 1869, he was looking for a peace agreement on terms that suited himself and his people. He created enough nuisance that he was eventually granted those terms.

CHAPTER 5

The Civil War

TOM STOPPED HIS HORSE BEFORE HE REACHED THE CREST OF THE hill. If he stretched, he could just see to the country beyond. He scanned it carefully, looking for signs of dust and smoke, anything that would reveal a human presence. The horse on the lead rope behind him nickered. A lone traveler with two horses might seem an opportunity to Apaches. This was the heart of Apache country. Behind him were the Gila Apache, around him the Coyoteros and ahead the Pinaleños. An armed company might be proof against them, a small party a sure target. One lone rider might make it, if he went unnoticed. That meant no campfires. He dared not raise any dust or expose himself on a ridgeline.

When he finally reached the end of the mountains, he would be fairly safe if the desert didn't kill his horses. There were Pima and Maricopa Indians who were friendly and who fed travelers. There would be grain for his livestock. Beyond them were Yavapais and Mojaves who might yet take his scalp. It was a long, dangerous ride at a dry time of the year growing hot. His horses had last year's grass to feed on but light winter rains had only brought a meager spring greenup.

The six hundred miles from Rio Grande to Rio Colorado were a long ride. His horses could feed and rest at night, but there wasn't much to feed on, not enough to keep a horse going for six hundred miles. He'd brought a second horse to carry a pack. In the pack he'd placed grain and feedbags. That would help. He hoped it would be enough. He'd been this way once before in 1860 with a party of men headed to the new diggings at Gila City, a gold rush. They'd followed Kearney's Route as he did now. The road ran through the mountains and along the Gila River. The trail had killed Kearney's horses in 1847. The Butterfield Overland Mail Road lay to the south. It was a good road without mountains and ran from waterhole to waterhole. Tucson lay on that route. Tucson was the only town left in what folks were beginning to call Arizona. After an Apache attack, the people departed and Mexican raiders burned Tubac. American prospectors abandoned Gila City. Confederates occupied Tucson, and, carrying dispatches between Union commanders, he couldn't go that way.

Tom Jeffords was a civilian, hired by Colonel Edward Canby, the Union commander at Fort Craig, New Mexico. The colonel had fought a great battle at Valverde south of Socorro in February 1862. They said he'd lost, since the Confederates bypassed him and headed north to Santa Fe. But the Rebels hadn't captured Fort Craig's supplies, and Colonel Canby and his subordinate, Colonel Kit Carson, sat astride their lines of communication. Tom Jeffords had seen the terrible condition of the invading army at Valverde. Colonel Canby saw it, too. The long trail had worn out the Confederates and they were in desperate need of supplies. Most of their horses and mules were gone and they'd had to burn many of their supply wagons. Nonetheless, on February 28, 1862, a reinforced company under Captain Sherod Hunter had taken Tucson. An envoy travelled with Hunter and was trying to bring Mexico into the fight on the side of the Confederacy. Colonel James Carleton was coming from California with a Union brigade called the California Column. Canby needed word of their plans, and Carleton needed to know the situation in New Mexico. After years of prospecting, Tom Jeffords knew the way.

Having received Canby's message, Colonel James Carleton found himself with a problem. He needed to get a message back to the Union forces on the Rio Grande. His messengers repeatedly failed to reach the beleaguered Union forces. They travelled the Butterfield Road through the heart of Chiricahua country, because by May 1862, it was free of Captain Sherod Hunter's Confederates. From Tucson, Carleton tried again. He was still in ignorance of the strength of the enemy before him. His messengers left Tucson on June 15, 1862, and three days later at Apache Pass, Chiricahua warriors discovered them and attacked at full gallop. The Indians killed the guide, Chavez, and Sergeant Wheeling, but Jones, mounted on a swift, sure-footed horse, was able to outride his pursuers. He reached the Rio Grande safely. The message he carried was heartening: "The Column from California is really coming."[1]

In the 1880s, Tom Jeffords wrote that in 1862 he returned to New Mexico and the Rio Grande with the lead companies of the California Column.[2] Since he didn't mention the Battle of Apache Pass in July 1862, usually thought of as involving the lead companies, it seems likely he was with Major Edward Eyre, who passed that way in June and met with Cochise, providing the chief with the information he needed to prepare the ambush that started the July battle. Major Eyre commanded a lead reconnaissance force. Before becoming Canby's long-range courier and returning with the California Column, Tom "saw the elephant" at Valverde, that is to say, he was a participant, if only as a civilian, in a major battle.

General Henry Hopkins Sibley, who had served with the 2nd Dragoons in New Mexico, envisioned the only strategic plan the South ever had to win the Civil War. He would take two regiments of Texas mounted militia and move on New Mexico, relieving Union forts of their supplies along the way. At Franklin (now called El Paso), he would get supplies from Southern-sympathizing merchants bringing them in from Mexico. New Mexicans would rise and join the cause because they disliked the Union. He'd capture more supplies and weapons at Fort Craig and Fort Union. In Colorado, he thought, numerous Southern sympathizers would join the cause. He'd then move west to Utah where the Mormons had only recently finished their war with the Union. They, too, would join the Confederacy, bringing in Nevada and its mines, then part of the Kingdom of Deseret, as Utah was known. From there he would move on lower California, where there were many Southern sympathizers. The Confederacy would be a transcontinental power with ports the Union could not blockade and rich sources of specie to support the war effort. The Confederacy would be unbeatable.

The Texas militia existed only on paper. The government of Texas had already used the presumed store of weapons, equipment, and horses elsewhere. Sibley spent months recruiting and training his force. In the end, some of his units were equipped with lances, not guns. Sibley should have moved in the wet summer when grass was high and waterholes full. It was winter before Sibley was ready to take the trail for New Mexico with two regiments. General Davey Twiggs surrendered the Union forts and they had been stripped of supplies. The merchants failed to come through with supplies. In August 1862, Lieutenant Colonel John Baylor took Mesilla, New Mexico, alerting the Union to the danger to their southwestern flank. Before long, he had also offended almost everyone, Mexican, Indian, and Anglo. The march across dry, winter Texas killed horses. The Apache stole many mounts from Sibley's command. When it arrived in Franklin, Sibley's force was in bad shape and had to recruit (that is, rest and let its horses feed on grass) and reorganize, turning mounted soldiers into infantry. New Mexico did not rise against the Union. General Sibley failed to realize that as much resentment as New Mexicans felt against the Union, they hated Texans far worse. On February 21, 1862, Sibley took the ground at Valverde, but failed to take the supplies at Fort Craig. After losing many mules, Sibley could no longer provide stock for his supply train. He burned many supply wagons. At Glorieta Pass, March 28, 1862, near Santa Fe, a force from Colorado turned the Texans back and they limped back home as beggars.

The Battle of Valverde began on February 17, 1862, with a reconnaissance in force against Fort Craig to test Union resolve. Sibley had marched his force over the one-hundred-mile Jornada del Muerte, crossing the desert away from the Rio Grande, avoiding deep ravines. He now crossed a river frigid with melting winter snow and faced the fort on the west bank looking down the barrels of "Quaker guns," logs painted to look like cannon. A Union force made up mostly of volunteers and militia met him and Sibley turned back, going south to cross to the east bank in an attempt to bypass Fort Craig.

The battlefield was extended, involving both banks of the Rio Grande and running from the crossing at Fra Cristobal miles south of Fort Craig on the west bank, through the east bank trails that ran over Mesa de Contadero in ravines deep with sand, to the three crossings at Valverde miles north of the fort. Colonel Canby had men in the fort, south of the fort, across the river on ridges above the ravines, and finally on both sides of the river at Valverde. He needed information to tie his battle together. He needed scouts to tell about the enemy's intentions. His force was split, defending in three directions, attempting to detect the main attack. Men like Tom Jeffords rode hard, under fire, carrying messages, orders, and combat information. In great danger, they made it possible for Colonel Canby to control his battle. Tom never spoke much about the battle, perhaps repulsed by the bloodshed, or perhaps he was embarrassed that he hadn't stood in the line under fire, but instead carried messages at higher pay than most soldiers. Nonetheless, his role was essential, even crucial, to the affray.

On February 20, detecting Confederate movement across the river south of Mesa de Contadero, Colonel Canby sent elements of two mounted regiments to face them. Both sides fought an uphill struggle through deep sand, facing each other across deep ravines with little effect. In the evening, Captain Paddy Graydon of Canby's Spies and Guides company crossed the river with two aging mules loaded down with explosives. He led them to the Confederate wagon park where the Confederate mules, unable to get to water for more than a day, bawled their thirst loudly. Paddy lit the fuses and smacked the mules' rumps to send them to the wagon park. But the mules had other ideas and chased him to the river, where, after he plunged in, they exploded. The explosion drove the remaining Confederate mules to break loose of their picket lines and head to the river seeking to slake their thirst. There, 150 of them deserted to the Union, leaving Sibley destitute of stock to haul his wagons, many of which had to be burned along with the precious supplies they carried.

Early on February 21, Confederate elements began crossing Mesa de Contadero through deep sand that delayed their cannon and reinforcements. They found themselves in an abandoned river-bed that formed a trench along the east side of the valley. Between them and the river crossings was a forest of cottonwood and the river. The cottonwood bosque was full of fallen and rotten, moss-covered tree trunks that made it difficult for cavalry to maneuver and which offered cover and concealment to Union forces. Meanwhile, south of the mesa, Sibley made a feint toward Fort Craig. Canby was left to wonder where the main attack would fall.

A Confederate battalion reached the upper ford at Valverde but found it guarded by a screen of Union cavalry and turned back. By 8:00 a.m., Union cavalry was crossing the lower ford in strength to take positions in the cottonwood bosque. Bolstered by the arrival of a cannon, the Confederates, in about equal strength, attacked and were driven back. As Confederate strength increased at Valverde, Canby continued to hold most of his force near Fort Craig.

At noon, the Union commander, Colonel Canby, finally recalled the force he had extended toward the Confederate camps back from the east side of the river south of the mesa. The main battle was developing miles away north and east of the river. By 12:30, a small Union force was contending with Confederates for the middle ford at Valverde. The Texans, growing in strength, were forging farther north around the Union's left flank. By midafternoon, Colonel Kit Carson was moving his New Mexico volunteers across the river at the middle ford. He would move to the Union right in an attempt to take the Confederate left flank and roll up their lines. Two more union regiments anchored the line right and left while Captain Alexander McRae's artillery battery stood to the Union center. The movement of Union troops to the south left the battery exposed. The Confederates attacked in some of the fiercest fighting of the day. Finally, McRae, fearing his battery lost, stood atop a limber, and fired his pistol into the ammunition. Explosion swept away the battery, attackers, and the few remaining defenders. The Confederates failed to take the battery but the Union lost its chance to roll up the enemy's flank. In the late afternoon, the Confederates descended on the upper forward, destroying Captain Theodore Dodd's company of Colorado volunteers.

At an unsustainable loss in manpower and supplies, Colonel Sibley had bypassed Fort Craig and the Union Army so that he could go on and take Santa Fe. Soon after, on March 27 to 29, 1862, at Glorieta Pass his forces met Colonel John Slough and the Colorado volunteers, who made a swift forced march to meet the Texans who had slain Dodd's company.[3] Colonel Sibley's force made its way back to Texas. The fighting between Union and Confederate in New Mexico was largely finished.

Promoted to brigadier general on March 31, 1862, Edward Canby departed for the east, taking with him most of the US Army regulars. In late summer 1862, General James Carleton arrived with the California Column. The Confederates would never again be a threat to New Mexico. Carleton was left with regiments of New Mexico and California volunteers both mounted and infantry. There were now more soldiers in New Mexico and fewer civilians than ever before. Carleton, a consummate Indian fighter who had ridden into battle with Kit Carson before the war, needed to keep his men occupied. New Mexico entered a period of the greatest military activity it had ever known.

On March 16, 1861, Arizona seceded from the Union as a Confederate territory. In July, Lieutenant Colonel John Baylor occupied Mesilla and declared himself governor. Confederate Arizona was New Mexico south of an east-west line drawn below Socorro. Control of

Mesilla gave Baylor control of Tubac and Tucson, the southern third of New Mexico. On February 24, 1863, the Federal government formally separated Arizona from New Mexico Territory along a north-south axis, the 110th line of longitude. The capital was Prescott in a newly opened mining district in central Arizona. Carleton was military commander of both territories. Given that Navajo, Chiricahua, and Coyotero Apache and the Utes lived and raided in both territories, this gave him the advantage of unified command. Carleton elected to use his military might to subdue the Indians.

In 1866, when many volunteer men were still bound by their enlistments, as the Civil War Army was still in existence, Tom Jeffords bought a house in Santa Fe. From 1862 to 1866, Tom was a scout for the army. Which campaign he participated in is not clear.[4] He might have been anywhere from Santa Fe to Tucson and might have fought in the Navajo campaigns, at Adobe Walls, against the Mescalero or Chiricahua and Western Apache.

Under General Carleton's command, officers reported killing hundreds of hostile Indians in Arizona, far more than at any other period in history. The Californians lost forty officers and men in battles. Carleton's men were better armed than the natives, and he placed his trust in "the gallantry of small parties against any number of Apache."[5] Typical of these small actions was an event in March 1864. Chiricahua raiders at Cow Springs, New Mexico, near the Arizona border, made off with a herd of government mules. Captain James H. Whitlock with Company F, 5th California Infantry, and a detachment of cavalry, pursued them. He held his men back until the raiders had a good lead. This proved, as he thought, to make them careless. They stopped masking their trail and headed directly for a large village in the Sierra Bonita Mountains, thirty-five miles northwest of Fort Bowie. Trailing and attacking in moonlight, Whitlock struck at daybreak on April 7, killing twenty-one warriors and recapturing the stock.[6]

In 1871, civilian raiders rocked the nation with the murder of sixty Apaches under the protection of the military at Old Camp Grant near the mouth of Aravaipa Creek and the San Pedro River. Some of the leaders of that shameful raid learned their craft riding with Captain T. T. Tidball in May 1864. Tidball's command consisted of men of Companies I and K, 5th California Infantry, ten Americans, thirty-two Mexicans, twenty Papagos from San Xavier, and nine Apaches Mansos also from San Xavier. They set out from Tucson to chastise the Apaches, marching at night, in silence, without fire for five days. Tidball completely surprised an Aravaipa Apache village and killed at least fifty natives, wounding many more. Tidball lost only one man. The 1871 raiders used the same route and techniques, achieving a similar degree of surprise and success. The people Tidball attacked were at war with the US. Those the Tucson raider hit were under protection.[7]

The Chiricahua could be equally cruel, and there were sadists among them that found their moment to come to the fore and wreak havoc on their enemies. These occurrences were more rare than Hollywood depicts. Apache abhorrence for dead bodies made scalp-taking rare and would also lead them to leave bodies, even of their own, unburied. The work of coyotes and scavengers may have accounted for many accounts of signs of torture. In June 1865, Captain Martin H. Calderwood observed firsthand the work of an Apache torturer.

> *Here I beheld one of the most sickening and cruel sights I ever witnessed during the whole of my campaign against the Apaches. The Indians had stripped naked the four women they had captured and after disemboweling them while still alive, had on the first sight of our approach lanced them through the heart. One of the lance heads had been pulled from its shaft and still remained in the woman's body.*[8]

Tom Jeffords is likely to have observed similar grisly corpses. It is a credit to him that this did not lead him to hate and fear all Apaches. By this time, he was in his mid-thirties, a mature man. As a lake captain, he'd learned calm and even-handedness in handling men. That requires a man to be able to see the situation from the other's point of view. It was raid and counter-raid. Both sides were killing women and children, though not usually as their primary targets. They were collateral damage in a war fought in village, farm, and ranch.

The war had its odd twists and turns. The volunteer forces promoted men to positions as officers who did not arise of the genteel circumstances of the officers of the antebellum. Paddy Graydon had been a soldier in the 1st Dragoons and took his discharge at Fort Buchanan to run the Boundary Hotel, providing everything a soldier wanted but couldn't find at the sutler's store, the precursor to the post exchange. When war came, the army offered Paddy a commission in the New Mexico Volunteers and the captaincy of the Spies and Guides Company, a semi-independent scouting organization. His men apparently idolized him, but his methods had little to do with the book.

In October 1862, while operating against Mescalero Apaches out of Fort Stanton near the Guadalupe Mountains, Graydon encountered the powerful chief, Manuelito, and some of his warriors. The chief asked for presents and Graydon supplied them on the understanding that Manuelito was headed for Santa Fe to parley for peace. With two men, seeming deserters, missing, Captain Graydon ran into Major Arthur Morrison who told him that he, Morrison, was under orders to "respect no Indians whatsoever . . . and that he would shoot the first Indians he saw." Morrison had not seen Graydon's missing men, and Paddy concluded the Mescalero had probably slain them. The captain again encountered Manuelito, along with Jose Pino and thirty-one warriors, who demanded whiskey and drew a weapon. Graydon and his men killed eleven. Major Morrison visited the site of battle some hours later and concluded that Graydon had gotten the Indians drunk and then slain them. The story of the Gallinas Massacre spread. Graydon distributed horses taken from the Mescalero to his men. Morrison complained that the horses were spoils of war that belonged to the Army.

On November 5, 1862, back at Fort Stanton, Dr. John Marmaduke Whitlock took Morrison's side, calling Paddy a "murderer and a thief." Colonel Kit Carson separated the pair once, but drawing weapons, they fired on and wounded each other. Paddy's men shot Whitlock to pieces. Within days, Paddy expired of his wounds.[9] As effective as it was against Indians, it was an army of lower discipline and standards of behavior than the regulars.

Nonetheless, this was the army that subdued the Navajo, who had been the scourge of New Mexico throughout the first half of the nineteenth century. The Spanish and then Mexican militia and regulars had made expeditions without any great success, as had the US Army in 1846 and in the 1850s. In 1864, Colonel Kit Carson campaigned against the Navajo and brought them to their first reservation, Bosque Redondo, on the plains east of the mountains. Carson did not choose the Bosque. That was General James Carleton, who wrongly thought the spot an agricultural paradise. It wasn't. Crops would not grow. He also stocked the reservation, at close quarters, with Indians of tribes hostile to one another. Colonel Carson pleaded with him to be allowed to go home on leave to tend to injuries. He begged for food to feed the Navajo and was refused. He told Carleton that any attempt to move the people in the winter of 1864–65 without wagons and food would result in many deaths. Carleton finally granted him leave. Later Carson was the commander at the Bosque. Although he tried to prevent much of the cruelty, his name is well known and he is remembered as the villain.[10]

Tom Jeffords emerged from the war well known as well, and respected as a scout and Indian fighter. He would continue, off and on, in this role when asked and when he needed money. The pay for a scout was quite high compared to soldiers' wages.

CHAPTER 6

Post-War Adventures

RELIABLE MAIL IS THE LIFEBLOOD OF COMMERCE. WITHOUT IT COM-
merce dies. It's not about keeping in touch with Aunt Tilly and a
sweetheart. Merchants use it to order and pay for merchandise. Mine
owners must have the mail to order and purchase equipment and to
communicate with investors to raise money to expand operations. Its
importance to the growth of a region cannot be understated. It goes
hand in hand with military protection and reliable freight service.
Of the three, it is the most important, even though the military also
contributes to growth by purchasing meat and produce, encouraging
farms and ranches. Tucson and Baja (southern) Arizona languished
from 1861 to 1867 for want of mail service.

On March 3, 1861, Congress elected to move the transcontinental Overland Mail service from the southern, all-weather route to
the Oregon-California Trail. The great Oxbow Route ran from St.
Louis to San Francisco by way of Arkansas and Texas, states that had
joined the Confederacy. The mail was at risk, not from Apaches, but
from Rebels. The war cut off Baja Arizona, and the territory remained
without mail service until June 1862, when the California Column
recaptured Tucson from Captain Sherod Hunter. At that point, the
mail was in the hands of military express riders coming over the desert
along the Gila River from Fort Yuma in California. Civilian mail was
an afterthought at best. The civilian population fell.

On the Oregon-California Trail, the first transcontinental telegraph was completed in 1861, connecting the eastern states to California by way of Omaha, Salt Lake City, and Carson. The Pony Express went out of business, no longer needed. This new form of communication had problems, to be sure, but it was fast and only cost one dollar per word, a bit higher than the thirty cents a word specified by Congress in the Telegraph Act of 1860. Bad weather affected the uninsulated wire when lightning took down sections. Buffalo rubbing on the poles also caused breaks in service. The Union rerouted lines in Missouri north to Chicago as Confederates sought to interrupt the line. Eventually, Native Americans would do the same, cutting the line and mending it with rawhide to make the break difficult to spot. None of this affected Tucson and Baja Arizona, which were left isolated.

Between 1863 and 1869, the United States completed its first transcontinental railroad following the Platte River Route and California Trail. Arizona did not have a railroad until 1882 and the isolation continued. Lieutenant John Bourke, who soon after became General George Crook's aide-de-camp, described backwater Tucson in 1869:

The "Shoo Fly" restaurant, which offered the comforts of a home to the weary wayfarer in Tucson, Arizona, circa 1869, was named on the principle of "lucus a non lucendo"—the flies wouldn't shoo worth a cent. Like the poor, they remained always with us. But though they might bedim the legend, "All meals payable in advance," they could not destroy the spirit of the legend, which was the principle upon which our most charming of landladies, Mrs. Wallen, did business.[1]

He went on to explain that:

[A]lways easy to procure, but there was no lack of bacon, chicken, mutton, and kid meat. Potatoes ranked as luxuries of the first class, and never sold for less than ten cents a pound, and often could not

be had for love or money. The soil of Arizona south of the Gila did not seem to suit their growth, but now that the Apaches have for nearly twenty years been docile in northern Arizona, and left its people free from terror and anxiety, they have succeeded in raising the finest "Murphies" in the world in the damp lava soil of the swales upon the summit of the great Mogollon Plateau.

There was plenty of "jerked" beef, savory and palatable enough in stews and hashes; eggs, and the sweet, toothsome black "frijoles" of Mexico; tomatoes equal to those of any part of our country, and lettuce always crisp, dainty, and delicious. For fresh fruit, our main reliance was upon the "burro" trains coming up from the charming oasis of Hermosillo, the capital of Sonora—a veritable garden of the Hesperides, in which Nature was most lavish with her gifts of homeny-juiced oranges, sweet limes, lemons, edible quinces, and luscious apricots; but the apple, the plum, and the cherry were unknown to us, and the strawberry only occasionally seen.[2]

In 1862–63, mountain man Joseph Walker led a gold-hunting party of thirty-four men into the mountains of central Arizona. William Bradshaw and his party entered the area of the Bradshaw Mountains about the same time. On February 24, 1863, Congress made Arizona a territory and President Abraham Lincoln appointed John A. Gurley as governor. Gurley died before taking office and his replacement, John N. Goodwin, selected the site for the territorial capital. On July 4, 1864, he founded Prescott near newly opened Fort Whipple on Granite Creek. The gold strike drew attention away from Tucson and Baja Arizona. Prescott remained the capital until November 1, 1867, when Tucson took over that role.[3]

From 1864 to 1867, the military escorted mail from Mesilla, New Mexico, on the Rio Grande, to Tucson twice monthly. The *Arizona Miner*, a Prescott newspaper, said that it was "notorious that the military express has never been molested." There were a few half-hearted attempts to start up a mail service but they were expensive, infrequent, and short-lived. Mail came from Albuquerque to Fort Whipple and on to Tucson.[4] In 1865, Sanford Poston, brother of Charles, father of Arizona, won the bid for a postal route from Albuquerque to Prescott to San Bernardino and from Prescott to Tucson and Tubac. Otherwise, mail came around the Horn or across the Isthmus of Panama to San Francisco where it was shipped by steamer to the Sea of Cortez and the mouth of the Colorado. From there it went upriver by paddle-wheel boat to Ehrenberg and across the desert to Prescott and on to Tucson. Mail was slow and irregular.

On March 16, 1867, the Post Office Department appointed Benjamin C. Truman to solve the Tucson–Mesilla debacle. Sanderson, Barlow and Co. accepted the contract and subcontracted to Tomlinson & Co. Soon express riders rode twice per week and service was reliable. A stagecoach, actually a two-horse buggy or buckboard, made the trip once per week. In mid-November, Apaches killed mail rider John Slater near Camp Bowie at Apache Pass. The company offered riders $150 to take the risk.[5] In April 1869, the Apache again attacked a mail rider:

> *A portion of the Eastern mail was brought in on Wednesday morning torn into fragments. The express rider was attacked by a party of Indians near San Pedro Crossing, who fired upon him, killing his mule; fortunately for him the attack was made in the neighborhood of the San Pedro ranches where he arrived in safety—having left everything behind—even his boots, which he doffed, that his flight might be unincumbered [sic]. Messrs. Reed and Anderson, coming over the road shortly afterwards, discovered the mail matter torn into fragments and scattered over the ground. They brought along with them to Tucson, such of it as they could conveniently collect—some two or three pounds.[6]*

Attacks were infrequent but never failed to create a stir. Shaw and Cook took over the contract from Sanderson and Barlow. In May

1868, Apache ambushed the eastbound mail coach driven by John Brownley and Charles "Tennessee" Hadsell, escorted by two soldiers, twelve miles east of Camp Bowie.[7] The job wasn't as dangerous as it must have seemed. A man rode alone through Apache country with little means of defending himself or drove a slow-moving stage with few to escort him. It required a brave man, even though the route was not as dangerous as legend had it. One or two riders killed and a stage lost was not twenty mail riders slain, but every rider knew he might be next.

In 1868, George W. Cook and John M. Shaw of Socorro, New Mexico, opened the Southern Overland US Mail and Express Line with passenger service between Santa Fe and El Paso and Mesilla and Tucson. Tom Jeffords was the supervisor of the line from Socorro to Tucson.[8] He stayed until March of 1869.[9]

Legend says that Tom lost twenty mail riders in this time and had trouble finding replacements. That would have made mail service highly irregular, which it was not. Attacks on mail riders were well reported in the newspapers when they occurred a few times per year. Jeffords is said to have learned the Apache language and then ridden into Cochise's stronghold to make a separate peace for the mail. This account comes from the movie *Broken Arrow* and from Elliott Arnold's novel, *Blood Brother*, on which it was based. Robert Forbes, who had dinner with Jeffords shortly before his death in 1914, further confused the story. By the 1960s, Forbes was referring to himself as Jeffords's friend. They had one meeting over dinner.

In the middle of dinner, Tom Jeffords excused himself and did not return. Forbes got much wrong. Jeffords may have driven a stage on the Butterfield Road, but not for Butterfield and not in the early 1860s. There is no record of him losing many riders nor is there a record that rider deaths decreased during his time as superintendent. They actually may have increased. Cochise understood the role of the mails and would have had no reason to decrease his attacks. Tom Jeffords may have been "yarning." He often did. Or, more likely, he grew tired of Forbes's colored preconceptions and departed when he could stand it no longer.

Accounts from late 1860s are incomplete. Tucson was a small, struggling town and there were few others in Arizona. The accounts available show one mail rider killed and two pursued by Apaches. In 1869, Cochise and his warriors attacked a mail wagon and killed its passengers, but this was after Jeffords's tenure as superintendent. There was uproar in the newspapers. The Army pursued Cochise for over a month and brought on a battle he did not want. In 1872, the chief allowed that attacking the mail wasn't worth the response. Various sources have quoted Jeffords as saying that he lost twenty, twenty-one, or twenty-two men. Cochise probably slew twenty-two Americans during Jeffords's tenure, but they weren't all mail riders. The government would never have continued the mail contract if there had been so many losses.

All of this makes it highly unlikely that Jeffords rode alone into Cochise's Stronghold to bargain for peace for the mail. The 1869 raid on the mail alone should tell us that. Nonetheless, Forbes wrote that:

> The situation became so bad that he determined upon a most dangerous contact with Cochise to make arrangements for the passage of his riders with mail through Indian territory. Alone, he rode into Cochise's camp in the Dragoon Mountain Stronghold and, dismounting and laying aside his weapons, made his way to Cochise's wickiup where the astonished chief asked him if he expected to return. Jeffords, speaking the language, stated that he came to talk with a brave and honorable man about his riders passing through Apache territory.[10]

Descriptions suggest that Cochise's stronghold was not the Stronghold Canyon that we know today but a far more forbidding eyrie called China Camp or China Meadow. High up the side of the Dragoon Mountains, behind the Sheephead formation, two stony pillars guard the entrance to a spring-fed meadow of thirty or forty acres. From between the pillars all of the San Pedro Valley from San Jose Peak in Sonora to beyond Tres Alamos in the north is visible. Half a mile to the east, the Sulphur Springs Valley is visible from the crest of the mountains. Cochise would have had perfect intelligence for everything happening in both valleys and thus control of southeast Arizona.[11] Tom Jeffords probably did not visit this place until he arrived with Lieutenant Joseph Alton Sladen and General Oliver Otis Howard in 1872.

In those days the US Post Office Department contracted with a variety of carriers to carry and deliver the mail along their assigned routes. They in turn subcontracted. The Post Office paid for these services and soon abrogated the contracts of those who couldn't maintain a regular service. The carrier had to succeed in regularly delivering the mail. Service often began with express or pony riders. This was not the famed Pony Express that operated on the Oregon-California Trail before the Civil War, though it was something similar and local lore often calls this service the pony express.

These companies seldom owned much in the way of equipment, facilities, or livestock. This was not the powerful and highly capitalized Southern Overland Mail, sometimes called the Butterfield Overland Mail. Butterfield built roads and stations, and he provided the stations with equipment for shoeing mules and repairing coaches. The Overland Mail owned coaches and mules and provided its men with the most modern weapons, Sharp's carbines. The Overland Mail carried letters along the entire route from St. Louis to San Francisco. The post-war companies had much shorter routes, filling in gaps. They owned little.

The company would contract with a station, which was no more than a ranch that was able to keep on hand a few animals for the express riders. Between Tucson and Socorro, only two riders per week made the trip in each direction. It was simpler and less expensive to contract. This meant that there were small ranches scattered like beads along the route. Going east from Tucson, there was a station at Cienaga or, as Butterfield had called it, Seneca, on Pantano Wash. The next was at San Pedro Crossing where Benson stands today, and then Dragoon Springs Station where Silas St. John's friends had died in 1858 and later Cochise had attacked Captain Sherod Hunter's Confederates. The Overland Mail had crossed the Willcox Playa to Ewell's Station, but the new route went six miles to the south to Sulphur Springs Station and then on to Apache Pass, San Simon, and Doubtful Canyon, also called Stein's, for Major Enoch Steen.

Sulphur Springs Ranch is interesting in that in 1876, Apaches murdered Nicholas Rogers and his partner, Orisoba Spence, for refusing to sell whiskey to the warriors. In 1872, it would serve as Jeffords's Chiricahua Agency. The ranch is only ten miles from east Stronghold Canyon. It is in the very heart of Apache country and at Cochise's very doorstep.[12] Although the earliest recordation on the property isn't until 1870, it is fairly certain that the station was in use when Jeffords was superintendent of the line.

There were other ranches nearby. Colonel Henry Hooker began herding cattle on open range between Sulphur Springs and the Sierra Bonita thirty miles to the north. He arrived in the area with a trail drive from Texas in the 1867, delivering cattle for Camp Goodwin and its captive Apache. He stayed on and founded the Sierra Bonita Ranch in 1872 although he'd already been ranching in the area for some years. It is said that he always wore a suit and would not ride a horse but instead drove a buggy. While the year is uncertain, he claimed to have run into Cochise by accident and survived. The times were such that if a rancher were to give a few beeves to Cochise and his people, the Indians were likely to tolerate him.[13]

The first stagecoaches in this era were described as buckboards pulled by two horses. A passenger might sit on the seat with the driver or lounge in the back in the bed. It wasn't a comfortable way to travel. The mail carriers demanded protection from the military, which was hard pressed to provide escorts. The Concord stagecoaches of the

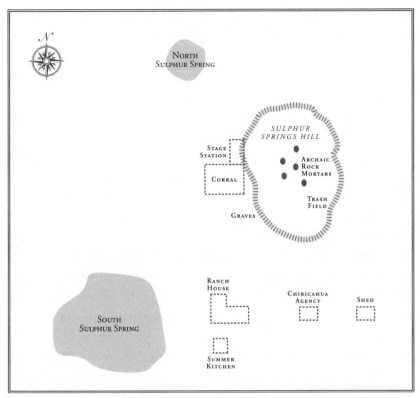

Layout of Sulphur Springs Ranch. In 1872–74, it was owned by Nicholas Rogers who partnered with Jeffords on the Brunckow Claim. Jeffords paid $50 per month for a 10x10 building. This had been a mail station. The hill at center was used by archaic Indians as a place to grind mesquite beans and acorns. Rogers and his partner, Orisoba O. Spence, who was awarded the Medal of Honor in combat with Cochise, were murdered by Apache in 1876.

movies and TV weren't put in use until the late 1870s. Some routes were still using ambulances or celerity wagons into the twentieth century. In a celerity wagon, driver and passengers all sat on the same level. They were designed to seat nine. Three faced rearwards behind the driver, three faced forward on the middle seat, and three faced forward on the last seat. The sides and top were canvas. Dog carts were also used. These were two-wheeled, one-horse wagons. A lightweight wagon would have been an advantage in Apache country. It would have moved much faster than a heavy Concord. At times when a driver was sick or when one couldn't be hired, as superintendent, Tom Jeffords probably drove the stage. There is no record of the Apache attacking him, but it could have happened.

A newspaper article in the *Daily New Mexican* of Santa Fe gives evidence of Tom's employment and what the times were like: "Mr. Jefferies, a conductor on the mail line between this place and Tucson, in Arizona, informs us of the exceedingly outrageous conduct of the Gila Apaches on the line of New Mexico and Arizona. During the entire season, thus far, these Indians have been constantly committing depredations in both of these Territories."[14]

If the newspaper was any more accurate with Mr. Jeffords's title than with his name, Tom was the conductor responsible for the mail and the express box, if any, and not, at least in July, for operations from Socorro to Tucson. He would have been something like a shotgun guard but more than that, the man signed for security of mail and express. The mail line may have promoted him later to superintendent.

The mention of Gila Apaches would indicate that the encounter took place somewhere between Mesilla and Doubtful Canyon on the New Mexico–Arizona border. As hostile as they may have seemed, it is unlikely that they wanted the stage. Unlike the movies, there would have been no prolonged chase of a fast-moving coach. The Apache could have taken the stage on a steep grade when the passengers dismounted to lighten the load. Or the Apache might have blocked the road, forcing the stage to halt, or shot one of the lead dray animals. As conductor, Tom might have taken over the reins to spell the driver during this encounter that boasts more of threat and warning than attempt to take the wagon.

The Apache occasionally chased mail riders and sometimes attacked near stations. We know of only two that the Chiricahua killed. Disruption of the mail always caused a stir and garnered attention in the press. One of the worst attacks took place after Tom left the stage line. The Southern Overland coach, a two-horse buckboard, left Camp Bowie for Tucson on October 5, 1869. The driver was Mr. Kaler and his passenger was John Finckle Stone, president of the Apache Pass Mining Company with sites near Fort Bowie. An escort of soldiers accompanied them, consisting of privates W. H. Bates, M. Blake, J. W. Slocum, and D. B. Shellabarger, of Company D, Twenty-first Infantry. About three miles west of Dragoon Springs, soon after passing a herd of cattle, they were attacked by many Apaches and all were killed by the first fire, stripped and mutilated, and the mail captured. The Apaches then attacked the herd, killed one drover, and took 150 cattle.[15] The uproar in Tucson was extreme. Typical of such was the letter of a young man to his sweetheart dated June 8, 1868:

> *Dear Marie*
>
> *I wrote you a long letter giving some account of the Indians in this territory but I expect you will not receive it because I believe it has been captured with a mail which the Indians have gobbled . . . but I am not quite shure [sic] weather [sic] my letter went by that mail.*[16]

He goes on to apologize for not saying anything personal or sweet. He was concerned that the mail might again be gobbled and didn't know who might read his letter. Apparently, he was worried that the Apaches might laugh.

The October 1869 attack on the mail led to a pursuit of Cochise that continued for most of a month. The day after attacking the mail, Cochise and his warriors attacked a trail drive from Texas, killing one man and making off with 150 cattle. A government train discovered the bodies of those killed with the mail and Cochise attacked them as well. Lieutenant William H. Winters mounted all the available troops at Fort Bowie, twenty-five men of Company G, 1st Cavalry, and took the field in pursuit. Scout Merejildo Grijalva, a former captive of Cochise, found the way. Winters soon reported that he was "hot upon the trail" of Cochise's band then driving their herd of cattle down the Sulphur Springs Valley toward Mexico. For twenty-two hours, without sleep, he and his men pursued Cochise to the Pedregosa Mountains near the Mexican border. There on the east slope at 8 a.m. on October 8, they attacked Cochise's rear guard, killing three of five warriors, and then barreled into the main body. Winters tried to stop the Apaches from escaping but the battle flowed back and forth for ninety minutes. Without success, the soldiers made a special target of Cochise.

Returning from a scout, Colonel Reuben Bernard took the field from Fort Bowie, forty-five miles away, with Troop G of the 1st Cavalry and a detachment of Troop G, 8th Cavalry, a force of sixty-one men. Along the way to the site of the engagement, he met Winters, by then returning with the recaptured cattle and two wounded. Winters had also taken some of Cochise's stock and killed twelve of his warriors. The *Prescott Miner* reported this action as the first time Cochise had been badly whipped since 1861. On October 18, he arrived at the site of Winters's engagement, and scout Grijalva picked up the trail, which did not lead to Mexico as expected but turned back north into the Chiricahua Mountains.

Bernard followed it through an abandoned camp to a rocky mesa deep in the Chiricahua Mountains at Chiricahua Pass between Rucker and Tex Canyons. There, on October 19, spotting Indians, he ordered his men to advance. Before they got halfway up the hill, the Apaches opened fire. In the barrage, Sergeant Stephen S. Fuller, 8th Cavalry, and Private Thomas Collins of the 1st were killed and Private Edwin Elwood wounded. A firefight ensued during which Bernard claimed his men picked off many Apaches. Bernard turned over command to Lieutenant John Lafferty of the 8th and went to the rear to attend to the trains and rear guard. The Colonel concluded that because of a precipice to his front, no successful advance could be made from his present position. He ordered a retreat to a new position to try the enemy right and left. Fire from the Apache was so intense that he was unable to recover his dead troopers. As the fighting continued through the afternoon, Lieutenant John Lafferty was badly wounded in the jaw while trying to recover the bodies. Bernard concluded he would need twice as many soldiers as he had to dislodge the Indians and gave up the assault. Thirty-one enlisted men received the Medal of Honor for this, one of the worst defeats ever inflicted on Cochise.[17]

Bernard took his wounded back to Fort Bowie, and on October 24 set out again for Chiricahua Pass. He found Cochise gone and was able to bury his dead. His scouts saw horses in a nearby canyon and soon a minor action ensued as the Apaches tried to gain his rear. The cavalry drove the Apache to a mountain top where the soldiers could not reach them. The Indians approached under flag of truce seeking terms, which Bernard said he refused.

This was Cochise's last large-scale action. The willingness to accept terms suggests that he was tired of war, tired of constantly being on the run. He probably wouldn't have seen it as a defeat, as Bernard tried to publicize it. He lost the herd to Lieutenant Winters and subsequently fought the army to a standstill. His losses probably came nowhere near Bernard's estimates. Reuben Bernard was a ruthless self-promoter who tried to gain traction at the expense of the dead hero, Lieutenant George Bascom. Cochise successfully escaped a larger force three times. He might have been tired of war, but he would continue to fight for three more years until he could negotiate a peace on his own terms. He rejected those offered by Bernard.

The significance to the mail coach wasn't lost on Cochise. In 1872, Cochise took General O. O. Howard's aide-de-camp, Joseph Sladen, to a high point in the Dragoon Mountains from which they could view the mail road. Below them they could see the buckboard carrying the mail between Fort Bowie and Tucson, driven by "Buckskin Alex." Cochise told Sladen that he could kill this man at any time and Sladen saw how easy it would have been for the chief. Previous to this, Cochise had shown the soldier how he had complete intelligence on the Sulphur Springs and San Pedro Valleys from his eyries high in the Dragoons and could even tell when the soldiers were leaving Fort Bowie two days ride away to head out on patrol. He wondered if, learning that he was at the mercy of these savages every time he drove the road, "Buckskin Alex" could ever be induced to make the trip again. Through Jeffords, Sladen asked why Cochise had not killed this man and the chief replied that it was because he drove a government "cart," and all the soldiers would be ordered out to avenge his death.[18] Cochise was inclined to leave the mail alone, but not because of any treaty with Jeffords.

Months before Bernard fought with the chief, Cochise had shown a willingness to talk. On February 3, 1869, Lieutenant Guthrie and Major Perry, along with sixty-two soldiers, three guides, an interpreter and a surgeon, met with Cochise in the Sulphur Springs Valley.[19] The writer of a letter to the newspaper, apparently Lieutenant Guthrie, recorded Cochise's conversation with the Chiricahua chief as follows:

Cacheis [Cochise]—What are you doing out here, Captain?

Major [Perry]—Come to see you and prospect the country generally.

C.—You mean you came to kill me or any of my tribe; that is what all your visits means to me. I tried the Americans once and they broke the treaty first, the officers I mean this was at the Pass. If I stop in, I must be treated right, but I don't expect they will do all they say for us. I won't stay Goodwin [Camp Goodwin near the Gila River in Pinal Apache country]; it is no place for Indians. They die after being there a short time. I will go in to Goodwin to talk to you, after I hear how you treat Indians there. I will send in two of my Indians who will let me know, (he did send in two squaws). I lost nearly 100 of my people in the last year, principally from sickness. The Americans killed a good many. I have not 100 Indians now. Ten years ago I had 1,000. The Americans are every-where, and we must live in bad places to shun them. I can't give you any mescal, as there is another scout on the other side, and we can't make fires to roast it. The Coyoteros are stronger than we are

*and steal stock from us; some of them say you come out to kill us, but
some Indians will lie. My Indians will do no harm until I come in,
which I may do inside of two months.*

M.—I heard you were wounded often, but you walk all right.

*C.—I was wounded twice. First, near Santa Cruz, in the leg
12 years ago. I had a bad leg for sometime afterwards. Next near
Fronteras, two years ago, in the neck. We are known as the Gamo
Apaches. I would like some bread and tobacco and a blanket.*

According to the writer, he got them. Guthrie went on to say
Cochise was about six foot, three inches tall, strongly muscled, with
mild, prominent features and a hooked nose. The writer thought him
about fifty years old.[20]

On December 20, 1869, the government licensed the firm of Jeffords and Brevoort to trade with the Gila River and Mimbres tribes
of Apaches on the recommendation of William Clinton, superintendent of Indian Affairs for New Mexico.[21] Tom Jeffords partnered
with Elias C. Brevoort as Indian Trader at the Canada Alamosa
Reservation. Brevoort was born in Michigan in 1822. During the war,
General Carleton had been anxious to capture one Elias Brevoort.
"One Elias Brevoort of Santa Fe, a spy and a traitor. Let him be where
he may, in the vicinity of Tucson; when caught, let him be tried by a
military commission and if he be found guilty of playing the spy or
traitor. Let him be hanged as speedily as possible."[22] It is unclear why
Carleton wanted him. Brevoort was associated with Sylvester Mowry,
also accused of treason for selling lead to Captain Sherod Hunter,
and with Captain Richard S. Ewell, who became a Confederate general. He may have been among those unfortunates who remained in
Arizona after the Confederates arrived who did business with them
willingly or under duress. In 1864, he was associated with a half-baked
scheme to link the Confederacy to southern California. In the early
1850s, Brevoort had been a Santa Fe trader. Kit Carson rescued him

when, returning to Missouri with a stash of silver, he inadvertently hired a crew of murderers who planned to rob him. In 1856, he was with Major Steen and Captain Richard Ewell at the founding of Fort Buchanan where he was post sutler and postmaster. He was one of that small group of civilians who had come to Arizona before the Civil War and was known to all the famous early settlers.[23]

The agent at Canada Alamosa was Lieutenant Charles Drew, an army officer well liked by the Apache. One reason for this, though nothing is certain, is that he drank with their chiefs. Drew had a reputation for insobriety. On March 8, 1870, Tom and Elias wrote a letter to either Drew or his commander, Captain George Shorkely, at Fort McRae. If the letter went to Drew, as seems likely, he soon took it to Captain Shorkely and made his defense. Drew claimed that Brevoort and Jeffords were attempting to intimidate him to cover their own misdeeds, presumably selling liquor to the Apaches. The letter reported that when Chief Loco returned from Fort McRae, very tired, he:

> . . . *wanted to get him some whiskey, when we told him, as we had repeatedly before, that we were not allowed to keep it, did not use it, and would not under no consideration give him any or procure it for him. He beged & beged [sic] & we continued to refuse when he became very excited and very angry and stated that he did not understand how it was we refused to get him whiskey & said to him that if this agent, or great father at Washington, knew we gave, or sold him or his tribe whiskey we would be removed from here, stating that when he was at Fort McRae (night of 2d) that you procured four bottles of whiskey, which he & yourself & perhaps some others drank, intimated that we were deceiving him &c. . . . We hope his statement may prove untrue though at the same time, the fact of his becoming so angry & being so much excited is almost proof that his statement is correct. We admit that it is a very strange affair, & requires an explicit explanation from you whether such is really the case, & if it will occur again in which*

case we are duty bound for our own protection to take notice of it through a different channel. . . . You will at once see the folly of your act if his statement be true & the critical position in which you have placed us. . . . You are probably not aware if any person who give or sells whiskey to an Indian subject himself to indictment—a fine of five hundred dollars & ten years imprisonment.[24]

On March 17, Lieutenant Drew sent the letter on to William Clinton with his defense.

I do not imagine that these gentlemen believe what they say and hence am at a loss to account for their action. I will state to you that there is not the slightest foundation for the story. So far from giving "Loco" whiskey, I took the trouble to go with him until he passed through Alamsita for the express purpose of preventing him from getting any. . . . After writing my letter to you in reference to the stories in circulation about these gentlemen, I told them what I had heard, and also that I had written you on the subject.

They denied it so emphatically that I left them under the impression that they had been misrepresented. On a second visit to Canada [Alamosa] they seemed very friendly and I was beginning to form a better opinion of them, although from the first they have exhibited a disposition to dictate to me in a manner strangely at variance with their position. This spirit has at length culminated in the insolent and bullying letter enclosed. Such language I cannot and will not tolerate, and am compelled therefore to request that their appointment be revoked.[25]

Captain Shorkely came to Drew's defense with the following letter:

I saw "Loco" in the evening of the 3rd instant soon after he came to the Post and he was there I thought under the influence of liquor.

Agent Drew took him to his quarters and kept him and his party over night [sic]. I again saw him the next morning and "Loco" was entire sober and was so when he left the Post. "Loco" may have been misunderstood by Jeffords and Brevoort as he denies their statement. From my personal knowledge of the condition of Lieut. Drew's Agency I have no hesitancy in stating that I give his statement full credence.[26]

It is not surprising that Shorkley would come to Drew's defense or that the military would close ranks to avoid embarrassment. More damaging to Brevoort and Jeffords is the statement of Fort McRae Post Trader Frank Frenger that he was the only one in the area legally allowed to handle and sell whiskey and he had seen Drew refuse Loco's request for liquor and had seen Drew warn others against providing it to the chief. Interpreter Robert C. Patterson stated that Loco had denied ever receiving liquor from Drew. Both of these men were dependent on the goodwill of the military for their livings. It is difficult to see how the letter from Brevoort and Jeffords could have brought them anything but predictable grief. Unless there was something behind their statements, it could not have served to intimidate Lieutenant Drew. By Special Order Number 1, dated April 15, 1870, Clinton revoked Jeffords's and Brevoort's license to trade with the Indians at Canada Alamosa.

On May 12, 1870, Brevoort and Jeffords defended their previous statements, stating that "we had personally seen the said Lieut. Drew give whiskey to Indians on a previous occasion, and that they had communicated to him privately, intending to rouse the said Lieut. Drew from the (we are pained to say) apparently drunken stupor, caused from almost constant dissipation or drunkenness since his arrival in the country & to bring him if possible to a true sense of his duties even at the risk of offending him." The letter formally alleged:

1st. That he did give whiskey to two Apache Indians out of a bottle. This was on or about the 12th day of January last.

2nd. That he has been under the influence of whiskey and drunk during the issuing of rations.

That he struck an Apache squaw for not interpreting for him, that he had been drunk with Loco, that he was always drunk, and so on, concluding with the revealing note that Lieut. Drew has publicly stated that he did not personally like Mr. Brevoort.[27]

Superintendent Clinton responded to these allegations by saying: "Lt. Drew has managed the Indians under his control quite as well as could be done by a man of more temperate habits, and he certainly is the first Agent who has had them under control, at least for many years."[28] The reference to more temperate habits is telling. Drew's proclivity for the bottle was known. To keep the peace on a reservation that was working well and to save military face, Brevoort and Jeffords had to go. Lieutenant Drew died soon after while on patrol of dehydration, which may have been a consequence of alcoholism.

CHAPTER 7

Friendship

IN DECEMBER 1872, GOVERNOR ANSON P. K. SAFFORD, AFTER AN
interview with Cochise on the new reservation, said Jeffords told him
he had known Cochise for about three years. That would point to
1869 or 1870. Governor Safford included other puzzling statements
in his account:

*He [Jeffords] is thirty-six[1] years of age; tall and well proportioned;
was born in the State of New York; came to Denver, Colorado, in
1857 and practiced law for a short time; has since spent much of
his time in the mountains prospecting for gold and silver; has been
among nearly all the Indian tribes of North America; has made
their habits and peculiarities a study, and is by nature well qual-
ified to deal with them. Several years ago he was Superintendent
of the Overland Mail Company, and during a short period of time
that he was in charge Cachise [sic] and his band killed twenty-one[2]
of his employees. He finally went to prospecting again and made
up his mind that if the Government could not subdue so bad an
enemy, he would try and make him his friend, and by the help of
other Indians, he visited Cachise [sic] in his own camp. This act
inspired Cachise [sic] with profound respect for his courage and
sincerity. Through Captain Jefferds [sic], Cachise [sic] was brought*

to Canada Alamosa reservation in 1871, and by him General Howard was led to his camp.[3]

Here is the origin of statements that Jeffords practiced law in Denver and was superintendent of the Southern Overland Mail, and also the first mention of twenty-one of his mail employees being slain by Cochise. Most of these statements are dubious. Jeffords had not been among all the Indian tribes and made a study of them. Tom arrived in Denver in 1858, not 1857, after building the road across the plains from Leavenworth, Kansas. This would have left very little time to practice law, since he was in Taos County, New Mexico, by 1859. Newspaper accounts of the time Tom was with the Southern Overland do not substantiate the count of twenty-one slain mail riders. Safford does not say that Tom Jeffords rode into Cochise's camp to make a separate peace for the mail, a story that appeared in Forbes's 1915 account, in the novel *Blood Brother*, and in the movie *Broken Arrow*.

Safford says that Tom went into Cochise's camp to secure permission to prospect in Cochise's country. Tom was prospecting between the time he left the Southern Overland in March 1869 and when he went into partnership with Elias Brevoort in December of that year. He and Brevoort needed time to work out their partnership and to gather goods, which they brought to the reservation in January 1871. The time for prospecting was very short. The story seems unlikely even if we allow that accounts of Cochise's ferocity are much overstated. People did approach Cochise and live. In 1909, former Army officer Henry Turrill repeated an account similar to Safford's story, stating that Jeffords met Cochise while "prospecting in the mountains in Cochise's country and was supposed to have effected friendly relations with Cochise."[4] Safford's letter might be the source of this information as it was published while Turrill was in Arizona.

Asa Daklugie, son of Juh, and informant for Eve Ball in the 1950s, had seen the movie *Broken Arrow*. He went on to state that Jeffords's relationship with Cochise began about ten years after the Bascom

Affair but that their meeting wasn't voluntary. Cochise's men had captured Jeffords, who was prospecting, and brought him to the chief. His courage led to an understanding that he could prospect on Cochise's land.[5] Daklugie said:

> There are stories of Jeffords having gone boldly to Cochise's stronghold alone. That is not as the Apaches know it. They say that Jeffords was captured by Cochise's scouts, but that he exhibited no fear. The Apaches were so impressed by his courage that instead of killing him they took him to Cochise. My father [Juh] knew both Cochise and Jeffords well, and he believed the latter account to be true. He knew that the two became very close friends; and in time Juh and Jeffords did, too. Cochise had shut himself off from White Eyes since the Bascom Affair, and accepting a white man as his friend was a tribute to a brave man. No greater praise could be given Jeffords than to say that he won the friendship of Cochise.[6]

Daklugie captured something of Jeffords's courage and an Apache rationale for why the chief and the white man became friends. Traits honed as a lake captain made the friendship possible. Courage and calm in a dangerous situation made an impression on the Apache.

In 1867, Colonel Henry Clay Hooker drove his first herd into Arizona. Years before he established Sierra Bonita Ranch in 1872, he was herding cattle on Cochise's range. Family legend maintains that Hooker always dressed as a gentleman in the latest fashions and, eschewing cowboy garb, wore necktie and swallow-tailed coat while tending steers. He did not ride but drove a buckboard with front- and rear-facing seats. In the rear seat sat a Mexican bodyguard serving as tail-gunner. At some point he found himself surrounded by Cochise's warriors, taken by surprise, and escorted to Cochise's camp. Hooker's clothing, the family says, much impressed the chief as he had never seen the like before. The colonel, an honorary appellate like Kentucky colonel, "never turned a hair" and stayed the night as Cochise's guest.

The Apache told him in the morning that he would have slain Hooker had he tried to run. Instead they became friends and Hooker provided beef when Cochise was camped nearby.[7] It was a wise policy trading a few beeves for rights to the range. As family legend, the story has little written to support it. It does illustrate a point. Not all white men who passed through Chiricahua land were slain. Cochise was approachable and could accept whites as friends. Hooker had something to give, beef, in exchange for Cochise's tolerance. And the colonel had courage. Jeffords had only his courage and his even-handed manner. A sergeant at Fort Bowie, who knew him during the years he was agent for the Chiricahua Reservation, described Tom as follows:

> *He was a dark, thin raw-boned man about six feet tall, tough and muscular. He was always jolly, rather witty, and hard to confuse. I remember we used to have dances at the post now and then—just the laundry women and the soldiers—and he used to come down. Once, one of the women complained that he stepped on her toe. With much apparent concern he asked, "Which toe madam?"*[8]

Historians often use culture to solve historians' writing dilemmas. They tell us the Apache behaved in a certain way because they respected courage, and couldn't abide being called liars or taken hostage in front of their men. There is some degree of credence in all of these statements, but probably these elements are little more so for Apache than for ourselves. Apache may have held that "scratching in Mother Earth for gold" was a crime above all others. That would make it extremely unlikely Cochise gave Jeffords permission to prospect. In 1861, Cochise and Mangas Coloradas tried to drive the miners at Pinos Altos from their land. There were other issues involved besides mining. On the other hand, modern Apaches may have acquired this cultural element by watching the movies. Cochise may have been willing to tolerate white men's activity as long as he received compensation. A meeting between Cochise and Jeffords in 1869 while Jeffords was prospecting is a possibility.

An Indian agent wrote that their friendship began while "having been a trader with the Apaches for some length of time."[9] Cochise may have met Jeffords while he was the trader at Canada Alamosa. The record shows that Cochise visited Canada Alamosa in October and November 1870, months after Jeffords lost his license to trade, to confer with William F. M. Arny, special Indian agent for New Mexico. On October 20, 1870, Arny recorded that Cochise said:

I want to talk first. I have come to hear you talk. If the Government talks straight, I want a good peace. My people do not know that there is a good peace here. They have to hide in the mountains and arroyos and keep out of the way. I want the truth told. A man has only one mouth and if he will not tell the truth, he is put out of the way. . . . The Mescaleros, Coyoteros, Mimbres, Mogollons are represented and I am head chief of them all.[10]

Cochise was proud and may have overstated the extent of his chieftainship. Or Arny may have wanted him to be chief over so many because this would simplify the process of making peace from his perspective. The Coyoteros, also known as White Mountain Apaches, the people of the Fort Apache Reservation, would in years ahead provide many Apache scouts to hunt the Chiricahua. Coyoteros are not Chiricahuas. Mescaleros lived east of the Rio Grande and weren't Chiricahua. These are not the names the Chiricahua use for themselves. It is significant that Cochise demanded peace on his own terms.

In August 1870, Tom Jeffords, then aged thirty-four[11], was living with Elias Brevoort at Pulvedero[12], New Mexico. They listed themselves as "general merchants." Pulvedero was north of Socorro and many miles north of the Canada Alamosa Reservation. They still had stocks from their time as Indian traders to sell. This was also north of

Cochise's usual haunts. Perhaps they took their stocks south by wagon instead of tending a regular store. History can't definitively place Tom at Canada Alamosa during October when Cochise was there. Cochise departed on November 16, 1870.

Fred Hughes was a clerk at Canada Alamosa in the early 1870s. He was there when Cochise again came in for parley in October 1870 and still there on September 28, 1871, three months after Jeffords had ridden boldly into his camp. Later he was Jeffords's clerk at the Chiricahua agency in 1872–73, living with the agent in a ten-foot-by-twelve-foot adobe rented from the Sulphur Springs Ranch. He should have known better than anyone else how the chief and the agent had come to know one another. Fred said that Jeffords met Cochise for the first time in 1870.[13] This is probably the first meeting that the two men, the chief and the frontiersman, both remembered. It would have been brief. Cochise was there to consider settling on the reservation, then in turmoil due to its planned closure and the proposed move to the Tularosa Valley. Jeffords would have been there trading, possibly illegally, just beyond the bounds of the reservation. Jeffords is supposed to have made such an impression that he became a favorite of Cochise, so much so that everyone knew it. It seems more likely that people knowing about their friendship followed dramatic events a year later in 1871.

Having met Cochise, Tom Jeffords would have known the sort of man he was, far less savage than traditional accounts of the time portrayed him:

> *In conversation, he was very pleasant, and to his family and those immediately around him, he was more affectionate than the average white man; he showed nothing of the brutish nature generally attributed to him. It was astonishing also to see what power he had over this brutal tribe, for while they idolized and almost worshipped him, no man was ever held in greater fear, his glance being enough to squelch the most obstreperous Chiricahua in the tribe.*[14]

Having met the chief, Tom Jeffords was willing to assume a dangerous mission.

In 1871, the superintendent of Indian Affairs for New Mexico, Nathanial Pope, sent out a month-long scout and peace mission. On the way back, about 160 or 175 miles west of Canada Alamosa, north of the Gila River in Arizona, his emissaries came upon Cochise's camp. The chief was raiding in Sonora with his warriors and no one knew when he would return. The Indians in camp were nearly naked, half-starved, and in constant fear of parties of troops. Soldiers had attacked them several times. They brought in about one hundred Indians, leaving behind Cochise's immediate family. Pope now needed someone to go back and invite Cochise to come in for a second peace parley. He had great difficulty in finding anyone willing to make the trip as it was dangerous. Indian Agent Orlando F. Piper obeyed Pope's order to seek out Cochise and sent Jose Maria Trujillo to find him, but Cochise refused to accompany him. With this failure, Piper sent Tom Jeffords. Piper hesitated. Jeffords was holding out for significant compensation, more than the agent was willing to pay. In the end, Jeffords left Canada Alamosa on June 7, 1871, and returned on the 28th without Cochise, who argued that "the country was filled with soldiers and he was now afraid to venture with his women and children . . . and as he could not take them with safety, he would not leave them."[15] Perhaps Jeffords went because he was already friendly with Cochise. Maybe he just had courage. After this, everyone knew he was the man who could ride into Cochise's camp and return alive. Jeffords provided his own mules and supplies and billed the government $300[16] for his effort. Cochise came in for talks at Canada Alamosa a few months later, and he called on Tom Jeffords to be his adviser and confidant. Friendship and trust had grown between the two men.

On April 30, 1871, a mixed militia of Tucson citizens and Indians from San Xavier del Bac made a raid on the Aravaipa Apache under military protection near Camp Grant on the San Pedro River.[17] Chief Eskiminzin had brought his people in with a request to settle, to be at peace, and to be fed by the government. Lieutenant Royal Whitman put them on half rations and requested advice from his superiors. No advice was forthcoming and the tribe remained in limbo under Whitman and the Army's protection. Apaches conducted murders and raids in the vicinity of Tucson. The Aravaipa, the closest Apache, were blamed and an expedition mounted that struck with complete surprise the peaceful camp at dawn. At least eighty[18] Apache died and many children were taken captive and sold into slavery in Mexico. That peaceful reservation Indians could be slaughtered in their sleep terrified other reservation Apache and fueled Cochise's caution at the time Jeffords visited. On June 4, 1871, Colonel George Crook assumed command in Arizona.

Nonetheless, overcoming fear, in late September 1871, Cochise came in to talk with Canada Alamosa Indian Agent Orlando Piper. Overawed and perhaps a bit frightened of the famous chief, the agent invited him inside his quarters to talk. "No, we will talk out here," said Cochise, perhaps recalling Lieutenant Bascom's 1861 invitation to come into his tent. Mexicans had slain his father and two of his brothers during talks and he remained cautious of all invitations. He was also cautious of proffered food and gifts, for similar offers had led to the deaths of many of his people in the past.

Cochise remained at Canada Alamosa or nearby from September 1871 through at least March 20, 1872. In October 1871, he granted an interview to Charles Coleman of the Las Cruces Borderer. On December 31, Agent Piper reported "Cochise and most of his band are here. They are very restless and suspicious."

In January 1872, Captain George Shorkely reported to his superiors that he had fallen in with Mr. Jeffords on his ride to Fort McRae and the two had talked of Indian affairs. Jeffords assured him that Cochise had not left Canada Alamosa but was nearby camped in the San Mateo Mountains twelve miles to the north. He was waiting for the "Big Talk" with Colonel Gordon Granger, military commander of New Mexico.[19] He went on to say that Mr. Jeffords would not oppose the move to Tularosa Valley: "[He took] pains to convince me of this. I am satisfied that he thinks it will advance his interests very much if the Indians go in peaceably and in consequence I think he will do what he can to get them there." Jeffords went on to note that the Indians were dissatisfied with the agent, Mr. Piper.[20] Shorkely attempted to dispel a growing distrust of Tom Jeffords. Army leadership saw him as siding with the Apache against his own people.

During this period, between September 1871 and the end of March 1872, Jeffords spent a lot of time in Cochise's camp. The military and those who worked with the Indians began to see him as the man who knew where he could locate Cochise and one who knew the chief's mind. He'd made a great impression on the Apache leader when he rode alone into Cochise's camp in June 1871. Now their relationship had time to grow, and by spring Cochise would be calling on Jeffords as his advisor. This may be the period Governor Safford referred to when he said that Jeffords had lived among the "tribes of North America" and studied their ways. Tom seems to have learned quite a bit and made many friends besides Cochise. He may have begun to pick up their language at this time, although many of them spoke Spanish.[21]

Distrust of Jeffords led to speculation that he was trading the Chiricahua ammunition and whiskey. It is possible, although there is no evidence. Smuggling was a common and minor crime along the border. It lacked the horror that Hollywood portrays. Cochise would have needed stolen Mexican livestock and goods to trade. Since he wasn't actively raiding, he would have lacked the means. Nonetheless, distrust would grow.

Assistant Surgeon Henry Stuart Turrill recounted his recollection on the March 20, 1872, meeting between Cochise and General Gordon Granger and Superintendent of Indian Affairs for New Mexico Nathanial Pope. When they arrived at the place of council no Indians were present, but soon Tom Jeffords appeared and assured them that Cochise would soon arrive. He did, with an escort exactly matching the general's and they took seats with Jeffords beside the chief. Turrill reported that he and Colonel Willard had made up their minds that they would account for Cochise and Jeffords if anything went wrong in the council.

This is a remarkable statement, showing how much some officers mistrusted Jeffords and the extent to which the Army viewed him as Cochise's man and ally. Friendship had blossomed and it was apparent. Turrill goes on to state:

> We had brought with us to the little Mexican town [Canada Alamosa] where we had left [with] our cavalry escort a lot of articles, which we thought would be acceptable to him and his people, as an earnest of our good faith. As General Granger mentioned these to him, and asked him to go to the town to receive them, his face lighted up for a moment; but he said no, he did not wish to go with the soldiers.
>
> Captain Jeffords turned to him and said, "If you want to go, I will pledge you my head that you will be safe; these men are talking straight to you."
>
> Cochise turned to him and said: "You believe these white men. I trusted them once; I went to their camp; my father and two brothers were hung.[22] No I will not go."[23]

Pope and Granger also invited Dr. Alexander N. Ellis to be part of the party that went to talk with Cochise. He recorded the chief as saying:

> I have no father and mother; I am alone in this world. No one cares for Cochise; that is why I do not care to live, and wish the rocks to fall on me and cover me up. If I had a father and a mother like you, I would be with them and they with me. When I was going around in the world, all were asking for Cochise. Now he is here—you see

him and hear him—are you glad? If so, say so. Speak. Americans
and Mexicans, I do not wish to hide anything from you nor have
you hide anything from me; I will not lie to you; do not lie to me. I
want to live in these mountains; I do not want to go to Tularosa.
That is a long ways off. The flies on those mountains eat out the eyes
of the horses. The bad spirits live there. I have drunk these waters
and they have cooled me; I do not want to leave here.[24]

Tularosa was a sticking point. The elevation was high, the weather
cold, the growing season short. The Apaches reported numerous
flies. More than this they thought the place haunted by evil spirits.
The Chiricahua fear the hoot of an owl; it is a harbinger of death.
According to Ed Sweeney, the Tularosa Valley is home to a significant
population of Mexican spotted owls.[25] This may be why they thought
it an evil place. After the Indian service moved Chihenne to Tularosa,
many departed and went to live on Cochise's Chiricahua Reservation.

Tom Jeffords and Cochise were friends and the word went around.
Soon everyone seemed to know. Washington sent Vincent Collier on
an unsuccessful peace mission. General Crook, the new commander
in Arizona, was busy subduing Apache by force. President U. S.
Grant sent General Oliver Otis Howard, the one-armed, Christian
general, to try to make peace with Cochise. He spent the summer of
1872 searching for the chief without luck and finally rode into Fort
Tularosa. There Fred Hughes, a clerk at the Indian agency, recalled, "I
had advised General Howard if he could find Captain Jeffords, to take
him with him on his mission, as Jeffords had already met Cochise and
the latter had taken quite a liking to him."[26]

General Howard had a slightly different recollection of how he
came to be aware of Cochise's friend, Tom Jeffords.

[Cochise] had never spared one [a white man], except a man the
Indians called Taglito, which means Red Beard. His real name

was Jeffords, and he was a white guide. How he alone came to be spared nobody knew. Of course, there couldn't be peace till Cochise agreed to it, so I told Victoria [Victorio] I had made up my mind to try and see this powerful warrior. Victoria was horrified. He seemed to think this out of the question, for no white man had ever seen Cochise and lived, except this same scout, Captain Jeffords. But where there's a will there's a way, and I did not give up, and kept at Victoria to help me.[27]

The general's aide-de-camp, Lieutenant Joseph Sladen, recalled hearing among the Coyotero Apache of a mysterious white man who had visited Cochise frequently and was on friendly terms with him. He also heard from Army officers and a rancher named Milligan that Jeffords could get in touch with Cochise.[28]

Sladen and General Howard's recollections of the general's first meeting with Jeffords differ slightly in reporting where the meeting took place but both capture the same character in the man. The general said:

[W]hen he entered my tent I did not wonder that he was called "Captain." He was very tall and fine looking, with clear blue eyes and a long bright red beard.

I said to him: They tell me that you have really been up in the Dragoon Mountains in the stronghold of the famous Apache chief—Cochise?"

"Yes, sir," he replied, "I have! Some people doubt it, but I assure you I made the old chief a visit last year."

"You are the first man," I said, "who has been able to get beyond his Indian spies. I want to go to see him; will you take me?"

Jeffords looked very steadily into my face with his fearless eyes and then he said: "Yes, General Howard, I will; but you must go with out [sic] any soldiers."

"All right," I said, "get ready to start as soon as you can."[29]

Sladen thought the meeting took place at Mr. Luther's store, the post sutler. He recalled that:

> . . . [a]fter a formal introduction, General Howard said: "I understand, Mr. Jeffords, that you know Cochise, and can find him. I have come here from Camp Apache to find you, and, if possible, to get you to go to him and induce him to come to me, for an interview."
>
> Jeffords eyed him closely, as if he would read his thoughts, and after a considerable deliberation, puffing the smoke of his cigar slowly as he thought, he took out his cigar, and said very deliberately: "General Howard, Cochise won't come. The man that wants to talk to Cochise, must go where he is."
>
> "Do you know where he is?" said the General. "I can find him," Jeffords laconically replied.
>
> "Will you go to him, with a message from me?" asked the General. "General," replied Jeffords, with the faintest appearance of a cynical smile: "I'll tell you what I'll do. I will take you to Cochise."
>
> Without a moment's hesitation, the General said, "I will go with you, Mr. Jeffords." "Very well," said Jeffords, "It must be you and I alone. When will you start, for it is a long journey, I assure you, and it may take weeks to find him." "I will start at once," said the General, "as soon as we can get ready. So we will call it tomorrow."[30]

Tom Jeffords had heard about General Howard's mission. He'd witnessed the missions of Vincent Colyer, Piper, Granger, and others and wasn't impressed. He wasn't about to get excited about another mission from the president that was going to solve all Apache problems once and for all. He had misgivings, and this explains his reticence. Jeffords made an instant impression on General Howard. There was something in his manner, something retained from having been a sea captain where he had to gain respect and obedience immediately, that the general witnessed. The general also made an impression on Tom, and he expressed it to historian Thomas Farish in 1913:

Jeffords later admitted that he had preconceived notions about General Howard. Before meeting the general, Jeffords acknowledged that "I was prejudiced against him on account of his well known [sic] humanitarian ideas, and, to my mind, posing as a Christian soldier." After this first meeting, Jeffords began to change his opinion of Howard; "I saw then that he was not only a brave man, and fearless as far as his person was concerned, but was really in earnest about trying to stop the destructive war which Cochise was waging upon my countrymen."[31]

They rode east with Victorio, who wanted to show the general Canada Alamosa. With them rode interpreter Jacob May, Captain Sladen, a packer named Zebina Streeter, and Chie. Chie, we believe, was Cochise's nephew, the son of Coyuntura, the chief's brother, who had been hanged by Lieutenant Moore at Apache Pass in 1861. Chie may have been the second boy taken hostage by Lieutenant Bascom when he held Cochise's wife and son. He had recently married a Chihenne woman.[32] Near Canada Alamosa they picked up Ponce, another relative of Cochise, living off the reservation. Ponce was a raider.

They travelled to Fort Bayard near the Santa Rita Copper Mines and then on to Silver City, where a mob wanted to hang Ponce and Chie. The general stood up to them and they headed west to Doubtful Canyon and Apache Pass. At the pass, the party became smaller as they left behind some of its members at Fort Bowie. At Sulphur Springs Ranch they stayed the night at the stage station of Nick Rogers. Here the road from Tucson, after passing north of the Dragoon Mountains, came south around the Willcox Playa, a usually dry lake, before it continued on to Apache Pass. In 1872 and 1873, the station would be the Chiricahua Agency. Ten miles due west from the station was what is known today as Stronghold Canyon, where Cochise died in June 1874.

The party headed southwest and rode up a spur over the crest of the Dragoon Mountains and down the western slope. They struck the bed of a crooked stream and followed it back eastward up into the mountains through a narrow gateway where rocks rose one hundred feet on each side. Beyond was a meadow of thirty or forty acres dotted with oak trees. From this eyrie the entire San Pedro Valley could be seen below. During his stay, the Apaches showed Sladen nearby roosts from which the Sulphur Springs Valley and the road between Tucson and Apache Pass could be viewed. The Apaches could see soldiers departing from Fort Bowie on patrol. No one could approach Cochise's camp without his knowing it. If anyone entered these valleys by day Cochise saw their dust and smoke. At night he saw their campfires. Today we call this place China Camp.[33]

Cochise wasn't home when the general's party arrived, but soon returned. Soon it was announced, "He is coming!"[34] "Soon a fierce looking Indian dubbed with vermillion and black and carrying a long spear came dashing at full speed on his horse down the ravine, and pulling his horse up suddenly on his haunches halted and jump[ing] from his horse, ran up to Jeffords and embraced him warmly."[35] This was Cochise's brother Juan. The remainder of the mounted party soon approached with great dignity. A young man, his son, and two women, a wife and his sister, followed the chief. He dismounted and, throwing his arms around Jeffords, greeted him with considerable warmth. Jeffords turned to the general and said, "General, this is the man; this is he."

Cochise greeted the general with, "*Buenos dias.*" Cochise asked, "Will the General tell me why he has come to me?"

The general replied: "The president has sent me to make peace between you and the whites."

"Nobody wants peace more than I do," he said. "I have done no mischief since I came from the Canada Alamosa, but, I am poor, my horses are poor, and I have but few. I might have got more by raiding on the Tucson road, but I did not do it."

"Give me," said he, "Apache Pass for my people and I will protect the road to Tucson. I will see that the Indians do no harm."[36]

The general argued for Canada Alamosa, but the chief would have none of it. Cochise wanted time to call his sub-chiefs in, and he wanted them safe from army patrols as they came. He might well worry. Some had been raiding. The general suggested sending Sladen to Fort Bowie, but the chief told him the soldiers would not listen to a mere lieutenant. The general would have to go. He argued that he did not know the way and a volunteer was needed to take him. Chie was unwilling for fear of the soldiers but finally relented and the general left Sladen and Jeffords alone with the Apache.

Jeffords and Sladen each told differing versions of a meal they shared with Cochise. Jeffords claimed that he didn't tell Sladen, who was digging in for seconds, what the meat was until after dinner. The young captain ate horse with much gusto. Something of Jeffords's quiet sense of humor is seen in this. Sladen said he didn't care for it and would have preferred antelope. Cochise set out to hunt up an antelope for his guest.

They moved several times to different locations and to different eyries from which the valleys and trails could be viewed, ending up at an alcove near the mouth of West Stronghold Canyon. Here Cochise showed Sladen his "home," a tiny rock shelter under a large boulder.[37] "I am forced to live in bad places," he said. Jeffords and Sladen spent time on top of the flat surface of the rock talking about the plan for peace and the trustworthiness of the general. Jeffords liked Howard and thought him a brave and honorable man who could be trusted.

When the general returned, he and Jeffords spent time with the chief, much of it atop the rock where the San Pedro Valley was laid out below. It was ten days before most of Cochise's runners found his sub-chiefs and gathered them. By then, he had bonded with both Howard and Jeffords.

Cochise took his people to a level, open meadow surrounded by oaks half a mile downhill from the alcove. There they sat on a circle of rocks while the women sat in a larger ring around them.[38] General Howard recalled:

> *The men inside the ring sat or knelt. Then followed a wonderful song in which all joined. It began like the growl of a bear and rising little by little to a high pitch, lasted ten or more minutes and then suddenly stopped. After this Cochise interpreted to the people the will of the Spirits, saying "The Spirits have decided that Indians and white men shall eat bread together."*[39]

His people agreed. Chie took a white flag as a symbol and flew it from Knob Hill, where it could be seen from all over the valley. Cochise decided that the general must call in the officers from Fort Bowie so that they would know the Apache were at peace with them. The next day they met a few miles to the north at Dragoon Springs, site of the old Overland Mail station, and the Apache chiefs and cavalry officers sat down together in peace.

General Howard did not make a written copy of his treaty and Cochise did not sign a paper, but kept their word. The warrior, Colonel George Crook, military commander of Arizona, requested a copy of the treaty many times, but none was forthcoming. Cochise was promised food, blankets, and supplies for his people. He would need them. Confined to a reservation, his people would not have game enough to hunt, and they were restricted from raiding, which had always made up the deficit. The chief probably agreed that his people would try farming, and Howard had undoubtedly agreed to feed them until they were successful at it. The reservation was defined by the western foothills of the Mule and Dragoon Mountains by a line running north from the Mexican border as far as Dragoon Springs. From there the boundary ran northeast to Stein's Peak, then south along the Peloncillo Mountains on the border with New Mexico south to the Mexican border and back to the point of beginning.

Jeffords did not let the general promise too much.

Later, the military, Sonorans, and Arizonans called one element into question. The general had told Cochise he had no authority to make a treaty for the Mexicans. The treaty was with the United States only. Howard said he had told Cochise that despite this, his people must stop raiding into Mexico. During 1873, this became a problem. Cochise said he had not made peace with the country to the south and could still raid in Sonora.

Nonetheless, peace had been made, and Cochise was willing to do everything in his power to make it work. In his first annual report to the Indian department, Jeffords wrote of General Howard: "I doubt if there is any other person that could have been sent here that could have performed the mission as well; certainly none could have performed it better."[40] Without Thomas Jefferson Jeffords and Cochise and their friendship, as well, peace would not have been possible. It would now be up to both of them to make it work.

CHAPTER 8

The Chiricahua Agency

GENERAL HOWARD AND COCHISE REACHED AN AGREEMENT IN October 1872, and the reservation was officially declared in December. The first year was full of challenges for Jeffords and Cochise. No one thought it could work.

Colonel (promoted to general in 1873) George Crook massed troops at Camp Grant[1] and sent his aide, Lieutenant John Bourke, to the reservation to interview Cochise and Jeffords. He requested a copy of the treaty, which was never forthcoming since it wasn't in writing. Crook thought that he must beat the Chiricahua into submission before they would behave:

The mere fact of their not having deprecated on our people . . . proves nothing, as it is Apache tactics after they have thoroughly aroused a neighborhood by their depredations to cease operations in that locality until the unwary citizen is thrown off his guard, when they commence their outrages with renewed vigor.[2]

Nonetheless, the general behaved honorably. The newspapers carried the same sentiment that Crook expressed. The Apache could not be trusted not to raid. The army had not yet soundly beaten the Chiricahua, the "Cachise Indians." The papers continued with new complaints. The reservation was too close, the land too valuable, too

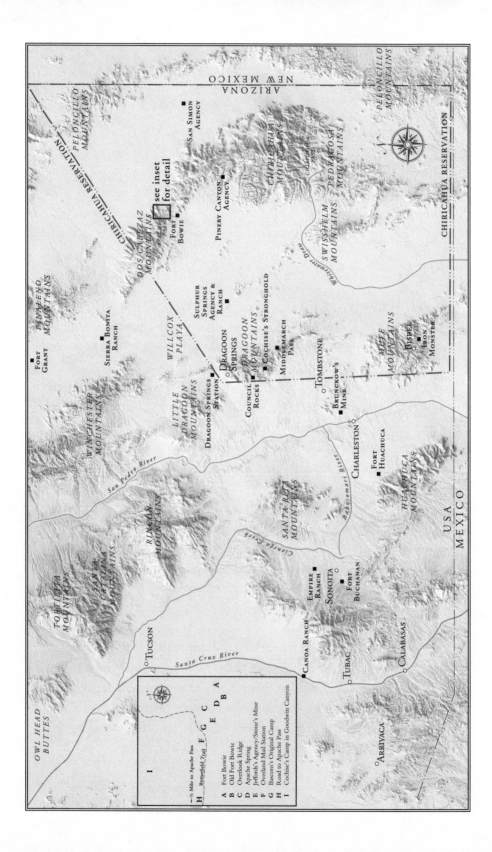

much of it had been given to the Indians. The Indians continued to raid. By the end of 1873, it was clear that raiding had stopped in Arizona, but there were complaints from Sonora, Mexico.

Soon Jeffords had other problems. In March 1873, Colonel Henry Hooker, the beef contractor, wrote that he could no longer supply beef since he hadn't been paid. The letter made it sound as though he had a personal issue with Tom, but it was not so. Tom stood as surety for the money. The Indian department believed, or so its representatives said, that the Army had made the treaty with Cochise and therefore was responsible to pay for rations and annuities from the military budget.

General Howard sent a telegram to Commissioner E. P. Smith who in turn sent a message to Herman Bendell, superintendent of Indian affairs for Arizona. On March 5, 1873, Secretary of the Interior Columbus Delano sent his own message to Bendell: "See that Chiricahua Reservation is furnished with all needful supplies. Do not neglect this duty."[3]

On Cochise's Chiricahua Reservation, the Apaches were free men living spread out in their mountain camps as they had always done. Their range was restricted, but their lives remained much as they had been. They were not prisoners of war forced to wear identity tags and to come in weekly in person to draw rations. Tom Jeffords did not force the Apache to live clustered around the agency where the agent could count them daily. Jeffords did not issue hunting passes to leave the reservation as other agents did. If the Apache left Cochise's reservation, they did so at their own peril. In the main, the people were happy with such treatment. Jeffords issued rations every fifteen days, often to a family head or even a chieftain for his entire band. He did not lack control. He visited the camps often and counted the Apache at those times and places.

Sergeant W. S. Grant, a friend of Jeffords's stationed at Fort Bowie, said of these times:

> *The Indians at that time wandered around over the Chiricahua Reservation as they pleased, living around the water holes and*

the agency in brush shacks, but never seeming to be permanently located. They were always stealing from the few people who passed through the country, and a few prospectors went out and were never heard of again. This was when the Indians were supposed to be peaceable.

Capt. Jeffords had in some way won the confidence of old Cochise, and they were great friends, which gave him free favor into all the Indian country. He could go out South anywhere and right into their camps, a thing which no other white men could do. If he was with the soldiers, the Indians could always be persuaded to come in and talk.[4]

Grant also said that Jeffords could speak to the Apache in their own language. He may have learned at Canada Alamosa and picked up more while running the reservation.

Tres Alamos resident Billy Ohnesorgen, a German immigrant, didn't care for Jeffords or the reservation.

I knew Captain Jeffords. He was Indian agent at one time—no good, a filthy fellow—filthy in his way of living—lived right among those damn things [Apache Indians]. Once in a while he would go down and haul one home with him. —was a blood brother or something of Cochise. He wasn't very bright. His clerk did all the work when he was agent. He could not even keep the Indians on the reservation. Jeff was a tall, lanky fellow of about six feet and his face was full of hair.[5]

Ohnesorgen had reason to dislike Jeffords. In November 1875, William Ohnesorgen undertook to drive a large flock of sheep, purchased in Chihuahua, back to his San Pedro ranch and decided to take them directly across the Chiricahua Reservation.[6] He passed a spring the Apache had improved with ditching and allowed his sheep to drink. The sheep broke down the ditching and the Apache warned him off. He did not heed, and the Chiricahua commenced to kill his sheep with rocks. Ohnesorgen billed the government for the amount of all the sheep he'd lost during the drive, and Jeffords called him on it.

Despite obvious dislike and disapproval, Ohnesorgen[7] does provide us with some of the reasons Jeffords was successful as agent. He was close to his people and stood up for their rights. He was sensitive to their customs and political relations. Understanding their relationships as he did, Jeffords did not form an Indian police force. Instead, he recruited people on an as-needed basis to assist him:

I do not consider it advisable to elect certain Indians as a police, for the reason that any Indian police are regarded with suspicion by other Indians, whereas, by calling upon any Indian to assist me in an emergency, it is considered by them that one Indian is as much compelled to preserve order as another, and consequently places every male Indian upon the same footing . . . [without] the jealousy and ill-feeling that would arise should certain men be appointed an armed police.[8]

That doesn't mean that Tom Jeffords wasn't tough on miscreants and offenders. Around July 6, 1873, he took stern action, as recounted in a letter to the *Arizona Citizen*:

Information was brought to this agency night before last, by some of our Indians, that the band of Natiza [Nednhi, the Juh-Geronimo band] had a captive boy at the Chiricahua Mountains, whom they had just brought from Sonora or Chihuahua. Captain Jeffords lost no time in proceeding to their camp to take measure for his recovery. He found the boy at the above mentioned rancheria, in the possession of an Indian named Heronimo [Geronimo], and without any ceremony took possession of him and brought him to this place. The Indians demanded ransom for the boy's release, but they did not find Captain Jeffords one of the ransoming kind; as I have said, he took the boy from them without ceremony, and they will have to charge whatever ransom they demanded.[9]

The Nednhi with their own chiefs and their territory in Mexico were a challenge for Jeffords. They came to live on the reservation, making up 250 of the 1,100 Indians Jeffords was feeding. If any of the Indians whose primary home was the reservation were raiding in Mexico, it would have been the Nednhi. We have to wonder how Jeffords took a Mexican child away from Geronimo so easily. Perhaps Jeffords was really brave and commanding. Perhaps the Nednhi worried about consequences from Cochise or perhaps Geronimo was more as Fred Hughes described him:

I always looked upon him as one of the most worthless and cowardly fiends on the reservation; on two different occasions, I saw squaws thrash him soundly. Upon one of these occasions I saw one drag him around by his hair, while the Indians stood looking and laughing and jeering. . . . I am inclined to the belief that the military have created Geronimo's chieftainship and kept him as such before the public.[10]

Tom sent Zebina Streeter[11], who had been the packer for General Howard, back to Canada Alamosa with an offer of a job to Fred Hughes[12] to become his clerk. Howard went on to Tucson and Jeffords stayed with Cochise to get things started. They set up the agency in a ten-foot-by-twelve-foot adobe building on Nick Rogers's Sulphur Springs Ranch, paying him fifty dollars per month for the privilege.[13] The building was much too small. Three men had to live in it, and it was where they stored all the supplies—blankets, pots and pans, tools, corn meal and flour, cotton cloth—to be distributed among the Indians. The weather damaged many of their stores since they were left in the open. Jeffords also hired Dr. Simon Freeman, post surgeon at Fort Bowie, as doctor for the reservation.

In August 1873, pressure from the Indian department resulted in Tom moving the agency to the San Simon Cienega.[14] Jeffords put the Chiricahua to work clearing land and building irrigation ditches so that they could farm. It's not clear that anyone involved in this experiment had any experience with irrigation farming. Tom Jeffords somehow got Cochise to cooperate and consolidate the people near the New Mexico line to make the attempt. It didn't go well. The Apache didn't like it and they all became sick. In the course of four months, four children died. Cochise concluded that the place, so unlike his mountain havens, was a home to evil spirits. Malaria[15] usually gets the blame, though the season was late for mosquito-born pathogens. By year's end Tom had moved the agency to Pinery Canyon, about twenty miles south of Apache Pass.

On October 10, 1873, Indian Inspector William Vandever visited Tom Jeffords's agency, while it was still at San Simon. The inspector didn't care for Tom's methods of Indian management. He couldn't find fault with the record keeping but implied that everything might not appear in the records. Moreover, the Indian service hadn't paid Tom and his employees in fourteen months.

The accounts as far as they were submitted to me [emphasis mine] by Mr. Jeffords and clerk appeared to be kept in proper form and were correct. Agent Jeffords informs me that since he has had charge of the Indians on this reservation he has received no money whatever for disbursement, and that only within a few days has he been notified of there being the sum of $4,400 placed to his credit in the US Depository at San Francisco. For 14 months neither Mr. Jeffords nor his employees had received any pay from the United States for their services and the sum now placed at his disposal is to pay only such indebtedness as has arisen since the 1st day of last July. Large arrearages of pay are yet due the Agent and his employees for which funds have yet to come to his hands.[16]

The Indian department was not making anything easier for Jeffords and Cochise. Vandever had his own ideas about how the reservation should be administered. In particular, according to the inspector, Jeffords needed to force the Indians to live near the agency where they could be counted regularly, and he needed to issue rations weekly and have the Indians report in person to draw them. Moreover, Jeffords should not feed Indians from other reservations.

Visiting Indians were a problem. About 350 Apache from Cochise's band, Chokonen, had come in and 250 Nednhi, the Juh-Geronimo band, had joined them. In addition another 250 or so minor bands lived on the reservation, possibly Bedonkohe. Jeffords was feeding more than 1,100 Indians. Many came from the Tularosa Reservation, the successor to Canada Alamosa, which the Chihenne hated. Coyotero, Cochise's old allies the White Mountain Apaches, came to the reservation as well. Some were on hunting passes from their agents. Others passed through the reservation on their way to raid in Mexico. Jeffords felt that the best policy was to feed them and let them settle on the reservation. If he didn't feed them, he argued, they'd be forced to raid more often in Mexico. Raiding was about feeding families, not glory like the Plains tribes. When owners reported stolen livestock to Jeffords, he recovered it from the offenders and returned it. He didn't make arrests or punish offenders. Cochise and his sons, Taza and Naiche, assisted with enforcement.

Vandever was not happy with this and spoke to the newspapers as well as sending negative reports to the commissioner of Indian Affairs. Of raiding he agreed with Tom "that most or all of it was occasioned by Indians from Tularosa and other distant places, who made headquarters at Chiricahua when they were not annoyed by the military forces." General Vandever blamed Jeffords for harboring the Tularosa Indians. The *Arizona Citizen* went on to say, "Commissioner Smith, undoubtedly influenced by the report of General Howard, thinks that Jeffords is the only man for the place; but General Vandever reports that several more competent for the position can be named. One of them in particular has more influence over Cachise than Jeffords."[17] Through the following years, Vandever continued to instigate for Jeffords's removal.

The attitudes of both Cochise and Jeffords during 1873 did not help the situation. Cochise had not made a treaty with Sonora, Mexico. General Howard was not empowered to treat for the Mexicans. While raiding stopped in southeast Arizona, it continued in Mexico. The newspapers reported:

> *Cachise told Gen. Vandever that he would take no steps to prevent this raiding and denied the right of government under the agreement—by divine aid—by and with General Howard, to use troops to stop it. Agent Jeffords told the proprietor of this paper in April last, that he did not care how many Mexicans "his people" (as he paternally called them) killed in Mexico; that for acts of treachery with those Indians, the Mexicans deserved killing, etc., etc.*[18]

Tom later said that this was a private opinion and not his statement of official policy for the agency. Late in the year, a Mexican emissary arrived with a long list of complaints of raiding and depredations. Agent Jeffords was able to deflect many of these accusations by pointing out that many of the depredations were assignable to Mexican bandits and Mexican Indians, to visitors to the reservation, and to Apaches from other reservations. Where ownership could be demonstrated, he recovered and returned livestock.

Chiricahua Ind. Agency, A.T.
September 25, 1873—Editor *Arizona Citizen:*

> *On the 22d inst, my Indians brought me information that there had been eight animals brought on this reservation from Santa Cruz, Sonora. I directed them to take them from the parties, bring them here, and turn them over to me, to enable me to return them to their proper owners. The animals are now at this*

agency awaiting their owners to come or send and get them. There are four bays, two greys, one cream color, and a sorrel colt; all small Mexican horses.

Thomas J. Jeffords[19]

In 1874, beef contractor Colonel Henry Hooker of the Sierra Bonita Ranch made a gift to Cochise and Jeffords of two very heavy blankets of a special design, each weighing ten pounds. Hooker family legend says that Cochise gave Colonel Hooker a special blanket crafted in Mexico. The family story says:

On one occasion Cochise presented Hooker, whom he called "captu" with a Mexican blanket of unique design. Its background was red, in the center was a large "C" in white with a black edge, a symbol of Cochise. On each end of the blanket was woven an H, for Hooker.[20]

This blanket is still in possession of the family. It may be one of three that Colonel Hooker had made. We have evidence that he called for two and presented them to the agent and the chief.

Two pair blankets made at the woolen mills in San Francisco for agent Jeffords and Cachise, were brought here by the bell train. We are not aware who the donor is. The blankets weigh twenty pounds to the pair.[21]

Cochise is said to have been buried in this, his favorite blanket. Who gave which blanket to whom is not nearly as important as the demonstration of affection shown between three men. It says something of how close they had become.[22]

In 1873, Jeffords called for establishing a missionary school at Pinery Canyon, but his recommendation fell on deaf ears. The department dropped the plan.[23] Perhaps it started with President Thomas Jefferson who dreamed of a country of free, yeoman farmers who could appreciate the idea of a republic. Only such men could form and keep a free republic. Americans believed and policy reflected the idea that Indians would become civilized only if we could teach them to farm. The purpose of a good agent was to keep the Indians in check, keep them counted, and teach them to farm. Moreover, if they began farming, the annuities were to stop and the Indians would be dropped from the budget. Indians of all kinds were showing themselves to be great stockmen. Their land in the west was more suited to grazing than farming. Unfortunately, cowboys were considered almost as wild and dangerous as Indians and stock raising was not to be encouraged.[24]

In January 1874, the following item appeared in the Prescott newspaper: "Major C.H. Veil, of East Phoenix, has been on a business trip through Southern Arizona and had the pleasure (?) of dining with those hightoned Apache rascals, Eskeminzin and Cachise."[25]

In his memoirs, Veil, a flour contractor, talked of meeting "old frontiersman" Tom Jeffords at his cabin in Pinery Canyon. He said that Jeffords had the reputation of having been in collusion with the Indians in the late "troubles" and of supplying them with ammunition. He described Tom as a crude backwoodsman. Having heard that in order to do business with Tom Jeffords he must bring something of the kind, Veil was prepared with a jug of whiskey. Jeffords poured out a cupful for himself and then a cupful for Cochise who was attended by two of his squaws. Veil described the chief as "one of the finest specimens of an Indian that I have ever seen, straight as an arrow and about six feet tall, not a spare ounce of flesh, and very dignified in his manner. The chief drained the cup without water and I began to think I would make my stay in camp as short as possible or, in other words, get away before the liquor had a chance to operate."[26]

Tom did not keep whiskey on the reservation and so built up a thirst.[27] He was not afraid to share whiskey with Cochise. The agent treated the chief as an equal. He insisted that Veil stay to dinner and Cochise stayed as well. We see Tom treating Cochise as a man, not as an Indian.

Levi Edwin Dudley succeeded Nathanial Pope as superintendent of Indian affairs for New Mexico.[28] When he learned that Cochise was lying very ill in his camp in the Dragoon Mountains, he felt it necessary to visit the chief for fear he might die. "I ascertained that the great chief retained in peace the wonderful power and influence he had exercised in war, and that he regarded his promises made to General Howard sacred and not to be violated upon any pretext whatever, I knew that it would be a calamity to the frontier to lose him from the ranks of living men."[29]

Dudley recalled that the camp was located on a high butte or foothill and commanded a view of the Sulphur Springs Valley as far as the Chiricahua Mountains. It was a place, he thought, well chosen for defense. On his first visit, he found Cochise lying down, a dying man, and presented the chief with a photograph of Dudley with General Howard by way of establishing his bona fides. The chief expressed the warmest feeling of affections for the general. Cochise soon tired and Dudley thought it best to return on another day when he could also talk to the sub-chiefs. Cochise summoned them. Dudley had asked Second Lieutenant Edward Livingstone Keyes along on the trip as his aide.[30] Keyes reported that Dudley fortified the old warrior with a soupçon of cognac from his pocket flask.[31]

After three days, Dudley returned.

During the second visit I found Cochise mounted on his horse in front of his wickiup, having been lifted there by his friends, showing his determination and strength of will. I asked why he did so, and he replied that he wished to be mounted once more before he died. The agent and myself both feared he might die while on his horse, and probably he would have preferred such a death.[32]

Dudley's fears for Cochise's life, and thus for the future of the reservation and the future of the Chihenne and Bedonkohe at Tularosa, which were more properly in his district, were allayed after meeting and talking with Jeffords and the chief. He felt that while Tom Jeffords did not answer all the requirements of an agent,[33] Jeffords was able to maintain discipline and, if necessary, would be able to bring the Chokonen and Nednhi to Tularosa. If anyone could teach the Apache to work (farm), Jeffords was the man.

On June 8, 1874, Cochise died, four days after Dudley's departure. His family believed a witch had cursed Cochise and thought they knew who it was, a crippled Chihenne who lived in the Chiricahua Mountains. Tradition required that they burn the man to preserve Cochise's life. Jeffords was at pains to rescue him, and Fred Hughes reports that he did. To this day, Cochise's descendants maintain that he was poisoned.[34] It may be so. Jeffords was with Cochise during his final illness and gave him the best medical attention available. The day before the chief's death, Tom was called away to issue rations. Cochise told Jeffords that he wanted his "brother" to take care of the Chihenne, his particular band. Jeffords said: "I am only one, and they are over three hundred, and they won't do what I ask them to unless they want to." Cochise said: "We will fix that." He called in his sub-chiefs and it was agreed that his oldest son, Taza, should be his successor and that they would do whatever Jeffords wanted them to do.

In saying good-bye, Cochise said: "Chickasaw, do you think you will ever see me alive again?" Jeffords replied: "I do not know; I don't think I will, for you have been failing very rapidly in the last three days, and I think that by tomorrow night you will be dead." Cochise said: "I think so too, about tomorrow morning, at ten o'clock, I will pass out, but do you think we will ever meet again?" Jeffords relied "I don't know. What do you think about it?" "Well," said Cochise, "I have been giving it a good deal of thought since I have been sick here, and I think we will." "Where?" asked Jeffords. "I don't know, somewhere up yonder," pointing to the skies. He never feared death, but rather courted it.[35]

There are two accounts of Cochise's funeral. Neither writer was there. The funeral was attended exclusively by Apaches. His family buried Cochise before Tom Jeffords could return. Lieutenant Edward Keyes, stationed at Camp Bowie, and who had been with Cochise just a few days before his death, provided a reasonable account that describes an affair consonant with Apache custom:

> *[A]t midnight they dressed the dead chieftain in his best apparel, braided up his hair, and painted his face. They wrapped him in two newly tanned deerskins, and around these wrapped the superb Navajo blanket[36] into which his name was woven when manufactured. A belt, with a revolver and hunting knife, was buckled around him and a loaded Springfield rifle was placed between his left arm and body. On a rude litter, he was then borne by his two sons, his three squaws, and the medicine man to the deep grave that had been prepared for him. A hole ten feet deep and four broad had been dug to receive his body. At a distance of six feet from the surface there was a ledge left shelving out at the sides of the interior of the grave. . . . The grave was then filled in, stamped down hard and level and cacti planted thereon, so that no one might have told an hour later that the ground had been disturbed.[37]*

Apache fear dead bodies and dispose of them as rapidly as possible. Another account mentions Cochise being mounted on a horse and held in place by one of his sub-chiefs while being taken twelve miles to the burial site. It seems unlikely any Apache would have stayed so close to a dead body for so long. At the burial site, Cochise's favorite horse was shot and buried with him. This is likely.[38] White men have speculated that the things buried with the dead are meant to accompany them to the other side. Apache knowledge of the afterlife is vague at best. They fear the return of the dead. Anything the dead were attached to in life goes into the grave with them so that they won't be drawn back to it. Apache will not speak the name of the dead.[39] Legend says that Tom Jeffords had a secret; he knew where the Apache had buried Cochise and wouldn't tell. He probably did. He was close enough in spirit to Cochise and the Chiricahua that he would have found it a strange invasion of privacy to tell.

Taza took over as chief. The Apache respected Jeffords. The newspapers began to admit that there hadn't been any raiding or murders in Arizona that could be attributed to the Chiricahua. In February 1874, even Inspector Vandever officially conceded that Chihenne Apache committed most raids, but instead of censuring the agent responsible on the Tularosa reservation, he blamed Jeffords for harboring them.[40] Tom continued to handle stolen livestock complaints as he always had. He recovered the animals and held them for their owners. He did not arrest or punish the perpetrators. Arizona had peace with the Apache.

There was new thirst for Apache land and complaints that the reservation was too big. It comprised valuable farming and ranch land. Minerals weren't mentioned, yet, but every corner of the reservation would prove to be mineral rich, and Tom Jeffords was well aware of it. The huge silver strike at Tombstone in 1877 was on the edge of the reservation. The major copper strike at Bisbee was within the boundaries, as were Pearce, Galeyville, Courtland, and Gleeson. Tom had an eye for minerals and staked numerous claims immediately after the reservation was broken up. In 1875, he laid claim to the abandoned Brunckow Mine[41] along with partners Sidney DeLong, sutler at Fort Bowie; Nick Rogers, who held the Sulphur Springs Ranch; and Estevan Ochoa and Randolph Tully, freighting magnates from Tucson. The mine was in the foothills of the Dragoon Mountains near the San Pedro River, just off the reservation. One source says Tom was actively working three mines in Pinery Canyon: the Southern Belle, Rarus, and Elizabeth Tilton. He may have noticed mineral outcroppings while the agency was at Pinery Canyon, but he could not have staked claims on reservation land.[42] In 1876, he would stake claims at Apache Pass and the Dos Cabezas Mountains.

The Southern Emigrant Road ran through Apache Pass and from there to Croton Springs, crossing the reservation. Contact between whites and Apaches was problematic. They had little to trade except livestock, some of it stolen. In return they wanted whiskey and ammunition, or at least so the Army and newspapers thought. On April 17, 1875, Lieutenant Galbraith C. Rodgers arrested two Mexicans at Camp Bowie who had exchanged whiskey for a stolen horse. Apache Pass had become the critical point. On May 14, 1875, Jeffords got permission to make the final move of the agency and settled into buildings erected by the Apache Pass Mining Company run by John Finckle Stone, who had been killed by Cochise in 1869. The agency was half a mile from Fort Bowie.[43]

All was not well on the reservation. Taza lacked his father's influence. A serious rift developed in the tribe. In the spring of 1876, the young chief took a band of men to the Dragoon Mountains where a fight broke out between his men and those of Eskinya. Three Chiricahuas died.[44]

Although warned by Jeffords, his sometimes partner was still selling whiskey on the reservation at Sulphur Springs Ranch. His primary customers were soldiers from Camp Bowie. His stock in trade was referred to as rot gut. It was expensive to transfer bottled whiskey by wagon. Distillers sold nearly pure alcohol by the barrel. In this form it would rot the gut, so barmen cut it by half with water, making it about the same strength as bottled whiskey. It lacked color and flavor and, since it wasn't aged, was hard to drink. They added chewing tobacco for color and bite, and burnt sugar or molasses for flavor. Chili peppers were a frequent addition, and some say snake heads as well. Although they sound horrible, none of the additives did nearly as much harm as the alcohol itself. Jeffords found tobacco and chili peppers in Rogers's blend.

On April 6, 1876, Pionsenay from Eskinya's band bought whiskey from Rogers for ten dollars a bottle. He came back the next day with a friend and bought more. Returning drunk to his camp, he got

Tom Jeffords's signature from the Brown Ranch visitor registor. This is the signature as it also appears on his letters but not the handwriting in the body of them. He was uncomfortable with cursive. ARIZONA HISTORICAL SOCIETY

Looking out across the San Pedro Valley from the entrance to Cochise's Stronghold (China Meadow). No one could approach Cochise across the San Pedro or Sulphur Springs Valley without his knowing of their coming a day or two in advance. From the Stronghold he could monitor comings and goings from Fort Bowie 40 miles away. DOUG HOCKING

The meadow at Cochise's Stronghold. Alice Rollins Crane described it as a beautiful place full of trees of all kinds and a flowing stream. She said that Jeffords made signal fires and called in Bronco Apaches (1895) or the Apache Kid (1914). ARIZONA HISTORICAL SOCIETY

Flat topped rock on the left is where Cochise, Jeffords, and O. O. Howard sat to discuss the peace. The dark spot at center is the tiny cave where Cochise slept. This is on the western slope of the Dragoon Mountains one mile south of West Stronghold Canyon. DOUG HOCKING

Half a mile from the peace rock is the circle of rocks where Cochise conducted a ceremony and had his sub-chiefs agree to the peace. The entrance to West Stronghold Canyon can be seen in the background. ARIZONA HISTORICAL SOCIETY

General Oliver Otis Howard whose peace terms with Cochise were never written down.

Foundations of the Chiricahua Agency at Sulphur Springs Ranch. Jeffords paid $50 per month to Nicholas Rogers for the use of this room. DOUG HOCKING

Ruins of the Chiricahua Agency at Apache Pass one half mile from Fort Bowie. Before Jeffords occupied the building, it was built by John Finckle Stone, who had a mine at Apache Pass. He was slain by Cochise in 1869. DOUG HOCKING

Photo was taken about 1914. The site is near the mouth of Huachuca Canyon along Reservoir Road, near the modern sergeant major housing area. In the early 1800s, Tom Jeffords built a sutler's store from adobe at a cost of $8,000. The 1888 map of Fort Huachuca shows a U-shaped sutler's store at this location. Today the site near Reservoir Hill has been bulldozed and only a few foundations remain. FORT HUACHUCA MUSEUM

Tom Jeffords in 1895 when Alice Rollins Crane talked him into sitting for a portrait. He holds the shotgun "that Cochise gave him." It is a modern, break down shotgun, not a muzzle-loader such as were common in Cochise's day. THE HUNTINGTON LIBRARY

Alice Rollins Crane in 1897.
ARIZONA HISTORICAL SOCIETY

Alice Rollins Crane on her way to
Alaska, 1898. SAN FRANCISCO EXAMINER

Owl Head Buttes from the stamp mill looking northwest. Tom Jeffords's ranch was between the two at center in 1892. His mines were on the tallest Owl Head on the left, to the south of it (left) and out of the photo to the right. DOUG HOCKING

Tom's house and dogs in 1913, shortly before his death. He was 81. The photo was taken by Thomas Farish. It is made of relatively expensive wood frame with glass windows, which were also expensive. ARIZONA HISTORICAL SOCIETY

THOMAS J. JEFFORDS
1832 —— 1914
FRIEND AND BLOOD-BROTHER OF COCHISE
PEACE-MAKER WITH HOSTILE APACHES
~ 1872 ~
ERECTED IN 1964 · BY
DAUGHTERS OF THE AMERICAN COLONISTS

Tom Jeffords's grave in Evergreen Cemetery, Tucson, along Oracle Road. DOUG HOCKING

Site of Tom's Ranch today. Identified from the shape of the hills in the background of 1913 photo. Nothing remains. The site was occupied by a ranch until very recently. DOUG HOCKING

Brunckow's Cabin, known as the Arizona Murder House. It is claimed that as many as 27 men were murdered here at different times. The building may have been seen by the Mormon Battalion in 1846 making this originally a Mexican mine. Brunckow and two partners were killed while working his mine in 1860. Marshal Milton Duffield restaked the claim and was killed here on June 5, 1874. Soon afterwards, Tom Jeffords, Sidney De Long, sutler at Fort Bowie, and Nicholas Rogers restaked the claim. J. W. Houten was slain here in 1879 while trying to jump a nearby claim. Tom continued assessment work on the claim into the mid-1880s with his brother John as guard. John received a shotgun blast to the head in nearby Charleston, but survived. ARIZONA HISTORICAL SOCIETY

This mine, which worked veins of ore near the surface, was close to Tom's ranch and may have been one of his. That it was worked so close to the surface strongly suggests Tom's ownership since none of his were said to have gone more than 75 feet underground. The ladder is probably from 1976; the area was worked because the price of gold was very high.
DOUG HOCKING

into a fight with his brother. Two sisters, apparently their wives, tried to intervene. Pionsenay killed them. On April 7, now morose, he returned once more to Sulphur Springs with Eskinya and Geronimo demanding more whiskey. Rogers refused. They killed him and his partner, O. O. Spence.[45]

On April 8, now realizing that they were in very great trouble, Pionsenay with four warriors went off the reservation to the nearby San Pedro Valley. There at the mouth of the Babocomari River, near where Fairbank stands today, they stole four horses, wounded a rancher named Brown, and killed another named Lewis.[46]

Learning of the matter, Taza sent for Tom Jeffords, who received word the night of April 7. The next morning he informed Captain Curwen Boyd McLellan, commander of Camp Bowie. McLellan and Jeffords understood the matter to be the result of a drunken row, with Jeffords telling the commander bad Indians who ought to be cleaned out had done it. [47] McLellan ordered Lieutenant Austin Henely to take the field with a wagon of rations and forty men of Company A, Sixth Cavalry. Jeffords and Streeter went directly to Taza's rancheria and joined Henely later. On April 9, at Sulphur Springs Ranch, word came that a considerable body of Chiricahuas had raided the San Pedro Valley. Packing a few rations in saddle bags, Henely went in pursuit, taking Jeffords, Taza, and Streeter. The pursuit continued through the Mule Mountains.[48] The *Arizona Citizen* reported:

On the April 10, Henely caught up with the fleeing Indians at the Iron Monster. They came up with the enemy strongly posted on a ridge in the San Jose mountains, on the east side of the San Pedro, about fifteen miles this side of the Sonora line. The position taken by the Indians was such that they could not be dislodged, being completely covered by rocks, so that none of them were seen during the engagement while they kept up a terrible fusillade on their assailants who were obliged to retreat from their unseen foes, with

*the supposed loss of one soldier, named Gardner, who was missing
but subsequently came into Sulphur Springs.*[49]

The position was very strong. Taza offered to take some soldiers
and outflank the position, driving the Indians from the rocks. Henely,
with wounded and dead, as he thought, and not wanting to divide
his command, declined. Allowing an Apache to command US cavalrymen would have posed difficulties. Out of food, Henely could not
conduct a siege and the soldiers returned to Camp Bowie.[50]

By mid-May, Jeffords had the difficulties under control. By May
10, things had calmed down so much that Eskinya felt he could return
to the reservation. He sought out Tom Jeffords, explaining that the
murders were the work of Pionsenay. After this, Pionsenay was considered a criminal and was not allowed to return to the reservation.
Eskinya railed against Taza's authority. Naiche, Cochise's younger son,
killed Eskinya.

John Wasson, editor of the Tucson *Citizen*, turned on Jeffords. In
a piece entitled "Jeffords a devil,"[51] he proceeded to list all of Tom's
"crimes." According to Wasson the story of Jeffords's service as agent
"unfolds a tale of this incarnate demon's doings for the last four years
which has so horrified us that if it lies within our weak power, we
propose bringing the late United States Indian Agent at Chiricahua
to justice." Furthermore, Jeffords "has been helplessly drunk at least
one half of his time and has grossly neglected his duty. That while in
charge of wild and dangerous Indians he has been in collusion and
interest with outside parties, has known of liquor and ammunition, in
vast quantities, being brought upon the reservation, and has at times
had temporary charge of such liquor and ammunition." Still more,
"in February last he also received a large quantity of gold which was
taken by the Indians from some Mexicans whom they had murdered
in Sonora." Zebina Streeter was identified as the middle man in these
transactions. Later, he rode with Geronimo and Juh and was, as the
newspapers called him, the White Apache.[52]

Tom wrote a letter answering these charges, but the *Citizen* declined to print it. The editor of the Prescott *Miner* took umbrage at this and published Tom's letter.[53] In addition to being owner of the *Citizen*, Wasson was also surveyor general of Arizona. He and Governor Safford called for Jeffords's removal. On May 3, 1876, Commissioner of Indian Affairs J. Q. Smith telegraphed John P. Clum,[54] Apache agent at San Carlos, telling him to proceed to the Chiricahua Agency and suspend Jeffords and take charge of the Indians and agency property there.[55]

Jeffords stayed on to assist Clum with the move and Taza worked with them. An executive order closed the reservation. The Nednhi, Juh, and Geronimo fled back to Mexico. Zebina Streeter went with them and became the White Apache. The Chihenne and Bedonkohe returned to Tularosa and the Mescalero Reservation in eastern New Mexico. Others scattered. Taza's band, the band his father had led, about three hundred in all, went peacefully to San Carlos. There were questions about the numbers Jeffords reported that he had been feeding. The Indian bureau wanted to know where all the Indians had gone. No wrong doing was ever found. Clum sent Taza with a delegation to meet the Great Father, the President of the United States, and on September 26, 1876, he died of pneumonia in Washington, DC. His younger brother, Naiche, took his place as chief.

Zebina Streeter was a New Yorker like Jeffords. He had grown up in California with the family of his father's second wife, a Mexican. He had served as packer with Jeffords since General Howard's expedition to find Cochise. He lived on the reservation with a Chiricahua woman. Jeffords referred to him as his translator and as "that little Mexican." In answering allegations that Streeter was his go-between for illicit deals, Jeffords had said that the little Mexican knew better than to come around the agency. Nonetheless, there seems to have been some sort of friendship between them. Perhaps Streeter just looked up to Jeffords. He began to raid with Geronimo and Juh. Streeter blamed Wasson, the newspaper editor, for Jeffords's removal. It is noteworthy that Juh raided Wasson's ranch at Fort Crittenden on two occasions.[56]

CHAPTER 9

Making a Fortune, 1877–1892

In the 1881 Tucson Business Directory, Tom Jeffords listed his occupation as "Capitalist." His brother John, then living with him, listed himself as a butcher.[1] Mining was among Tom's capitalistic enterprises. It often came with grief, feud, and bloodshed. The location of claims was inexact in country that had yet to be surveyed. Assessment work had to be done on claims each year in order to maintain them and eventually to have them patented. Claims crossed over each other and men filed counter-claims alleging the assessment work hadn't been done and the claim was therefore abandoned. In 1880, Jeffords, through his partner, S. R. DeLong, filed notice in the Tucson newspaper on a claim in the Santa Rita Mountains south of town.

Mining Notice

This is to caution all persons against purchasing a certain Copper Mine, unless from the undersigned and associates, located in two locations of fifteen hundred feet each, on May 24th, 1877, as the "Omega" mine, and the "Omega" mine first Easterly extension, situated on Western base of the Santa Rita Mountains, about thirty miles a little East of South from Tucson. The necessary lawful work required by law to hold mining claims has been done upon each of those locations, year by year, from date of location. On February

4th, 1877, one Birgin located 1,500 feet taking in part of each location, calling his location the "Gibraltar." Persons purchasing or intending to purchase the "Gibraltar" will do well to examine title, as myself and associates claim to be the legal owners, and shall not part with our title unless for a consideration until legal remedies are exhausted.

SR DeLong
Fort Bowie, AT, Nov. 12, 1880

Tom Jeffords returned to prospecting and mining even before he left the Chiricahua Agency. He and his partners laid claim to the Brunckow Mine[2] in 1875. Prospecting and mining are two distinctly different activities, especially where "hard rock" or lode mining is concerned. Mining law grew up out of the rules enacted by mining districts or towns in the California Gold Rush of 1849. A prospector would locate rich sand or gravel along a stream where nature had deposited gold already separated from quartz. All the prospector had to do was recover it from loose sand. When he found a good spot, he built a sluice to help him with this. Water passing over ridges in the sluice would cause heavy gold to sink and lighter sand to wash away until only gold was left.

In lode mining, the prospector searched for the original ledge that gold or other minerals had come from before washing down to a stream. A vein might grow larger or pinch out entirely. The prospector would stake a claim. The 1872 Mining Act granted extralateral rights to lode claims, and fixed the maximum size of lode claims as fifteen hundred feet (457 m) long and six hundred feet (183 m) wide. The prospector would set a monument in the middle of his claim and append a notice. He would then walk off the distance and place monuments on his four corners. He would run fifteen hundred feet along what he hoped was the direction of the vein. Each year, he had to do one hundred dollars' worth of assessment work. This meant that he had to dig into or otherwise improve the property showing "color," samples of minerals from the rock. He could lay additional claims, if he could afford it, but he would have to do assessment work on them as well. If he did not, others would stake claims around his, hoping the vein ran their way. After five years, the prospector could file for a patent, that is, he could have the government transfer the claim to him as real property. Even before that, he could sell the claim to a miner who had the money to continue the assessment work or develop the prospect into a mine. A prospect becomes a mine when the mine owner takes out ore, rock with enough mineral in it to make it profitable to process.

Surveyors became important in mining districts. The prospectors usually got there first, and their "legal" descriptions were naturally vague. One of Tom's claims, the Bowie Mine, stated that the center was approximately one mile south of the Fort Bowie flagpole. The Brunckow claim was a half mile from the San Pedro River. On October 18, 1875, Tom located, or claimed, the Brunckow along with Sydney DeLong and Nicholas Rogers. On December 2, 1875, he also located the nearby John Randolph mine. On January 19, 1882, the partners sold a one-tenth share of the First Easterly Extension of the Brunckow for two thousand dollars.[3] As the papers noted, it was undoubtedly a mine of value and they intended to continue development.[4] Vague legal descriptions made claim-jumping easy, and it could also occur accidentally. In 1881, Tom would contend in court with the Dean Richmond Claim, which overlapped his own. The claimant also held that Tom hadn't kept up his assessment work:

> *The rival claims now are the Bronkow[5] and First Easterly Extension of the Bronkow, covering 3000 feet, 1500 feet each way from the "deep" shaft of the old location, which was 3600 feet long, and the Dean Richmond claim, which laps about 'alf and 'alf in each of the first mentioned claims. There was a lively struggle between these applicants for a patent, before the Land Office.[6]*

Tom brought his brother, John, in as a guard to prevent additional shenanigans. John had a temper and the Brunckow a bad reputation. Frederick Brunckow, a German mining engineer who worked with Charles Poston's Sonora Exploring and Mining Company, discovered the Brunckow in 1857. In July 1860, Mexican workers killed Brunckow and two of his partners. Six years later, Milton B. Duffield, former United States marshal, relocated the mine. In June 1874, Joseph T. Homes, who also claimed ownership, killed him on the property. The next year, Sydney DeLong, Tom Jeffords, and Nicholas Rogers, later killed by Pionsenay, relocated the mine.[7] The newspaper would eventually claim there had been twenty-seven murders on this site.

In September 1881, while serving as guard, brother John went into nearby Charleston.[8] Once there he met up with friends and they began "tossing the ruby." He proceeded to the hotel of Mr. Flores, a Frenchman, demanding dinner although it was past the dinner hour. Flores declined to provide food and John became rowdy. There were ladies present. Flores asked John to tone it down or leave. John Jeffords yanked out his six-shooter and fired on Flores, missing him. Flores scrambled for his shotgun charged with buckshot and fired, striking John in the head. Still game, John continued to fire his six-shooter, but, blinded by blood, missed. Having emptied his weapon, John ran, but Justice Holt apprehended him and "Billy the Kid" Claiborne disarmed him. Initially, according to one newspaper, John was dying, but the next day the rival paper said he was up and around and feeling much better, his wounds superficial.[9] John would get into difficulty on another occasion while working for Tom.

In the summer of 1876, Fred Hughes returned to the Chiricahua Agency to assist Tom, Taza, and John Clum in moving the Chiricahua to the San Carlos Reservation. Even while this was happening, Tom, Fred, and Charles O. Brown, a Tucson businessman, on July 14, staked a claim to the Harris Lode in Apache Pass. This was the same Harris Lode that John Finckle Stone had been working in 1869 when he was killed by Cochise. Stone's buildings became the Chiricahua Agency.

Tom had been sitting on top of the lode while he was agent and now that the reservation was no longer a hindrance, he filed a claim. A year later, on May 16, 1877, Tom, Estevan Ochoa, and Sydney DeLong, sutler at Fort Bowie, filed on the Lone Harris nearby. On July 15, 1877, Tom, Brown, George Smerden, and DeLong filed on another Apache Pass mine in the same vicinity.[10]

George Warren, another prospector, is famed for having located the fabulous Copper Queen Mine, the source of Bisbee's wealth and fame. He is the prospector who appears on the Great Seal of the State of Arizona. George lost his mother as an infant, which may help explain his subsequent alcoholism and insanity. Apaches killed his father and took George captive and raised him. After the Apache traded him to a group of prospectors for a twenty-pound bag of sugar, he became friends with Jack Dunn, an Army scout out of Fort Bowie, and Lieutenant John A. Rucker, a cavalry officer. In 1877, the cavalryman and the scout grubstaked Warren to search for minerals at deposits they'd detected in the Mule Mountains, near the Iron Monster. George was to stake claims and the three would share the proceeds. George staked claims but failed to include Dunn's or Rucker's names. One of his claims became the famed Copper Queen Mine on which Phelps-Dodge built an empire. George had a drinking problem and was soon recognized as both the Father of Bisbee and the town drunk. Legend has it that on July 3, 1880, in Charleston, while drinking, George bet his share of the Copper Queen on a race between himself and a horse. He lost. On November 20, 1882, for five dollars, in a quit claim deed,[11] Warren sold his one-ninth share of the Copper Queen to Tom Jeffords and Tom Fitch, the lawyer who defended Wyatt Earp and John Henry "Doc" Holliday on a charge of murder over the gunfight near the O.K. Corral. The *Tombstone Republican* proclaimed:

More litigation. . . . A case was filed today in the District that promises to be of great interest. Thomas J. Jeffords and Thomas Fitch claim an interest already settled for and disposed of in the

Copper Queen Mine. Plaintiffs have brought suit to recover a judgment decreeing a certain deed dated March 12, 1880, from George Warren to George W. Arkins void. [12]

Apparently, they were successful. On January 4, 1885, Tom sold his share by quit claim for seven hundred dollars.[13] George Warren died drunk and insane.

Tom also had mining interests in Sonora, Mexico. The Altar district is southwest of where Nogales stands today. The *Citizen* reported: "The principal work recently done in the Altar District is at the Cienega, perhaps the richest neighborhood for gold and silver in the State. The developments within the past year have been mainly by Messrs. Tully & Ochoa and Capt. Jeffords of this city, and under the direct supervision of Mr. Rainey, who is also a partner." [14]

In Tombstone, Tom was associated with the Yellow Jacket and Head Center. He also served as a Constable. On August 1, 1877, Ed Schieffelin discovered the lode at Tombstone. Stories indicate that he was doing assessment work for Tom Jeffords on the Brunckow Claim at the time. Tombstone is eight miles east of the San Pedro River and a thousand feet higher in elevation in the Tombstone Hills. In Tombstone, water has always been a problem. Wyatt Earp was involved in the building of the Tombstone Aqueduct, a ten-inch cast-iron pipe, which brought drinking water twenty-five miles from the Huachuca Mountains. The mines also needed water for milling.

Gold often comes from the earth pure. It doesn't combine chemically with much of anything. Not so other minerals. They combine with water, sulfur, and chlorine, just to mention a few.

In lode mining, large infusions of cash were needed to drill and blast the rock and lay track for cars to bring it to the surface and money for timber to shore the mine and keep it from collapsing. Once the ore was on the surface, money was needed to mill it, crush it, and wash away the unwanted rock. This was done with stamp mills. A set of giant stair steps were built in a hillside and a stamp mill imported.

This was a set of vertical hammers than ran day and night crushing ore to powder. Mills powered their hammers with water and used it as well to wash away the lighter stone from the mineral. The material left behind, heavy in minerals, now needed to have its chemical bonds cracked and the mineral made pure. In the early days, this was often done in a smelter furnace. Usually, the prospector lacked the money needed. Partnerships were set up and investors from the east coast were invited in to take the risk. It was high risk. At any time the ore might give out, the mine might flood, the price of the mineral might collapse, or a new technique of extraction might be developed that ran more inexpensively, making the price of mineral less expensive in the market than the cost of current extraction methods.

A string of towns grew up along the San Pedro River. Richard Gird, partner to Ed Schieffelin, built a dam and brought water to his mill at Millville eight miles from Tombstone and only one mile from the old Brunckow mine. In Millville, Gird allowed no drinking. Intoxication around the massive machinery of the stamp mills could prove deadly. Across the river, only two yards wide and knee deep, Charleston grew in answer to a need for a place to drink, and Cow Boys[15] and other ruffians spent their time in its confines. Drovers came up the trail from Texas driving cattle to feed the Army and reservation Indians in Arizona. Once there, they found little work and turned to rustling, carousing, and robbery.[16] Farther north, downriver, was Boston Mill and then Contention City. The mines transported heavy ore, a great deal of which was waste rock, at high cost to these river towns. Woodcutters stripped the hills bare of trees for shoring and fuel to fire the smelters.

High in the mountains, water seeps into cracks in the rock and descends into the earth until it reaches an impervious layer of rock. It then flows along that layer until it emerges from the earth at a spring. If the impervious layer is tilted, the water emerges under pressure as an artesian well. Tom Jeffords saw possibilities in this concept. In 1879, the Tucson *Citizen* proclaimed:

Tombstone—practical wagon route to the "Empire," "Grand Central," "Contention," and the mines in that vicinity—good influence, indeed, and if these companies take the later est. which is accredited them in the future of the burgh, it certainly ought to succeed. That town is upon the only level spot in the district (or among the mines) of sufficient size to admit of any considerable village, and in that respect has a decided advantage. They depend upon teams for their water at present, but Capt. Jeffords we have hurled at us, is to do away with that inconvenience as soon as his artesian machine can be put to work on a neighboring hill. Alternate lots are given away to those who put houses upon them within a stipulated time. Selected lots are held at $100 or more; twenty or thirty houses already built.[17]

In the 1880s, at the five-hundred-foot level, the Tombstone mines flooded. The mining companies brought in huge Cornish pumps to draw the water out. With plenty of water on hand, though none of it potable, mills were built in Tombstone and the river communities died. Tom wasn't done with artesian water. He worked for years to bring drinking water to Tucson with the approval of the Tucson city council: "April 11. Full Council present. Minutes read and approved. On motion it was ordered the Council proceed to the consideration of the application of T.J. Jeffords for a franchise for supplying the city of Tucson with flowing artesian water."[18]

Tom Jeffords was to be granted an exclusive contract for twenty-five years to provide water for culinary and domestic purposes within Tucson provided he start drilling wells within six months. In December 1879, the paper reported that [the] grand bore, the only one regarded with interest is going down steadily. A depth of 450 feet has been reached.[19] Thereafter, all did not go well. A single well proved insufficient to provide the water needed. There wasn't enough pressure. There wasn't enough money. Tucson remained without water. The question of the forfeiture of the bond of TJ Jeffords as principal and RN Leatherwood and Samuel Hughes as sureties, then came up, and it was declared that owing to non-completion of the water works within the required time, that the bond of $5000 be forfeited and the City Attorney be ordered to collect the same.[20]

It's not clear that Tom ever forfeited the bond, although he did lose the company. In June 1881, the city attorney, R. H. Hereford, gave the opinion that the city had no right to the bond as the city hadn't given any consideration and the city hadn't lost anything.[21] This would have been a lot of money in those days; five thousand dollars was a small fortune. Tom had money and at least some of his many ventures were paying off.

In May 1880, Tom Jeffords, along with partners S. W. Carpenter, Marcus Katy, and J. C. Handy, were sued for one hundred dollars by John Jenkins (or Jennings) and Joseph Garmen for work done on the Bon Ton Mine. The partners failed to show up at trial and the judge held for the plaintiffs in the amount of $143.50.[22] Tom also partnered on the Head Center and Yellow Jacket mines in Tombstone with Dr. J. C. Handy. On August 16, 1879, Moody, Farish and Associates of San Francisco bought the mine for thirty thousand dollars.[23] Tom's share might have been as much as ten thousand dollars, a sizable sum in the 1880s.

The expense of setting up a mine included setting up a stamp mill and smelter. The owners of prospects set up complex partnerships with local folks who had money, imported big-money partners from the coasts, or they sold the mine to those with the money to develop it. Prospectors seldom got rich. The machinery of stamp mills was expensive. Mines played out all too rapidly. Mill owners moved the machinery from place to place. Buildings are usually part of the real estate, but they were torn down by the owners of the machinery inside so that it might be moved, the machinery, the hammers, being personal property instead of real property. They left the southwestern countryside littered with giant stair-steps, the foundations of stamp mills. In late 1883, Tom apparently had money, for he bought a stamp mill at sheriff's auction, which is to say the mill and real property had been seized for unpaid taxes. Tom's old partner, Dr. J. C. Handy, got the real property in the same sale.

Dec. 25th, 1883
Mr. Colin Cameron

Dear Sir,

Yours of the 22nd instant at hand in which you inform me of your visit to the Smelter in the interest of Dr. Handy and the unpleasant reception you met with from my brother while there (that I regret). It was due undoubtedly to the manner they treated him in Tucson in connection with the personal property, being the Smelter complete, Tanks and all its connections, in fact everything except the real estate that belonged to the Yankee Smelting Co. that I purchased at Sheriffs Sale and paid cash for and have had John there in charge since the purchase. My Brother tells me that you have bought the Real-Estate. If so I wish you would give me written permission to let my property remain there until I can get it out of your way. I have written John of this date to commence taking the machinery down as soon as he gets his letter which will be about the same time you get this.

Yours Very Truly,
T.J. Jeffords[24]
Office of Jeffords & Franklin
Attorneys at Law
HR Jeffords[25]
SM Franklin

Despite Tom's efforts to cool the situation, brother John's hot-headed behavior clashed with an equally hot-headed Dr. Handy. The doctor's biographer said: "He [Handy] was unable, however, to accept anyone who questioned his opinions or who did not follow his directions as a physician. Those who crossed him aroused his animosity. His aggressive personality and vindictive spirit made him enemies among some of Tucson's citizens and in the end proved to be his undoing. . . . He was frequently involved in public and private disputes."[26] The case went to court and Handy lost. He filed again and finally, five years later, on June 5, 1888, ended up paying Tom $600 in court costs when Tom again prevailed.[27]

The doctor lost sympathy when he publicly disgraced his wife by calling her a common slut and a morphine fiend. She was from an old and prominent Tucson family, the Penningtons,[28] and this did not sit well. The doctor filed for divorce and threatened anyone who would take Mary's case.[29] In the end, he was shot on the streets of Tucson and his killer was never indicted.

On September 1, 1881, while serving as sutler (post trader) at Fort Huachuca, Tom filed on the Grand Misery claim near the Black Bear Mine in Ash Canyon, Huachuca Mountains.

On May 24, 1877, Tom's old partner, S. R. DeLong, filed on a copper mine, the Omega, at the north end of the Santa Rita Mountains about thirty miles south and a little east of Tucson. Prospectors thought copper claims valueless at the time, but by the 1880s America had begun to wire itself for electric lights and telephone. In 1880, the Gibraltar claim overlapped the Omega. This was an attempt to jump the claim.[30] The price of copper rose and DeLong formed a company to provide money and skill for mining. Tom owned shares in this new mine of great expectations. "The stock has been divided into 300,000 shares, of which 120,000 are held by parties in Philadelphia, as stated, 150,000 by Tully, Ochoa & Co. (Hon. S.R. DeLong being the Company) and 15,000 each by Messrs. Jeffords and [Fred] Hughes," reported the *Citizen*. The partners from Philadelphia were supposed to set up a smelter: "The smelter of class and capacity agreed upon has been ordered of Rankin, Brayton & Col, San Francisco, who furnish much of the mining machinery used for the reduction of copper ores in their country, and as by the nature of the contract, it must be on the ground by the 8th of January coming."[31]

All did not go as planned. Apparently, the smelter wasn't forthcoming. The Arizona owners sued the Philadelphia owners. In 1883, workers took exception to Fred Hughes's management of the mine. Some of the mine machinery was blown up and damaged:

The latest developments of this outrage, are the following: at the place where the water pipe was blown up, several more fuses were found ready for use. A lot of blood was discovered and a trail made by a burro or a pony. It is conjectured that the wounded man, Cameron had probably been placed on the animal and taken to his cabin, as the tracks go in that direction, and blood was discovered in several places, especially in one where the wounded man was probably laid down for a while and where there is considerable blood.[32]

On October 10, 1885, the Omega was sold at a sheriff's sale.[33] Between labor disputes and disagreements over construction of the smelter, perhaps the owners ran out of money. The Philadelphia Mill Site went with the mine to satisfy a judgment of less than two thousand dollars. Maybe the mine was played out, although the area contained a wealth of copper.

In 1879, Tom Jeffords obtained a license as an Indian trader at Apache Pass near Fort Bowie.[34] In 1880, he sought the position of Indian agent for the San Carlos Reservation. His application to serve as the sutler for Fort Huachuca[35] was accepted, and he had to give up both of the former appointments. New rules from the War Department forbade serving as both an Indian trader and a sutler. Tom's other activities—scouting for the Army, mining, prospecting, serving as Tombstone constable, developing Tucson's water resources—interfered with his duties as sutler, and his tenure was marred by intrigue and complaints.

A council of post officers elected the sutler and sent their recommendation to the Secretary of War for confirmation. The sutler was the post trader, a precursor to the modern Post Exchange, supplying soldiers' needs for polish, needle and thread, household goods, supplemental foods, and alcohol. The sutler's store also served as post canteen. Soldiers went there to play cards, shoot pool, socialize, and drink—especially drink. The sale of alcohol was the most lucrative part of the business. Sutlerships were extremely lucrative franchises, most grossing in excess of fifty to sixty thousand dollars.[36] A post trader expected profits at a rate of twenty-five hundred dollars per company per annum. Fort Huachuca was a two-company post, averaging about fifty men per company, although they were authorized one hundred. A sutler would have expected to make a five-thousand-dollar profit. Tom and the officers at Fort Huachuca expected the post to grow to four companies or maybe even eight. Twenty thousand dollars was a lot of money in 1880. In addition, the postmaster position, which went along with the sutler store, brought in $508.44, with only two companies in residence.[37] In addition, posts were economic hubs where settlers came to make purchases. Tom dropped the Indian trading position and the application to be an Indian agent. The Secretary of War signed his appointment, and he accepted on May 4, 1880.

In 1881, two presidential orders made life harder for the post trader. One prohibited holding the sutlership and an Indian trader license at the same time. The second prohibited the sale of alcohol on posts. Most commanders compromised, not wanting their men to mutiny, and allowed liquor within limits. An untoward event could lead to a crackdown or serve as an excuse to replace a sutler.[38] For a year and a half, things went fairly well for Tom at Fort Huachuca.

On December 19, 1881, seventy-three men at Fort Huachuca signed a petition complaining about high prices and inferior goods in the sutler's store. The Post Council decided in favor of the petitioners and ordered that the store be equipped for a five-company post. The council also set prices on specific goods, including beer, wine, and liquor.[39] This created real problems for Tom Jeffords, who also acted as a high-risk banker for the soldiers. Pay was irregular, so the sutler extended credit. Unfortunately, transfers were also frequent and soldiers skipped out on debt. High prices covered some of this loss. Price controls were debilitating for the sutler, but the position still offered promise. Expanding the store to be adequate for five companies may seem ridiculous and a significant cost in overstock, but Jeffords and the military expected the post to grow. Jeffords was not the only one who wanted the position.

On June 30, 1882, officers voiced similar complaints. The post adjutant instructed Jeffords to appear before the Post Council. In an irregular move, the new post commander, Captain Madden, also came to council and effectively instructed the officers to remove Tom as sutler. The council named M. W. Stewart to replace him. Stewart and Madden were mining partners. Tom fought back, showing that supplies in his store were adequate for the average of ninety-seven men assigned to the post. Nonetheless, he offered to expand the store. He also obtained help from political allies. On October 16, H. H. Hubbard, the post quartermaster, sent a telegram to the Adjutant General[40], in other words to the attention of the commanding general of the Army, urging him to save Jeffords, who was being treated unfairly. Tom retained his position. He built a large and commodious store[41] at a cost between eight and nine thousand dollars.[42]

M. W. Stewart was not the only one seeking the position. Dr. J. S. W. Gardiner tried unsuccessfully to insert his assistant, A. C. Bernard,[43] into the sutlership. Captain Bernard declined, after which Gardiner approached Tom with an offer to invest seven thousand dollars and post a twenty-thousand-dollar bond for a one-third share of the profits. General Crook court-martialed Captain Morrow, the new post commander, for drunkenness on duty. He may have been under the influence of a drug given him by Dr. Gardiner. In September 1883, the vortex of Crook's anger over the incident also swept up the sutler and Tom was removed. His tenure as postmaster lasted from May 6, 1880, until January 18, 1884.[44]

On July 8, 1888, the Tucson papers noted that Captain Allen C. Bernard and Tom Jeffords had set up a house in Tucson decorated with Apache artifacts. It was supposed to be museum-like and worth seeing.

Tom Jeffords's interest in the mines never slackened and extended into Mexico. In August 1891, the newspapers noted, "Captain Jeffords is just in from the Quijotoa district. Business at the mines there is very dull, very little doing. About 40 or 50 Papago Indians are engaged in dry washing[45] for gold, evidently with some success, as Mr. Jeffords saw $110 worth of gold dust in F.A. Steven's store."[46] This was not Tom's only venture into Mexico. Not only did he visit the mines in Sonora, he was also running for the office of Pima County sheriff, when he got "quite full:"

It would not be much loss to the community to have a Democratic candidate turn his toes to the pansy blossoms, still the personal and individual loss would be felt. One, however, a candidate for the nomination for Sheriff, whose initials are Captain Jeffords, while in bathing with a party of friends last evening came near declining any nomination. In fact the Captain got fuller than he has been for a long time. It appears that he and Sheriff Paul,[47] Colonel Muir, Len Harries and one or two others who had been down south on a business trip, concluded while returning home that they would have a bath in Silver Lake.[48] They had a fine time in the beginning, but Captain Jeffords, who is not an expert swimmer, lost his hold on the towline and went under. He yelled like a Democratic stump speaker, and this brought the Sheriff, Colonel Muir and Len Harries, who at once conveyed him to the shore. The Captain was so full of Lake water that his companions had to roll him around on a barrel for some time in order to restore his breathing qualifications.

When the Captain had expurged [sic] about four barrels of water from his interior he arose, and brushing off his long whiskers with a blue silk handkerchief, remarked: "Well, gentlemen, that is more water than I ever took at one time before." The jest was greatly appreciated by his companions, and has doubtless cost him several dollars for lemonades.[49]

This wasn't the last time Tom was asked to run for office. In 1888, he was urged to run for sheriff of Cochise County.[50] Tom Jeffords became involved in many lines of work. In 1889, Tom tried his hand at cowboying by breeding and training colts at Ed Bullock's ranch at Agua Caliente in the Rincon Mountains near Tucson. In the past he had supplied mules to the Army on various occasions.[51] George Oakes said that in 1906, Tom was serving as Tucson's jailer. During the 1870s and '80s, Tom was generous in giving to the Tucson public schools.[52] Since he had also wanted a school for the Chiricahua, perhaps this is a reflection of his own lack of schooling.

In 1884, he joined the newly formed Arizona Pioneers Society, which has since merged with the Arizona Historical Society. The Pioneers would only accept those who had arrived before 1870. Even then they recognized that there was something special about people who had survived Arizona in the early days.

Col. Chas. D. Poston:

Dear Sir:

I hereby acknowledge your invitation to attend a meeting of the "Arizona Pioneers." I am in full accord with the object of the meeting. I presume I may be regarded as a pioneer. I came to the territory first in 1860. In 1862, when I saw Tucson, the population did not exceed one hundred, outside of the California column of soldiers. It was at this time that I first met Hiram Stevens, W.S. Ouray and Wheat. Tucson was a very small place then. The Apache was in full possession of the country from the Rio Grande to Tuc-son. In those days, the Pioneers had about all they could do to save their hair, but they were men of determination, and came to stay, and the present general prosperity of the territory shows plainly that they were men of foresight, as well as of industry and enter-prise. I regret my inability to be with you in person, but I assure you my best wishes are for the complete success of the association.

Very Truly Yours,
T.J. Jeffords
Tombstone, Jan. 30, 1884[53]

Tom's clerk from reservation days, Fred Hughes, was also a member of the Pioneers and as such served as the president of the society. He was also Pima County Clerk and president of the Territorial Legislature. In 1898, Pima County reduced his salary, making it difficult for Fred to make ends meet. He took to gambling to make up the deficit and this naturally had the opposite effect. As president of the legislature, Fred introduced legislation to provide the Pioneers with three thousand dollars. As president of the Pioneers, he signed for the money and fled to Sonora. After a year, he was induced to come back and turn himself over to the law. He did time at Yuma Territorial Prison but had too many political friends to remain there for long and was soon released on a gubernatorial pardon. He died sitting on his own front porch when struck in the forehead by lightning. The strike probably wasn't related to his past.

The government continued to call on Tom Jeffords as Indian expert, scout, and peacemaker. In 1879 and early 1880, he joined Archie McIntosh and Captain A. S. Haskell on a mission into Mexico. Geronimo and Juh[54] turned themselves in at the San Carlos Reservation. It is said that Juh had come to respect Jeffords.[55]

Tom Jeffords was called upon to quell disquiet on the San Carlos Reservation and ended up being blamed for an uprising. His old foe,

General William Vandever, Indian inspector, accused him of importing whiskey.[56] The *Arizona Miner* took Tom's side: "General Vandever, the old dotard, telegraphs . . . that late Indian Agent Jeffords is responsible for the late uprising of the Warm Springs [Chihenne] Indians, who recently left the San Carlos reservation, and that Jeffords can be convicted by Indian testimony of furnishing the Indians with liquor. It is curious that the Indian Department, and especially men like Vandever should be mixed up with such men, men who would stoop to incite Indians to leave their reservation and commit deeds of horror. Birds of a feather flock together."[57] Nonetheless, the Army, General Miles and General Crook, and the political establishment would call on Tom time and again for assistance with the Apache.

In August 1881, the Cibeque Apache on the Fort Apache or White Mountain Reservation were dancing with medicine man Nochaydelklinne to an early form of the Ghost Dance meant to bring back dead warriors and drive out the whites. Colonel Eugene Carr, 6th Cavalry, took eighty soldiers and twenty-three White Mountain Apache scouts to arrest the medicine man. Things did not go well. The medicine man was killed and the Apache scouts revolted, killing five cavalrymen and an officer. An overwhelming number of Apache on the high ground forced Colonel Carr's retreat to Fort Apache. Nana, Geronimo, and Naiche at San Carlos were unnerved and broke out to head for Mexico. Arizona was terrified. The Apache fought a rearguard action all the way to Mexico. Even the Tombstone Militia, including Virgil and Wyatt Earp, was called out to face the Chiricahua who passed nearby.

Summoned to Camp Thomas, near the San Carlos Reservation, to quell disturbances,[58] valiant Captain Jeffords, "whose great influence with the wild and murderous Apaches led to his selection by the military authorities as a valuable coadjutor in subduing the hostiles," was called into action.[59] He succeeded in bringing some of them back to the reservation and in calming those who remained at San Carlos. He was paid $150 per month as an interpreter.[60] This was one of the occasions on which he was called away from his post as sutler.

In June 1886, he joined General Miles in helping the Chiricahua at Fort Apache to form a delegation to go to Washington with a view to their removal from Arizona and in selecting two Indians to go with Lieutenant Gatewood into Mexico to treat with Geronimo and Naiche.[61] The Apache continued to respect him and trust him. Tom Jeffords played a significant role in ending the Geronimo War and in keeping the Apache who remained on the reservations calm. His contribution has been overshadowed by military operations in 1886 and by his own role in making the peace with Cochise.

CHAPTER 10

Owl Head Buttes, 1892–1914

IN 1892, AT THE AGE OF SIXTY, TOM MOVED TO THE OWL HEAD Buttes. The Owl Heads are at the northwest corner of the Tortolita Mountains about thirty miles north of Tucson. The closest town was Red Rock, a train station, on the Southern Pacific Railroad[1] about fifteen miles away. There in the sheltered space between two of the buttes, where water was close to the surface, he built a frame house with glass windows and a picket fence. It was reminiscent of his childhood home in the Western Reserve. He imported the timber he used from distant mountains and sawmills. Glass, too, was expensive. Tom's business dealings of the 1870s and '80s had left him comfortable but not wealthy. No longer involved in large business dealings or politics, Tom faded from public view. Since he was not a letter writer or keeper of journals, we catch only glimmers of his time in semi-retirement. He continued to prospect and to work several small mines.

The life of a mining district is a rollercoaster ride with peaks of prosperity and valleys of despair. The price of minerals rises and falls with demand. New means of digging and of extraction make once valueless ores profitable. Investors return to work even the tailings of old mines. At one point ore of less than 10 percent mineral might be thrown away as too expensive to work. New methods might make ore of even 0.1 percent usable. A man could carry enough gold to make him wealthy for life. Wealth in copper would take many wagons to transport, so when a railroad was built nearby the value of lesser mineral claims, like copper, increased. The Owl Head District was originally worked for gold and silver in the 1880s. The area was quiet until the price of copper rose and folks recalled that there was untouched copper in the area. The Owl Head District was organized in January of 1880:

1. This District shall be known as the Owl Head District.

2. The boundaries of the Owl Head District shall be as follows: Commencing at Big Cottonwood Springs on the road from Old Camp Grant to Adamsville, in Pinal county, A.T. thence westerly in a straight line to Wheat's Station on the road from Florence to Tucson, thence southerly along said road to a point four miles southerly from Point of Mountain Station, thence due east to a road from Tucson to Old Camp Grant, thence along said road to its intersection with the road from Big Cottonwood Springs, thence northerly along said road to place of beginning.

3. The mining laws of the United States and of the Territory of Arizona are hereby adopted as the laws of this District.

4. Locations may be fifteen hundred by six hundred feet. . . .

5. Eight hours work shall constitute a day's work on the claims; two hundred and forty cubic feet of rock excavation or twenty days' work shall be lawful assessment work on each claim, and mine owners shall be allowed five dollars for each day's work on a claim.[2]

These rules allow the same size for a claim as was stated in the General Mining Act of 1872. The size of the claim was about twenty acres. This was not enough for real development as a mine, so secondary claims were filed around the original provided that they showed "color," that is, minerals on the surface. The only limit of the number of claims was how much assessment work a man could do or pay others to do for him.[3] Tom filed more than twenty claims in the Owl

Head District. Assessment work lapsed on some of them and they were thus up for grabs by other prospectors at various times.

In 1882, there was a five-stamp mill three miles west of the principal mines.[4] In 1973, the Arizona Department of Mineral Resources studied the Jesse Benton Mine, Apache Mines, Morajeski Mines, Silver Hoard Group, and the Big Mine. At one time or another, these were Tom Jeffords's claims. Between 1882 and 1892, the district shipped five hundred thousand dollars' worth of silver. Between 1892 and 1894, Captain Jeffords staked twenty claims and held them until 1912. The state's report explains, "A basic dike . . . cuts the Precambrian granite comprising most of the area. . . . Within the dike zone copper oxides are present and these are associated with iron and manganese oxides. In the structurally related fissures it is here where most of the silver values occurred along with some values of gold . . . enriched near the surface and most of the workings in the area are shallow."[5] Tom Jeffords worked the gold and silver deposits near the surface. His mines were shallow but brought him an income. The *Arizona Daily Star* reported, "Although his mining enterprise was small, it was enough to sustain him and his hired Mexican employees. A well existed on his land along with a smelter used to refine the silver and copper he found."[6]

Around 2010, the *West Southern Arizona News Examiner* reported on Tom Jeffords's activities at Owl Head Buttes and the following is taken from a news clipping:[7]

> *He [Tom Jeffords] had a mining claim and dug for gold and silver on the [Owl Head] Buttes themselves and sometimes with some hired Mexican laborers. He used dynamite, picks, and muscles and some of his actual mines were up to 50 feet deep. That was hard work. He also found enough to live on, though he lived a very simple lifestyle with no extravagances. . . . The mines were mostly located on the east side of the Middle Butte, which was actually the remains of a volcano's "plug," the rest of that volcano having*

eroded away. These mines slanted down into the reddish-brown rock for 10 feet to 75 feet depending on which excavation it was. Rattlesnakes were usually found in these abandoned diggings, sometimes by the dozens, as they clearly like to hibernate there as well as escape from the hot summer days. . . . At the outside of these diggings were green and blue rocks that were clearly copper oxides. There are still built-up paths from most of these sites running north and onto what is now state lands. I traced them down to an area several hundred yards north to a flat area where there was some refuse and pieces of what appear to be a large shack, lots of funny colored, crushed rocks. It was likely a smelting operation to get the valuable metals from the rocks by crushing and smelting.[8]

That might have been where Tom's story ended, except for a strange woman, Alice Rollins Crane, who sought him out in 1895, and set him on a last great adventure. From his interaction with this woman, we learn something of Tom's sense of humor that reflects back on many of the conflicting statements Jeffords made about himself. Like many frontiersmen, Tom would let a tenderfoot believe what he or she was inclined to believe and might even help them along. Although he was unusually reticent, he did take great pride in being an Arizona pioneer and having lived through tough and dangerous times. He stretched the truth just a little in explaining how tough those times were. In Alice he found a woman, then in her mid-thirties, who was a charming deceiver. All of her statements about herself contradict each other. We don't even really know when or where she was born.[9]

When she arrived in Arizona at the end of 1895, she had recently wed Colonel Loren Crane of Los Angeles, a respected engineer.[10] She had come to Arizona to gather material for a new book that would deal with the Indian question, devoid of theories and replete with facts. She had begun to collect these seven years prior when she lived among nine Apache tribes. The newspapers said she was known to the literary world as Alice Rollins, a writer of short stories and poems.[11] Later she added the Dakota to the list of tribes she had lived with. The *Arizona Weekly Journal-Miner* reported, "Many of her works are incomplete. Among these is a reply to Helen Hunt Jackson's 'Ramona' and 'Amorean.' She has decided, however, to leave these half-finished and devote her energies to the completion of the interesting work on which she is now engaged."[12] Indeed the works remained half-finished, if they existed at all, and no work on the Indian problem was ever forthcoming. Perhaps she intended to publish, but her other behavior suggests deceit.

In 1877 in Illinois she married Frank Higbee, a traveling sales-man, and they had a son, Fred.[13] They divorced in 1880, only to marry again on Christmas Eve. They divorced for the last time in 1890.[14] This would have meant that Alice had young Fred to drag along when she lived among the Indians. It is difficult to imagine an Indian agent allowing a lone white woman to visit, let alone live on, the reservation. The consequences would have been brutal even if the Indians accepted her. She went west after the divorce from Higbee and somehow found time to court and marry Colonel Crane within the nine years she was living among the Indians. In 1912, she described her visit to Jeffords in 1895 as her first visit to Arizona.[15] This seems to square with the facts. In fairness, she did publish an article that refuted the idea that no sites in the United States deserved serious archaeological attention. She wrote that La Casa Grande, in Arizona, deserved attention, and that even in the sixteenth century, the local native people had no idea of its origin or tradition concerning its builders.[16] The local people did and do have a tradition about the origin of the ruins. She described Montezuma's Castle 150 miles north of Casa Grande. Archaeologists were already at work in the Southwest. In November 1895, Alice gave away what might have been the greatest story of her career by telling it to the Tucson papers instead of writing it herself.

Introduced to Tom Jeffords, she enticed him to take her on a tour of the key sites in southeast Arizona that related to Cochise's treaty with O. O. Howard. We can well imagine the thirty-something woman wrapping the sixty-three-year-old frontiersman around her finger. She even got him to pose for a photographic studio portrait. More than anything, she wanted to see Cochise's stronghold and his grave. She also took along a newfangled Kodak camera. Tom escorted her to Cochise's stronghold, which she described as being on the west side of the Dragoon Mountains accessed by a narrow canyon surrounded by towering rocks and high up in the mountains. By her account it was a veritable Shangri La with a wide variety of trees growing in a meadow. They stayed overnight.

She begged Tom to make a signal fire and call in the Apache. He warned that it might be worth her life and built one large and three small fires spaced out at ten-foot intervals. Despite the rain the smoke rose in straight columns.[17] Sure enough, Nol-gee, a Bronco Apache, one who escaped from General Miles at Bowie in 1886, popped up from behind a nearby rock and greeted Tom as Red Whiskers. She asked about the Apache Kid and was told they hadn't seen him in a long time. The Kid was a White Mountain Apache, Nol-gee said, and very bad, so they didn't like him. When she retold that tale in 1914, Nol-gee became the Kid. Tom made a bed for her in an abandoned adobe structure and told her she was in great danger. He stayed up to reminisce all night with Nol-gee. Still in danger the next morning, they fled without break-fast through a secret canyon leading to the east known only to Tom Jeffords. As they went, he showed her Cochise's grave.[18]

Alice took photos on her trip, so we know that Tom took her to the place where he, O. O. Howard, and Cochise talked peace on top of the big flat rock. A surviving copy of that photo is in possession of Captain Sladen's family. The site is on the western flank of the Dra-goon Mountains, north of the stronghold. She failed to mention this place in her account. She gathered accounts of Cochise's treaty from Sladen, Jeffords, and O. O. Howard. Only the Sladen account sur-vives.[19] Alice never published her book on the Indians and Cochise. As she gathered primary accounts, this is regrettable.

Ben Jaastad recalled George Oakes talking about Alice. By the time Jaastad knew her, she was divorced from Crane and married to Count Morajeski, actually a Polish peasant. In 1912, she described Crane as having died rather than divorced, but the record is clear, and he was still alive at the time.[20] As a countess, Alice demanded that everyone call her Madam: "The madam told me she was writing a book about Chief Cochise, and I suppose she was forever pestering Jeffords and he having a pretty good sense of humor stuffed her aplenty and one of these tales was about Cochise's gun. But the Morajeskas were good to Jeffords, took good care of him the rest of his days."[21]

In January 1898, Alice Rollins Crane headed out for the Klondike Gold Rush. During this escapade, Colonel Crane divorced her for desertion. She went as a representative of a magazine syndicate and as agent for the Los Angeles women's mining syndicate.[22] In the Yukon, she took on her new husband, Count Victor Morajeski.[23]

In Los Angeles, she formed a syndicate of women who paid her way to the Klondike. This was an expensive proposition. Boat fare to Alaska was costly. From Skagway one ascended White Pass and at the top crossed into Canada. The Canadians posted guards to ensure that people had enough supplies, several tons, to survive the winter. It took many trips up the pass to carry all of this material. Presumably, Alice, as a woman, hired men to carry her supplies. Getting to the Klondike was a heroic proposition. Her syndicate also provided money to purchase mines when she arrived. She would own them in her own name and pay dividends to the syndicate. She did make the purchases and managed the mines though no dividends were ever paid. In San Francisco she told the press that a secret syndicate of New York magazines was paying her way:

> Mrs. Crane admits frankly that she has been "dying to tell all about it," and, for fear that she might be tempted too strongly to show the contract, she has kept it "locked up tightly in a safe deposit box in the bank ever since it came." By this contract, which is to

last for one year, Mrs. Crane is to receive $100 a month, besides her expenses: and in addition, she will receive extra pay for all she writes. . . . Five hundred dollars toward her expenses will be advanced to her before she starts through the pass. Her articles are to be of an historic and descriptive character. . . . In addition to all this Mrs. Crane is backed here by the Alaskan Mining syndicate of men and women. She carries with her valuable letters to people all along the way who will render her any assistance she may need. [24]

By the time she reached Seattle, the Smithsonian was also supporting her effort. Eventually, she did provide the Smithsonian with ten photographs of Indians, though it is unclear whether this was as a result of any contractual arrangement.

In San Francisco, on January 19, 1898, Miriam Michelson interviewed Alice Rollins Crane for the *San Francisco Call*. Alice was on her way to the Klondike Gold Rush, her first foray into the Canadian wilderness. Her expenses were being paid by a women's mining syndicate in Los Angeles.

"My expenses are paid by a small syndicate of five magazines, to which I shall send matter. Then I am commissioned by the ethnological bureau of the Smithsonian Institution to gather data regarding Indian folk lore and all the details to be got by living intimately with them."

"Really living with them?" I repeated, with uncomfortable recollections of Piute wickiups and Piute ladies and gentlemen.

"Oh, yes. Why, I've lived with a dozen different tribes of Indians—the Apaches, etc." She checked the Indians' names off on her large, strong fingers.

"Why, I'm the only white woman that ever lived with the Apaches in any other way than as a captive. I used to think they let me stay with them 'cause they liked me so much. But after a long while the old chief told me he thought I was crazy! . . . But my son

was my companion, my friend. He worked with me, illustrated my matter, lived with me in the desert and the brush. And then when I went to Los Angeles, thinking he needed a couple of years schooling, he took cold. Think of it, after lying out nights and sleeping in the rain as we'd done, he took cold from a draughty window in the schoolhouse and died of la grippe three years ago. He would have been nineteen if he had lived. For the first year I couldn't get reconciled to it, but now I understand," she added gently, "that he's only gone ahead. We're believers in evolution, he and I."[25]

A writer in Dawson City described her as being in the service of the Smithsonian Institution, a unique inhabitant who wore a buckskin skirt and bloomers of the same material with leather leggings: "She likes frontier life, and expects to die with her boots on."[26]

Two years later, returning from Dawson, Alice was interviewed by the newspaper in Seattle. She clung to the idea that she had been sent by the Bureau of Ethnography at the Smithsonian and again, as in the past, claimed she was going to publish. In the Yukon, she bought and sold claims and took ten photographs of Indians.

Seattle, Aug. 27 [1900]—Mrs. Alice Rollins Crane wife of Colonel L. P. Crane, a retired army officer of Los Angeles, arrived to-night from Dawson. She went north two years ago with a commission from the bureau of ethnology of the Smithsonian Institution to make a collection of folk lore and mythology of the Indians. She will soon publish several books, as well as a play entitled "Official Life in Dawson."[27]

She returned to face divorce from Crane. The books and articles promised and the ethnographic material, other than ten photographs, does not appear to have been forthcoming. That the mines she was to purchase for the syndicate in Los Angeles were to be held in her own name should have raised red flags that she was running a confidence game. She returned briefly to the Owl Heads as a guest of Jeffords. Evidently he was quite fond of her, as he deeded her three of his mining claims,[28] although the record only shows two, Golconda Mining Claim and the Last Chance. He sold them to her for ten dollars.[29] Soon after, she returned to the Klondike and took up residence with Captain William Galpin. Together they planned to publish a book, an anthology of other folks' short stories. Alice succeeded in getting it published, but only her name appeared on the cover.[30] When Galpin found out, he was enraged, and she said he tried to kill her. She ran to the protection of Count Morajeski. Galpin sought revenge elsewhere.

Captain Galpin wrote to the Los Angeles syndicate explaining to them that Alice had purchased mines and was managing them. The mines were making money, but she wasn't paying any dividends. The syndicate fired Alice and hired Galpin as her successor.[31]

She spent time in Nevada and made a home in Los Angeles. In 1912, she returned to Arizona and spoke to the Phoenix newspapers. She told them that when she had made her first trip to Arizona in 1895, she had gathered material for an interesting story, which she had already written but which she would not print until after the death of Captain Jeffords. That's a change from her earlier accounts of a work about Indians for which she had spent nine years living among them collecting data. Needless to say, no such articles or books were ever forthcoming. She also related to the newspaper that she had become manager of a mining company after she arrived in the Klondike and that its investors were in New York and Philadelphia. During that trip the bureau of ethnology appointed her as a special commissioner to study the Indians of Alaska and those who lived across the Bering Strait. This is quite a change from her 1898 claims that Smithsonian sent her to the Klondike. Now she said she had returned to look after the mining property she had acquired at the time of her previous visit to Arizona.[32] That would have been in 1900, when she acquired two claims from Tom Jeffords. For many years, according to one newspaper, she had been writing and collecting material for stories, which she had not yet offered for publication; she was preparing to have some released as motion pictures.[33]

It was assessment work on valuable claims in the Owl Heads, she told the papers, which brought the count and herself to Arizona.[34] She would soon have twenty-three claims and they would form the basis of the Owl Heads Mining and Trust Company. It appears that she acquired most of these claims from Tom as he had been working the area since 1892, and she had only just returned. Alice and the count offered shares to investors in Los Angeles. In the meantime, Alice and Victor had problems of their own.

Alice wrote a new will and left Count Victor out of it. He was enraged. In September 1913, he knocked her down and pushed her face into the mud of an irrigation ditch. She was hospitalized. In court, he claimed self-defense as Madam had a butcher knife in one hand and an ax in the other. It must have been an interesting brawl as it roused the entire neighborhood.[35] On September 24, she sued for divorce, which the court granted on the grounds of non-support.[36] They weren't fanatical about divorce and continued to live and work together throughout the remaining ten years of their lives.

After the divorce, Victor and Alice continue to partner on mining claims, and he even agreed to leave his claims to her in the event of his death.

I undersigned, Victor Morajeski resident of Owl Heads Mining District, Pinal Co., Arizona divorced husband of Madame Alice Morajeska resident of said District county and state on May 7, 1915 do hereby promise said Madame Alice Morajeska to bequeth and cause to be given to said party my half interest in all mining claims as now appearing on record under the name of Madame Alice Morajeska since the year 1909 also all moneyed interest which might accrue from proceeds of said mining interest in the future after all just debts funeral expenses and other incidentals are deducted from said interest.

This is my personal wish in case of any death as written and signed this 7th day of May 1915.[37]

Thomas Farish, Arizona State Historian, interviewed Tom Jeffords before his death in February 1914. Farish visited with Tom at his homestead in the Owl Heads and took photographs that show a stooped, white-haired man attended by his five dogs. Jeffords was too old to work his mines and seems to have transferred all of them to the Morajeskis, who promised to bring him in for shares in the Owl Heads Mining and Trust and make him wealthy. At this point, he was destitute and Victor, who had become his friend, looked after him. Madam would attempt to claim one thousand dollars from his estate for this care.[38]

On February 19, 1914, Tom Jeffords passed away at his ranch in the Owl Heads attended by two Mexican workers. Victor Morajeski escorted his body to Tucson where the Pioneers Society took charge of funeral arrangements. Tucson photographer Albert Bushman photographed the body in the casket lying in state at the Pioneers' rooms.[39] At 2 p.m. on Sunday, February 21, the Reverend L. W. Wheatley conducted the funeral. Herbert E. Nixon sang. John F. Jeffords, Tom's younger brother, telegraphed that he could not come. He was too ill at the Soldier's Home in Los Angeles. The newspaper said that all of the Pioneers turned out and they provided both honorary pallbearers, men who were too old for the job, and actual pallbearers.[40] Among them were Tucson merchants and leaders Sam Hughes and E. N. Fish, as well as Fort Bowie sutler and Arizona historian Sidney B. DeLong. George W. Oakes, who fought the Cheyenne, served along with Frank Hereford, his son Ken, A. B. Sanford, and Ed Vail,[41] an owner of the Empire Ranch, the largest in Arizona. The Pioneers interred Tom Jeffords at Evergreen Cemetery in Tucson along Oracle Road where he rests today.

In life, respect for Tom Jeffords held back a tide of legal problems. Assessment work was not up to date on the many claims and an important well. Prospectors and mining companies jumped the claims. Thieves robbed his house and took a large ore cabinet with glass doors, a filing cabinet for legal documents, a swivel chair, dining room chairs, gold scales in a glass case, merchant's scales and weights, and many other items.[42]

A few days after the funeral, Victor Morajeski paraded around Tucson showing off the shotgun Cochise had given to Tom. He showed it to Sam Grant, George Oakes, and Ben Jaastad. Although Grant and Oakes seemed to sit up and take notice, Grant winked at Jaastad and gave a shake of his head. Victor presented them with a modern take-down twelve-gauge shotgun, which he said he would give to the Pioneers Society.[43] George Oakes later commented on the shotgun: "Cochise died in '74 and if he had a gun it was a muzzle loader. The Indians would shoot pebbles and gravel when they ran out of lead. If an Indian gave away a gun you could bet it was no damn good, and if Tom ever got a gun from Cochise I'll bet he either buried it or threw it away first chance he got."[44]

Furthermore, Oakes was pretty sure he knew where Tom bought the weapon. Tom Jeffords had a sense of humor and would let a tenderfoot believe what he wanted. His old friends counted this a pretty good joke.

Madam Morajeski was away for a year and returned to look after Victor and their claims in the Owl Heads. By then she had disposed of fifty-one per cent of her holdings in the Owl Heads Mining and Trust Co., which she said was composed of well-known operators, some of whom were connected with the Phelps-Dodge people. At that time, Phelps-Dodge was the copper mining giant operating out of Bisbee and Jerome. She claimed that extensive development work was about to begin.[45]

By January 15, 1916, at least some of the investors were tired of waiting for development to begin. Three Los Angeles men known only as Dunbar, Wilson, and Green began litigation and sent their man William Carpenter, who stayed with Victor Morajeski at his

Owl Head Butte cabin, a crude affair with a back wall of canvas. Victor went to Red Rock, fifteen miles away, to phone Alice and tell her there was trouble. "Arriving at the cabin, Mr. Dick and the countess found no one but on searching the vicinity they discovered the count's watch and his rifle and a little later a pool of blood and indications of a struggle. The stock and barrel of the rifle were also covered with blood stains." They found Victor at Tom Jeffords's cabin two miles away. Carpenter had beaten him badly and choked him. Carpenter struck him violently on the head from behind. "When his hair was shaved away it was found that a charge of shot had been poured into the back and side of his head. . . . The mining property, which the Morajeskas have owned for several years is said to be quite valuable and negotiations for its sale for a large sum are now pending."[46] Tom's property may have been valuable but it never really played out. It was mined again in the 1920s, and in the 1930s when men scratched whatever they could from the earth, and yet again in the 1970s, when the price of gold went through the roof.

Tom Jeffords was a great man respected and loved by the Arizona Pioneers and the Chiricahua Apache. As George Hand said, "He always arrived with friends and was always welcome." He was brave, but he didn't shoot a pistol out of badman John Wesley Hardin's hand. Elliott Arnold wrote that in his novel. He also claimed that Tom was Cochise's blood brother. Arnold didn't invent that. The newspapers did around the time of Tom's death. It might even be something Alice Rollins Crane originated. Nonetheless, Cochise and Tom were as close as blood brothers and the chief called him brother. The "mystical ceremony" that joined them arose from white imagination. Tom didn't have a sweetheart in Tucson and didn't marry an Apache bride. Arnold and Jimmy Stewart can be thanked for these additions to legend. But Tom did live among the Apache, and he stayed in their homes. The Civil War, the frontier, and his time as Chiricahua agent stole away the years when he might have sought a bride. Instead he sought wealth, finding and losing it several times. Upper-class snobs, like Indian Inspector Vandever and some West Pointers, looked down on him and couldn't accept his blunt honesty in doing what was right. Jeffords didn't ride into Cochise's Stronghold to make a private peace for his mail riders, but he did ride in alone to request that Cochise come to a peace parley.

The movies and novels capture Tom Jeffords's courage and determination but fail to give us a complete understanding of a very special man. He was a tall, thin frontiersman with a reddish beard, rather crude in his habits but never without friends. Lacking in education, he supported Tucson schools and promoted a school for the Chiricahua. Early in life, sailing as an officer on the Great Lakes, he learned to win men's trust and respect while gaining wisdom in dealing with men of other cultures and social classes. This enabled him to win the friendship of Cochise and the trust of his tribe. Although not quite accepting him, the Army turned to Tom Jeffords time and again as scout and as the man the Chiricahua trusted who could convince them to keep the peace. He was an Arizona Pioneer of distinction who set aside his own best interests in favor of those of his country. He accomplished the impossible winning the trust and friendship of Cochise. Will they meet again someday? I think they already have somewhere up yonder. They're smoking around a campfire and sipping a bit of bad whiskey as they talk about the old days.

Bibliography

Archival Material Codes

AHS Arizona Historical Society, Tucson
AG Adjutant general, a military title for an officer serving as the secretary to a commander
BIA Bureau of Indian Affairs
Biofile A collection concerning an individual
LR Letters received
LS Letters sent
MS Manuscript
NARA National Archives and Records Administration
NMS New Mexico military headquarters
RG Records Group. NARA assigns all national agencies a number; 353 is Army; 75 is Indian Affairs.

Sources

Arizona Historical Society, Tucson, Arizona
    Brevoort, Elias C., Biofile, Box 15
    Brown reminiscences, 1934, Autograph Album, MS 210
    Constitution, Bylaws and List of Members of the Society of Arizona Pioneers, organized February 1884
    Harte, Bret, Collection
    Hughes, Fred, Biofile
    Hayden File
    Jeffords, Thomas Jefferson, Biofile, Box 66.
    Sonnichsen Papers, MS1475, Box 66
Cochise County Recorder's Archive, Cochise County, Arizona
Fort Bowie National Historic Site, Arizona
Fort Laramie National Historic Site
National Archive and Records Administration

Internet Sources

Ancestry.com, Jeffords Family Tree, http://trees.ancestry.com/tree/67016979/family

Ancestry.com, Rollins Family Tree (Alice Rollins Crane), http://trees.ancestry.com/tree/73715158/family

Maritime History of the Great Lakes, http://maritimehistoryofthegreatlakes.ca

Newspapers

Arizona Citizen
Arizona Daily Citizen
Arizona Miner
Arizona Republican
Arizona Sentinel
Arizona Silver Belt
Arizona Weekly Journal-Miner
Bisbee Daily Review
Buffalo Commercial Advertiser, Buffalo, New York
Buffalo Daily Express, Buffalo, New York
Buffalo Daily Republic, Buffalo, New York
Daily News, Kingston, Ontario, Canada
The Democracy, Buffalo, New York
El Paso Herald
Missouri Republican
Mohave County Miner
Morning Express, Buffalo, N.Y.
New York World
The Oasis
Sandusky Daily Register, Sandusky, Ohio
San Francisco Bulletin
Tombstone Epitaph
Weekly Arizona Miner
Weekly Arizonian

Journal Articles

Cammack, Sister Alberta. "A Faithful Account of the Life and Death of Doctor John Charles Handy," *The Smoke Signal* 52 (1989).

Cramer, Captain Harry G. "Tom Jeffords—Indian Agent," *Journal of Arizona History* 17 (Autumn 1976), 265–300.

De Stefano, William. "Tom Jeffords Capitalist," Arizona–New Mexico Historical Convention, Tucson, April 1995.

DeVault, Tracy. "Finding Ewell's Station," *Desert Tracks* (January 2016).

Fontana, Bernard L., J. Cameron Greenleaf, Charles W. Ferguson, Robert A. Wright, and Doris Frederick. "Johnny Ward's Ranch: A Study in Historic Archaeology," *Kiva*, 28:1/2 (Oct.–Dec. 1962), 1–115.

Forbes, Robert H. "Letters to the editor," *Journal of Arizona History* (Summer 1966).

Ford, Dixon, and Lee Kruetzer. "Oxen: Engines of the Overland Emigration," *Overland Journal*, XXXIII: 1, Spring 2015.

Harlan, Mark E. "Historians and Archaeologists: Proposals for Connecting in a Common Past," *New Mexico Historical Review* 82 (Fall 2007).

Irwin, Bernard John Dowling. "The Apache Pass Fight," *Infantry Journal*. XXXII: 4 (April 1928).

———. "Why the Apaches Made War," Irwin articles, 1876–1934, for publication, Tucson, AHS.

Kessell, John L. "So What's Truth Got to Do with It? Reflections on Oñate and the Black Legend," *New Mexico Historical Review* 86 (Summer 2011).

Lyon, Juana Frazer. "Archie McIntosh, the Scottish Scout," *The Journal of Arizona History* VII (Autumn 1968): 103–22.

McChristian, Douglas C., and Larry L. Ludwig, eds. "Eyewitness to the Bascom Affair: An Account by Sergeant Daniel Robinson, Seventh Infantry," *Journal of Arizona History* 42 (Autumn 2001).

Miller, Anne. "When the Right Road Goes the Wrong Way, Evaluating Historical Evidence," Meeting of the Southern Trails Chapter of the Oregon-California Trails Association, Temecula, CA, March 28, 2014.

Mulligan, Raymond A., "Sixteen Days in Apache Pass," *Kiva* 24 (1958): 1–13.

Oberly, Hubert, and Colonel Martin L. Crimmins. "Why the Apaches Made War: Officer Oberly, of Brooklyn, Tells What He Knows About It," *New York World*, July 1, 1886.

Oury, William Sanders. "A True History of the Outbreak of the Noted Apache Chieftan Cachise in the Year 1861," Tucson: *Arizona Star*, June 28, July 5 and 12, 1877.

Robinson, Daniel. "The Affair at Apache Pass," *Sports Afield* 17 (August 1896): 79–83.

———. "A Narrative of Events Pertaining to C. F and H Companies of the Seventh Infantry while Serving in New Mexico and Arizona from October 1860, to April 1862," Fort Laramie National Historic Site.

Robinson, Sherry. "Renegades and Refugees: Lipan Apaches at the Mescalero Apache Reservation, 1879–1881," *New Mexico Historical Review*, 91/1 (Winter 2016).

Sacks, Benjamin H. "New Evidence on the Bascom Affair," *Arizona and the West*, IV: 3 (Autumn 1962).

Safford, A.P.K. "Something About Cachise," *Arizona Citizen*, December 7, 1872.

Seymour, Deni J. "Evaluating Eyewitness Accounts of Native Peoples along the Coronado Trail from the International Border to Cibola," *New Mexico Historical Review*, 84/3 (Summer 2009).

———. "The Canutillo Complex: Evidence of Protohistoric Mobile Occupants in the Southern Southwest," *Kiva*, 79 (Winter 2009).

Seymour, Deni J., and George Robertson. "A Pledge of Peace: Evidence of the Cochise-Howard Treaty Campsite," *Historical Archaeology*, 42(4), (Winter 2008): 154–79.

Soldier at Fort McLane. "Apache Pass," *Missouri Republican*, December 27, 1861.

Sonnichsen, C. L. "Who Was Tom Jeffords?" *Journal of Arizona History*, 23 (Winter 1982).

Sweeney, Edwin R. "Cochise and the Prelude to the Bascom Affair," *New Mexico Historical Review* 64 (Autumn 1989): 427–46.

Torrez, Robert J., "The San Juan Gold Rush of 1860 and Its Effect on the Development of Northern New Mexico," *New Mexico Historical Review*, LXIII: 3, Summer, 1988.

Tyler, Barbara Ann. "Cochise Apache War Leader, 1858–1861," *Journal of Arizona History*, VI (1965).

Utley, Robert M. "The Bascom Affair: a Reconstruction," *Arizona and the West* 3 (Spring 1961): 59–68.

Valputic, Marian E., and Harold H. Longfellow. "The Fight at Chiricahua Pass in 1869 as described by L. L. Dorr, M.D.," *Arizona and the West* 13 (Winter 1971): 369–78.

Young, Roy B. "Graves Lie Thick: Murders At The Brunkow Mine," *Journal of Wild West History Association*, II/3 (June 2009).

Books

Aleshire, Peter. *Cochise: The Life and Times of the Great Apache Chief.* New York: John Wiley & Sons, Inc., 2001.

Altshuler, Constance Wynn. *Chains of Command: Arizona and the Army, 1856–1875.* Tucson: The Arizona Historical Society, 1981.

———. *Latest from Arizona! The Hesperian Letters, 1859–1861.* Tucson, Arizona: Pioneers' Historical Society, 1969.

Arnold, Elliott. *Blood Brother.* New York: Hawthorne Books, 1947.

Ball, Eve. *Indeh: An Apache Odyssey.* Provo, Utah: Brigham Young University, 1980.

Bailey, Lynn R., and Don Chaput. *Cochise County Stalwarts, A Who's Who of the Territorial Years, Volume 1,* Tucson: Westernlore Press, 2000.

———. *Cochise County Stalwarts, A Who's Who of the Territorial Years, Volume 2,* Tucson: Westernlore Press, 2000.

———. *Henry Clay Hooker and the Sierra Bonita Ranch.* Tucson: Westernlore Publications, 1998.

———. *White Apache: The Life and Times of Zebina Nathaniel Streeter.* Tucson: Westernlore Press, 2010.

Banford, Don. *Freshwater Heritage: A History of Sail on the Great Lakes, 1670–1918*. Natural Heritage, 2012.

Betzinez, Jason, and Wilber Sturtevant Nye. *I Fought with Geronimo*. Lincoln: University of Nebraska Press, 1959.

Bourke, John G. *On the Border with Crook*. Lincoln: University of Nebraska Press, 1971.

Bourke, John Gregory, and Charles M. Robinson III, ed. *The Diaries of John Gregory Bourke, Vol. 1, Nov. 20, 1872 to July 28, 1876*. Denton, TX: University of North Texas Press, 2003.

DeLong, Sidney. *History of Arizona*. San Francisco: The Whitaker & Ray Company, 1905.

Downs, John P., and Fenwick Y. Hedley, eds. *History of Chautauqua County, New York, and Its People*. New York: American Historical Society, 1921.

Farish, Thomas F. *History of Arizona*, Volume 2, Chapter 10. Phoenix, AZ: Filmer Brothers. 1915.

Frazier, Donald S. *Blood and Treasure: Confederate Empire in the Southwest*. College Station: Texas A&M Press, 1995.

Garrard, Lewis H. *Wah-to-yah and the Taos Trail*. Norman: University of Oklahoma Press, 1955.

Gregg, Josiah. *Commerce of the Prairies: Life on the Great Plains in the 1830s and 1840s*. Santa Barbara: The Narrative Press, 2001.

Gustafson, A. M., *John Spring's Arizona*. Tucson: University of Arizona Press, 1966.

Hand, George, and Neil B. Carmony, ed. *Whiskey, Six-guns and Red-light Ladies: George Hand's Saloon Diary, Tucson, 1875 to 1878*. Silver City, NM: High Lonesome Books, 1994.

Howard, Gen. Oliver Otis. *Famous Indian Chiefs I Have Known*. New York: The Century Co., 1908 (Kindle version).

Hunt, Aurora. *Major General James Henry Carleton, 1814–1873, Western Frontier Dragoon*. Glendale: Arthur H. Clark and Company, 1958.

Karamanski, Theodore J. *Schooner Passage: Sailing Ships and the Lake Michigan Frontier*. Detroit: Great Lakes Book Series, Wayne State University Press, 2000.

Large, Moina W. *History of Ashtabula County, Ohio*. Indianapolis: Historical Publication Co., 1924.

Lingenfelter, Richard E. *Steamboats on the Colorado River: 1852–1916*. Tucson: University of Arizona Press, 1978.

Lockwood, Frank C. *Pioneer Days in Arizona*. New York: Macmillan, 1932.

Ludwig, Larry L. "An Archaeological Survey of Possible Bascom Affair Sites," MS, 1993. Fort Bowie NHS.

Masich, Andrew E. *The Civil War in Arizona: The Story of the California Volunteers, 1861–1865*. Norman: University of Oklahoma Press, 2006.

McChristian, Douglas C. *Fort Bowie, Arizona: Combat Post of the Southwest, 1858 to 1894*. Norman: University of Oklahoma Press, 2005.

Michno, Gregory. *Encyclopedia of the Indian Wars: Western Battles and Skirmishes 1850–1890.* Missoula: Mountain Press, 2003.

Michno, Gregory, and Susan Michno. *Forgotten Fights: Little-Known Raids and Skirmishes on the Frontier, 1823 to 1890.* Missoula, MT: Mountain Press Publishing Co., 2008.

Morgan, Phyllis S. *As Far As the Eye Could Reach: Accounts of Animals Along the Santa Fe Trail, 1821–1880.* Norman: University of Oklahoma Press, 2015.

Mulligan, Raymond A. *Apache Pass and Old Fort Bowie.* Tucson: Tucson Corral of the Westerners Press, 1965.

Parsons, George W., and Lynn R. Bailey, ed., *A Tenderfoot in Tombstone, the Private Journal of George Whitwell Parsons: The Turbulent Years, 1880–82.* Westernlore Publications, 1996.

Pfanz, Donald. *Richard S. Ewell: A Soldier's Life.* Civil War America, Chapel Hill: University of North Carolina Press, 1998.

Poston, Charles D. *Building a State in Apache Land.* Tempe: Aztec Press, 1963.

Prezelski, Tom. *Californio Lancers: The First Battalion of Native Cavalry in the Far West, 1863 to 1866.* Norman: University of Oklahoma Press, 2015.

Roberts, Virginia Culin. *With Their Own Blood: A Saga of Southwestern Pioneers.* Fort Worth: Texas Christian University Press, 1992.

Russell, Don. *One Hundred and Three Fights and Scrimmages: The Story of General Reuben F. Bernard.* Washington, DC: United States Cavalry Association, 1936.

Schubert, Frank. *The Nation Builders: A Sesquicentennial History of the Corps of Topographical Engineers 1838–1863.* Fort Belvoir, VA: Office of History United States Army Corps of Engineers, 1988.

Schuetz, Mardith K. *Archaeology of Tom Jeffords's Chiricahua Indian Agency.* Las Cruces, New Mexico: COAS, 1986.

Sides, Hampton. *Blood and Thunder—An Epic of the American West.* Garden City: Doubleday, 2006.

Smith, Brad. *The Stagecoach through Apache Country: A History of the Stagecoach Companies and Stage Stations in Northeastern Cochise County, Arizona Territory: 1857-1880.* Willcox, AZ: Sulphur Springs Valley Historical Society, 2013.

Spude, Katherine Holder. *"That Fiend in Hell" Soapy Smith in Legend.* Norman, University of Oklahoma Press, 2012.

Sweeney, Edwin R. *Cochise: Chiricahua Apache Chief.* Norman: University of Oklahoma Press, 1991.

———, ed. *Cochise: Firsthand Accounts of the Chiricahua Apache Chief.* Norman: University of Oklahoma Press, 2014.

———, ed. *Making Peace with Cochise: The 1872 Journal of Captain Joseph Alton Sladen.* Norman: University of Oklahoma Press, 1991.

Taylor, John. *Bloody Valverde: A Civil War Battle on the Rio Grande, February 21, 1862.* Albuquerque: University of New Mexico Press, 1995.

Tevis, Captain James Henry, and Betty Barr, ed. *Arizona in the 50s.* Albuquerque: University of New Mexico Press, 1854.

Theobald, John O., and Lillian Theobald. *Arizona Territory: Post Offices and Post-masters.* Phoenix, AZ: Arizona Historical Foundation, 1961.

Thompson, Jerry. *Desert Tiger: Captain Paddy Graydon and the Civil War in the Far Southwest.* El Paso: Western Press: University of Texas at El Paso, 1992.

———. *Civil War in the Southwest: Recollections of the Sibley Brigade,* College Station: Texas A&M University Press, 2001.

Thrapp, Dan L. *The Conquest of Apacheria.* Norman: University of Oklahoma Press, 1988.

———. *Encyclopedia of Frontier Biography.* Spokane: Arthur H. Clark and Company, 1988.

———. *Victorio and the Mimbres Apaches.* Norman: University of Oklahoma Press, 1974.

Time Life, Inc., eds. *The Old West: The Gamblers.* Alexandria: Time Life Books, 1978.

Traywick, Ben. *Tyzaalton (Red Beard),* Tombstone: Red Marie's Bookstore, 1987.

Twain, Mark. *Life on the Mississippi.* New York: Harper and Bros., 1917.

Utley, Robert M. *Frontiersmen in Blue: The United States Army and the Indian, 1848–1865.* New York: Macmillan, 1967.

Viola, Herman J., ed. *The Memoirs of Charles Henry Veil: A Soldier's Recollections of the Civil War and the Arizona Territory.* New York: Orion Books, 1993.

Waldman, Carl. *Atlas of the North American Indian, Revised Edition.* New York: Checkmark Books, 2000.

Washburn, Wilcomb E., and Robert M. Utley. *Indian Wars.* New York: Mariner Books, 2002.

Williams, William W. *The History of Ashtabula, Co., Ohio.* Philadelphia: Williams Bros., 1878.

Worcester, Donald Emmet. *The Apaches: Eagles of the Southwest.* Norman: University of Oklahoma Press, 1992.

Young, Otis E., Jr. *Western Mining: An Informal Account of Precious-Metals Prospecting, Placering, Lode Mining, and Milling on the American Frontier from Spanish Times to 1893.* Norman: University of Oklahoma Press, 1970.

ENDNOTES

Introduction

1. Sweeney, Edwin R., ed., *Making Peace with Cochise: the 1872 Journal of Captain Joseph Alton Sladen*, Norman: University of Oklahoma Press, 1991, p. 33.

2. Rank in the nineteenth century. The military had no retirement plan until very late in the century so men stayed on the rolls until they died. The elder men often went on invalid status and weren't with their regiments. Congress allocated one colonel, one lieutenant colonel, one major, ten captains, and twenty lieutenants per regiment. However, some of these officers served as adjutants (an adjutant general is the general's secretary), quartermasters (supply officer) and on detached duty recruiting and instructing in military schools and on special missions. The military also employed a system of brevet rank. A brevet officer was entitled to be addressed by his brevet rank and to fill a position commensurate with his brevet rank. General Custer, for instance, should be addressed as a Major General, his brevet rank. He was paid as a lieutenant colonel but filled the position of a colonel since the colonel of the regiment was away. He was entitled to fill the position of a major general as long as there was no one present senior in rank to himself. Brevet rank was awarded like medals are today for performance in combat. Confusing the issue further is the fact that so many officers were brevetted to senior rank during the Civil War, many of them in state volunteer formations. Many regular officers argued that volunteer brevet rank didn't count. In addition, men were addressed by rank they had held as sea captains and rank they held or were thought to have held in the militia. Thus, we have many men addressed as colonel, major, and captain for whom the origin of their rank is uncertain.

3. Traywick, Ben, *Tyzaalton (Red Beard)*, Tombstone: Red Marie's Bookstore, 1987.

4. Ibid.

5. Arnold, Elliott, *Blood Brother*, New York: Hawthorne Books, 1947.

6. Kessell, John L., "So What's Truth Got to Do with It? Reflection on Oñate and the Black Legend," *New Mexico Historical Review* 86 (Summer 2011), pp. 377–78.

7. Thomas Jefferson Jeffords, Biofile, Box 66, Letter, January 30, 1884, Arizona Historical Society.

8. Forbes, Robert H., "Letters to the editor," *Journal of Arizona History* (Summer 1966), pp. 87-88.

Chapter 1: Growing Up

1. I've based the account of Eber on the sort of conditions emigrants encountered.

2. Was Eber Jeffords poor? He was a Jackson Democrat and Jackson appealed to poor farmers. A grandson shows up in the Who's Who of Ashtabula. Eber and his sons do not. This suggests that they weren't tradesmen or in politics and not among the principal men of town. Four of the sons went to sea, suggesting there was a need to find employment with others. Eber finally bought a farm about 1850. Going west to Chautauqua and leaving family suggests an economic need. How would he have gotten there? He seems unlikely to have had the money to take a stage. He might have worked on the Erie Canal, but the canal was being built in many places at once and he'd have been stuck in one place. He'd have lacked funds for an outfit so it seems likely that he'd have driven another man's wagon as a hired hand.

3. Information on oxen comes from Morgan, Phyllis S., *As Far as the Eye Could Reach: Accounts of Animals Along the Santa Fe Trail, 1821–1880*, Norman: University of Oklahoma Press, 2015; and Ford, Dixon, and Lee Kruetzer, "Oxen: Engines of the Overland Emigration," *Overland Journal*, XXXIII: 1, Spring 2015, pp. 4–29.

4. Gregg, Josiah, *Commerce of the Prairies: Life on the Great Plains in the 1830s and 1840s*, Santa Barbara: The Narrative Press, 2001.

5. We're not sure if Almira's family was named Wood or Woods. I could find no trace of ancestors beyond her parents. She was born in 1808 in Chautauqua, which would have made her parents among the first settlers. This lack of traceable family may indicate that they were poor, and their early arrival at Chautauqua likely makes them backwoodsmen.

6. The frequency of childbirth is one indicator of love between husband and wife. The daughters all grew up and married, and they named their children after father and siblings, another sign of love and respect. All of the children grew to adulthood, a sign that the family was well regulated and cared for, especially in the early nineteenth century when child mortality was high.

7. Census records show the brothers as sailors and captains. Ship registries show James and Tom as ship captains in their early twenties. That was an accomplishment. Had their father owned the vessels, this might have been expected. He did not. So they must have gone to sea young and been very competent and mature.

8. Large, Moina W., *History of Ashtabula County, Ohio*, Indianapolis: Historical Publication Co., 1924, p. 560.

Chapter 2: Lake Sailor

1. http://images.maritimehistoryofthegreatlakes.ca/47432/data?n=3. *Morning Express Buffalo*, Tuesday, October 14, 1851, and *Buffalo Commercial Advertiser*, Tuesday, October 14, 1851.

2. http://images.maritimehistoryofthegreatlakes.ca/56198/data?n=1 *Sandusky Daily Register*, August 27, 1852.

3. http://images.maritimehistoryofthegreatlakes.ca/27749/data?n=6. *The Democracy*, Buffalo, July 8, 1854.

4. *Daily News*, Kingston, Ontario, November 6, 1855.

5. Lewis, Walter, personal communication, March 1, 2014.

6. http://images.maritimehistoryofthegreatlakes.ca/37538/data?n=1 *Buffalo Daily Republic*, September 8, 1859.

7. *The Democracy*, Buffalo, Thursday, September 7, 1854.

8. *Morning Express*, Buffalo, Tuesday, October 14, 1851.

9. *Buffalo Daily Republic*, Thursday, November 1, 1855.

10. *Buffalo Daily Republic*, Friday, November 2, 1855.

11. *Buffalo Daily Republic*, Friday, September 21, 1855.

12. *Buffalo Daily Republic*, Saturday, July 5, 1856; *Buffalo Morning Express*, January 11, 1856.

13. Sonnichsen Papers, MS1475, Box 66, Letter from Richard Wright to Mrs. Jacques, April 5, 1976, Arizona Historical Society.

14. It is clear that Richard Wright believed himself to be referring to Thomas Jeffords. He didn't mention James. This is almost the earliest that Tom could have been in command. It is also clear from the records that there were many more runs or voyages than are recorded and that ship's captains changed frequently. Tom Jeffords was known as captain throughout the rest of his life. In the nineteenth century it was not uncommon for a man to be granted a military title although he had never commanded troops or ships. There is no way to be absolutely certain that the Captain Jeffords referred to is Tom, but the preponderance of opinion points to Tom commanding a ship.

15. There is little support for this claim, which seems to ride on the misidentification of a member of another branch of the Jeffords family, a very distant cousin. That branch of the family had strong ties to southern Ohio and ultimately to Sandusky.

16. Time Life, Inc., eds., *The Old West: The Gamblers*, Alexandria: Time Life Books, 1978. This source says the nearly all of the gamblers were dishonest and that the captains of vessels were mostly at a loss to control them.

17. Twain, Mark, *Life on the Mississippi*, New York: Harper and Bros., 1917.

18. Pike's Peakers, those who went to the Colorado Gold Rush at Pike's Peak (Colorado Springs) and Aurora and Cherry Creek (Denver), were called Fifty-niners in deference to the Forty-niners, although most went west in 1858. Eastern Colorado was then part of Kansas and the area south of Pueblo was in Taos County, New Mexico. Colorado was made up of parts of Kansas, New Mexico, and Utah.

Chapter 3: Going West

1. This is an error that has been followed by some others. The middle name Jefferson has been confirmed by many sources.

2. I have used "fort" and "camp" interchangeably. The military distinction between the two is that the construction and maintenance of camps was paid for out of the regimental budget and a fort was paid for out of Army budget. Finding out which budget was paying for a post at any given time is a tedious research challenge. The newspapers of the time regularly used the terms interchangeably. Before the Civil War, most posts were known as forts and afterwards, most were called camps. After 1886, when the Apache Wars ended, surviving camps became forts. So Camps Grant, Bowie, and Huachuca became forts.

3. Fort Thorn was a settlement and military outpost located on the west bank of the Rio Grande, northwest of present day Hatch. It is doubtful that Jeffords carried dispatches from Fort Thorn, which was active from 1853 to 1859 and reoccupied by Confederate troops from 1861 to 1862. Colonel Canby, the New Mexico commander, was headquartered farther north at Fort Craig, south of Socorro. It's possible Tom was prospecting near Thorn and that this led to the confusion. Thomas Farish, who wrote between 1914 and 1920, is often off on small points. He did not have access to the archival material we do today. His main point is that Tom Jeffords carried dispatches between the Union commander on the Rio Grande and the Union commander at Fort Yuma on the Colorado River nearly six hundred miles away through territory occupied by Confederate forces.

4. Farish, Thomas F., *History of Arizona*, Volume 2, Chapter 10. Phoenix, AZ: Filmer Brothers, 1915, p. 133. Farish interviewed Tom Jeffords shortly before Jeffords's death.

5. Tom Jeffords said he built, or laid out, the road to Denver following the 1858 Pike's Peak Gold Rush. We don't know his role in road building, whether he was a laborer or gang boss, or whether navigational skills got him a position with the surveyors. He expressed an almost proprietary pride in the building of the road that suggests he might have worked in a supervisory capacity of some kind.

6. Dried buffalo dung.

7. Morgan, Phyllis S., *As Far As the Eye Could Reach: Accounts of Animals Along the Santa Fe Trail, 1821–1880*, Norman: University of Oklahoma Press, 2015. The author collected accounts from familiar works like Josiah Gregg, *Commerce of the Prairies*, and Lewis H. Garrard, *Wah-to-yah and the Taos Trail*.

8. Moiling refers to the process of separating gold flakes and nuggets from sand.

9. There have been stories that Tom Jeffords went to work as an apprentice lawyer reading law in an uncle's office. I can find no trace of such an uncle in Tom's family tree. The man in question seems to be from the southern Ohio family that passed through Sandusky. Tom's lack of education would seem to disqualify him from reading law.

10. His name appears on the voting register as Thos. J. Jefferds.

11. It is an assumption that Tom partnered, but he needed someone to show him the ropes and he needed a claim.

12. From one slope of the Continental Divide, water flows to the Pacific Ocean, and on the other to the Atlantic.

13. Torrez, Robert J., "The San Juan Gold Rush of 1860 and Its Effect on the Development of Northern New Mexico," *New Mexico Historical Review*, LXIII: 3, Summer, 1988, pp. 257–72.

14. Letter from Tom Jeffords to Charles Poston, January 30, 1884, Box 66, Biofile, Arizona Historical Society, Tucson.

15. In 1860, Arizona had three towns: Gila City, Tucson, and Tubac. Tucson and Gila City were on the Butterfield Road; Tubac was thirty miles south of Tucson. Cooke's Wagon Road went south into Mexico and returned from Santa Cruz, Sonora, to Tubac and Tucson. Leach's Wagon Road avoided Tucson by following the San Pedro River to near its junction with the Gila but wasn't much used. Kearney's Route was suitable for pack animals. As a courier in the Civil War, Tom would have found all routes except Kearney's under Confederate control. It seems likely that he used Kearney's Route along the Gila River.

16. "A Candidate's Escape at Silverlake," *Citizen*, June 28, 1884.

Chapter 4: Apaches

1. Account of Captain Frank Perry, *Arizona Weekly Miner*, March 20, 1869. Perry met Cochise in the Dragoon Mountains on or about February 3, 1869. According to Edwin Sweeney, Cochise was closer to five-foot-ten and at least sixty years old. Edwin Sweeney, ed. *Cochise: Firsthand Accounts of the Chiricahua Apache Chief.* Norman: University of Oklahoma Press, 2014: 126, n8 and n9.

2. Seymour, Deni J., "Evaluating Eyewitness Accounts of Native Peoples along the Coronado Trail from the International Border to Cibola," *New Mexico Historical Review*, 84/3 (Summer 2009), and "The Canutillo Complex: Evidence of Protohistoric Mobile Occupants in the Southern Southwest," *Kiva*, 79 (Winter 2009).

3. Pinal, Aravaipa, Tonto, Coyotero, Cibeque, and a few more bands.

4. The White Mountain Apache were once known as Coyotero. The Cibeque Apache live among them on their reservation. Apache groups were named by where they lived and what they ate. Politically, there is only the local band and beyond that traditional alliances and tribes within which groups intermarried. The Chiricahua intermarried with the Coyotero but thought of the Coyotero as "not Chiricahua." Their languages are so closely related that there is little distinction.

5. Robinson, Sherry, "Renegades and Refugees: Lipan Apaches at the Mescalero Apache Reservation, 1879–1881," *New Mexico Historical Review*, 91/1 (Winter 2016), p. 17.

6. Sweeney, Edwin, *Cochise: Chiricahua Apache Chief*, Norman: University of Oklahoma Press, 1991, pp. 25–36.

7. Hodge, Colonel Hiram C., "The Chiricahua Reservation," *Arizona Citizen*, May 18, 1875.

8. Sweeney, *Cochise*, pp. 37–58.

9. Sweeney, Edwin R., ed. *Cochise: Firsthand Accounts of the Chiricahua Apache Chief*, Norman: University of Oklahoma Press, 2014, pp. 124–26.

10. "Letter from Camp Goodwin," *Weekly Arizona Miner*, March 20, 1869.

11. Sweeney, Edwin, ed., *Making Peace with Cochise: the 1872 Journal of Captain Joseph Alton Sladen*, Norman: University of Oklahoma Press, 1991, p. 148 n83 and n62.

12. Siphon Canyon curls west around Overlook Ridge and leads down and east to the San Simon Valley. Goodwin Canyon lies over a low ridge one mile or so to the north of the Overland Mail Station. Apache Spring is at the head of the canyon. The Butterfield Trail runs east to west using Siphon Canyon as a road as far as the mail station. Two miles west of the mail station, climbing out of Siphon Canyon, is Apache Pass. Old Fort Bowie, established in 1862, is on a hill to the south of the spring. East of it, on the mesa, below Overlook Ridge, is the new fort.

13. Pfanz, Donald, *Richard S. Ewell: A Soldier's Life*, Civil War America, Chapel Hill: University of North Carolina Press, 1998, pp. 108–9.

14. *Daily Missouri Republican*, June 3, 1860.

15. Michno, Gregory, *Encyclopedia of the Indian Wars: Western Battles and Skirmishes 1850–1890*, Missoula: Mountain Press, 2003, p. 137.

16. Also known as Chiricahua Pass.

17. Ball, Eve. *Indeh: An Apache Odessey*. Provo, Utah: Brigham Young University, 1980, p. 25.

18. Bernard was breveted to colonel during the Civil War and after the war served as a captain in Arizona. It is unclear if he retained his brevet rank of colonel after the war. If he had earned it in the regular army, he would have been entitled to be addressed as colonel. If he earned it, in a state volunteer organization, perhaps not.

19. Reuben Bernard's biographer, Don Russell (*One Hundred and Three Fights and Scrimmages: The Story of General Rueben F. Bernard*, Washington, DC: United States Cavalry Association, 1936) says that Bernard was in Tennessee on leave about the time of the election of 1860. Unit records show a man on leave from October 1860 to March 1861. A man on leave would have returned to his unit over the Santa Fe Trail from Fort Leavenworth. The trail was closed in the winter. Bernard's account is fantastic. Sidney DeLong (*History of Arizona*, San Francisco: The Whitaker & Ray Company, 1905: 26–29) tells of Lieutenant Bascom leading a patrol of twelve dragoons including First Sergeant Bernard. There is no record of such a cross attachment. They were from two different forts ninety miles apart. Bernard had his own officers. We know from the record that Bascom set out with fifty-four infantrymen of company C, 7th Infantry. There are so many factual errors that it seems unlikely that Bernard was in Arizona at the time, and much more likely that he was in Tennessee or Missouri.

20. There are several versions of this story coming to us from Colonel Thomas Devin, Captain Bernard's commander in 1869. Altshuler, Constance Wynn. *Chains of Command: Arizona and the Army, 1856–1875*. Tucson: The Arizona Historical Society, 1981, p. 18. Sidney R. Delong came to Arizona with the California Column in 1862 and stayed on as the longtime sutler, post trader, at Fort Bowie. He

knew Captain Reuben Bernard quite well and provides a comprehensive version of Bernard's hero-story in DeLong, Sidney R. *History of Arizona*, San Francisco: The Whitaker & Ray Company, 1905, pp. 26–29.

21. This oversight alone should tell us that Bernard was not at Apache Pass and only heard about the events later.

22. Poston, Charles, *Building a State in Apache Land*, Tempe: Aztec Press, 1963.

23. The following are the primary sources I have relied on for the Bascom Affair. You'll find them quite different from later histories but very consistent between themselves. Robinson, Daniel, "A Narrative of Events Pertaining to C. F and H Companies of the Seventh Infantry while Serving in New Mexico and Arizona from October 1860, to April 1862," Fort Laramie National Historic Site, provides a very thorough treatment of what occurred at Apache Pass in February 1861 by an eyewitness. A synthesized and expanded version is found in McChristian, Douglas C. and Larry L. Ludwig, eds., "Eyewitness to the Bascom Affair: An Account by Sergeant Daniel Robinson, Seventh Infantry," *Journal of Arizona History* 42 (Autumn 2001). Bascom's reports are found at NARA, Bascom, George, to Lieutenant Colonel Pitcairn Morrison, 14 January 1861. NARA RG 353, Film 1120, Rolls 13–14. General Irwin, then an assistant surgeon, was also an eyewitness and his account is found at Irwin, Bernard John Dowling. "The Apache Pass Fight," *Infantry Journal*, XXXII: 4 (April 1928). William Oury arrived late but gives a very knowledgeable account that has often been discounted because of his role in the Camp Grant Massacre (Oury, William Sanders. "A True History of the Outbreak of the Noted Apache Chieftain Cachise in the Year 1861," Tucson: *Arizona Star*, June 28, July 5 and 12, 1877). Constance Wynn Altshuler provides the newspaper accounts from 1861 as well as accounts of threats by Cochise's warriors against the Overland Mail Station in Apache Pass in *Latest from Arizona! The Hesperian Letters, 1859–1861*, Tucson, Arizona: Pioneers' Historical Society, 1969. The theft of mules from Dragoon Springs Station and Ewell's Station was reported in the *Daily Missouri Republican*, June 3, 1860. Donald Pfanz (*Richard S. Ewell: A Soldier's Life*, Civil War America, Chapel Hill: University of North Carolina Press, 1998) tells of Captain Ewell's attitude toward Cochise.

24. Nothing anywhere in the military record suggests that Sergeant Bernard and twelve dragoons were under Bascom's command. In the version of the story that Bernard told to Sidney DeLong, sutler at Fort Bowie, where Bernard was assigned in 1868, Bascom was sent out in command of Bernard and twelve dragoons. No mention was made of Bascom's own company, nor can orders be found showing dragoons assigned to Bascom. Reuben Bernard, who wasn't there, described Bascom as an inexperienced, arrogant fool, who bungled his way into an intolerable situation. The four officers, all of them senior to Bascom, who were there, thought he'd done well. So did the commander of the Department of New Mexico. Those who compare his effort to that of Ewell, the year before, have little to go on. Ewell confronted Eskiminzin, demanding the return of Mercedes Quiroz. Eskiminzin

demanded the return of hostages and two wagonloads of goods. Ewell made the trade and got the girl. Some might call this shameful as it encouraged future kidnappings. Bascom was willing to trade, but Cochise never offered Felix Ward, nor did he ask for wagonloads of goods.

25. One boy was probably Cochise's son Naiche. His son Taza would have been too old. The other was probably Chie, Coyuntura's son, who was about the right age. He would later accompany Jeffords and General Howard to arrange peace with Cochise.

26. Ward spoke Spanish. So did Cochise, though perhaps not well.

27. The only practical way to unload a muzzle-loading musket is to fire it, and that wastes powder and shot. These weapons were dangerous to leave loaded. So officers didn't order them loaded until they faced a need. Bascom didn't see such a need. He wasn't expecting trouble. Sergeant Robinson reported that the sentries didn't have loaded weapons. Robinson, Daniel, "A Narrative of Events Pertaining to C. F, and H Companies of the Seventh Infantry while serving in New Mexico and Arizona from October 1860, to April 1862," Fort Laramie National Historic Site.

28. If everyone had been firing, no one would have remembered Johnny Ward's two shots. This is more confirmation that Johnny had the only loaded weapon.

29. Bascom and Colonel Morrison released the woman and boys at Fort Buchanan.

30. Sweeney, *Cochise, Chiricahua Apache Chief*, p. 164.

31. Robinson, Daniel, "A Narrative of Events Pertaining to C. F, and H Companies of the Seventh Infantry while serving in New Mexico and Arizona from October 1860, to April 1862," Fort Laramie National Historic Site, p. 7. This is the best evidence available for Lieutenant Colonel Pitcairn Morrison's orders to Lieutenant Bascom, since no written record survives other than writings that indicate Morrison was pleased with Bascom's performance.

32. Pfanz, Donald, *Richard S. Ewell: A Soldier's Life*, Civil War America, Chapel Hill: University of North Carolina Press, 1998, pp. 108–9.

33. The author grew up on the Jicarilla Apache Reservation and attended far too many funerals. He has had a difficult time tracking down the fate of old friends who have passed because of reluctance to speak their names.

34. Roy Bean would later become Judge Roy Bean of Texas.

35. Michno, Gregory, and Susan Michno, *Forgotten Fights: Little-known Raids and Skirmishes on the Frontier, 1823 to 1890*, Missoula: Mountain Press, 2008, pp. 175–76.

36. Ibid., 181.

37. Ibid., 184–85.

38. Probably under Cochise, since Doubtful Canyon was a favored ambush site.

39. Masich, Andrew E., *The Civil War in Arizona: The Story of the California Volunteers, 1861–1865*, Norman: University of Oklahoma Press, 2006, p. 283.

40. Stone, Paul S., "Stein's Peak Cañon Fight," *San Francisco Bulletin*, June 1864. E. R., "Steen's Peak Cañon Fight," *San Francisco Bulletin*, June 6, 1864.

Chapter 5: The Civil War

1. Hunt, Aurora, *Major General James Henry Carleton, 1814–1873, Western Frontier Dragoon*, Glendale: Arthur H. Clark and Company, 1958, p. 226.

2. Arizona Historical Society, Tucson, Thomas Jefferson Jeffords, Biofile, Box 66, Letter January 30, 1884.

3. Based on Taylor, John, *Bloody Valverde: A Civil War Battle on the Rio Grande, February 21, 1862*, Albuquerque, University of New Mexico Press, 1995, and Frazier, Donald S., *Blood & Treasure: Confederate Empire in the Southwest*, College Station: Texas A&M University Press, 1995; and Thompson, Jerry, *Civil War in the Southwest: Recollections of the Sibley Brigade*, College Station: Texas A&M University Press, 2001.

4. The military seldom recorded the names of civilian scouts in Post Returns.

5. Masich, Andrew W., *The Civil War in Arizona: The Story of the California Volunteers, 1861–1865*. Norman: University of Oklahoma Press, 2006, p. 62.

6. Ibid.

7. Ibid., p. 63.

8. Ibid., pp. 64–65. *Arizona Enterprise*, June 13, 1891; Capt. M. H. Calderwood to J. F. Calderwood, June 27, 1865, in *Dutch Flat Enquirer*, August 12, 1865.

9. Thompson, Jerry, *Desert Tiger: Captain Paddy Graydon and the Civil War in the Far Southwest*, El Paso: Western Press: University of Texas at El Paso, 1992, pp. 52–58.

10. Sides, Hampton, *Blood and Thunder—An Epic of the American West*, Garden City: Doubleday, 2006.

Chapter 6: Post-War Adventures

1. Bourke, John G., *On the Border with Crook*, Lincoln: University of Nebraska Press, 1971, p. 57.

2. Ibid., p. 59.

3. Prescott again became the capital in 1877. On February 4, 1889, the capital was finally moved to Phoenix where it remains.

4. Smith, Brad, *The Stagecoach through Apache Country: A History of the Stagecoach Companies and Stage Stations in Northeastern Cochise County, Arizona Territory: 1857-1880*, Willcox, AZ: Sulphur Springs Valley Historical Society, 2013, p. 46.

5. Ibid., p 48.

6. "Apaches and Mails," *Weekly Arizonian*, April 11, 1869.

7. Smith, *The Stagecoach through Apache Country*, p. 49.

8. Ibid.

9. Ibid., p. 50.

10. Forbes, Robert H., letter to *Journal of Arizona History*, 7:2 (Summer 1966), pp. 87–88.

11. Sweeney, Edwin, ed., *Making Peace with Cochise: the 1872 Journal of Captain Joseph Alton Sladen*. Norman: University of Oklahoma Press, 1991, p. 148 n83.

"Letter from Camp Goodwin," *The Weekly Arizona Miner*, March 20, 1869. Both Sladen and Lieutenant Guthrie describe a stronghold on the western flank of the Dragoon Mountains near Middle March Pass. Sladen provides the description of the meadow and a stream. China Camp matches the description, as Sweeney notes.

12. The first record of this site held by Cochise County shows a homestead claim filed in 1870, on a spot halfway between Dragoon Springs and Apache Pass. Soon after, Nick Rogers is recorded as having purchased the ranch.

13. Bailey, Lynn R., *Henry Clay Hooker and the Sierra Bonita Ranch*, Tucson: Westernlore Publications, 1998.

14. *The Daily New Mexican*, July 27, 1868.

15. Valputic, Marian E., and Harold H. Longfellow, "The Fight at Chiricahua Pass in 1869 as described by L. L. Dorr, M.D.," *Arizona and the West* 13 (Winter 1971), pp. 369–78; and *Prescott Miner*, October 30, 1869.

16. Letter dated June 8, 1868, AHS.

17. Michno, Gregory, *Encyclopedia of Indian Wars: Western Battles and Skirmishes 1850–1890*, Missoula: Mountain Press Publishing Co., 2003, pp. 238–39; and Russell, Don, *One Hundred and Three Fights and Scrimmages: The Story of General Reuben F. Bernard*, Washington, DC: United States Cavalry Association, 1936, pp. 71–79.

18. Sweeney, *Making Peace with Cochise*, p. 72.

19. Guthrie met with Cochise on the eastern flank of the Dragoon Mountains near Middle March Pass and noted that Cochise emerged from a site on the western flank before coming through the pass, a site that was six miles off. This is a match for China Camp and not for east Stronghold Canyon. The writer has little doubt that Cochise died at east Stronghold Canyon but his favored eyrie seems to have been the place now known as China Camp. There he had a meadow for horses and a flowing stream, and could survey both the San Pedro and Sulphur Springs Valley. No one could approach within twenty miles without his knowing it.

20. "Letter from Camp Goodwin," *Weekly Arizona Miner*, March 20, 1869.

21. Sweeney, *Cochise*; Farish, *History of Arizona*, *II*, p. 228; C. L. Sonnichsen, "Who Was Tom Jeffords?" *Journal of Arizona History*, 23 (Winter 1982), p. 388; RG123, Indian Depredation Files, Tom Jeffords File 9695.

22. Brevoort, Elias C., 1823, Biofile, Box 15, AHS, Tucson. Copied from Official Report of War of Rebellion, Series I; Vol. 50; Pt. 1; p. 930.

23. De Stefano, William, "Tom Jeffords, Capitalist," Arizona–New Mexico Historical Convention, Tucson, Arizona, April 1995.

24. Thrapp, Dan L., *Victorio and the Mimbres Apaches*, Norman: University of Oklahoma Press, 1974, p. 106. LR NMS, Roll 557, C1150, Jeffords and Brevoort to Drew, March 8, 1870. There are several points of interest concerning this letter. The grammatical errors are not typical of letters attributed to Tom Jeffords of whom it has been said he was so eloquent that he must have been a lawyer. The letter is likely the work of Brevoort and suggests that other Jeffords letters were also the work of others, of clerks and lawyers. It has been speculated that Tom read the law

in Denver under his uncle. There was a lawyer named Jeffords in Denver in 1859 but he was not Tom's uncle. Tom did have an uncle, Thomas Jefferson Jeffords, born in 1811, who was a lawyer, but he remained in Monroe, New York, and it is unlikely Tom ever met him. Jeffords Family Tree, Ancestry.com.

25. Ibid., Drew to Clinton, March 17, 1870.

26. Ibid., Shorkley to AAG, District of New Mexico, March 29, 1870.

27. Ibid., C328, Jeffords and Brevoort to Clinton, May 12, 1870, with endorsement by Clinton.

28. Ibid., Clinton endorsement.

Chapter 7: Friendship

1. He was forty.

2. Elsewhere stated at twenty and twenty-two men Cochise had killed, fourteen of them Jeffords's employees. Authors may be borrowing from Governor Safford or Jeffords may have provided the figures. Twenty-two men might have been killed while Jeffords worked for the mail. Fourteen of them may have been associated with the mail in some capacity, i.e. passengers, drivers, riders, military escorts, and station attendants. The latter were especially vulnerable.

3. Letter to the editor of the *Miner* from Governor Anson P. K. Safford, December 21, 1872, "Something About Cachise."

4. Sweeney, Edwin R. *Cochise: Chiricahua Apache Chief*. Norman: University of Oklahoma Press, 1991, p. 295. Turrill, Henry Stuart. "A Vanished Race of Aboriginal Founders," speech given in Tucson, February 14, 1907, AHS.

5. Sweeney, *Cochise*, p. 296.

6. Ball, Eve, *Indeh: An Apache Odyssey*, Provo, Utah: Brigham Young University, 1980, pp. 27–29.

7. Forrest, Earle R., "The Fabulous Sierra Bonita," *The Journal of Arizona History*, VI (Autumn 1965), pp. 137–38. Bailey, Lynn R., *Henry Clay Hooker and the Sierra Bonita*, Tucson: Westernlore Publications, 1998, pp. 43–45.

8. Grant, W.S., "Captain Jeffords," Oral History, November 5, 1926, AHS.

9. Ibid., RG75, T21, R15, Piper to Pope, February 7, 1871.

10. Sweeney, Edwin R., ed., *Cochise: Firsthand Accounts of the Chiricahua Apache Chief*. Norman: University of Oklahoma Press, 2014, pp. 138–39. NA, RG75, M234, R557, Arny to Parker, October 24, 1870.

11. He would have been thirty-eight. Census takers make errors. Since he was living with Elias Brevoort, there is no question that it is the Thomas Jeffords born in 1832. Perhaps they asked Elias Tom's age.

12. Pulvedero, Spanish for "dusty," is north of Socorro.

13. Hughes, Fred, *Arizona Daily Star*, January 20, 22, 27, 1886.

14. Ibid., January 31, 1886.

15. Thrapp, Dan L., *Victorio and the Mimbres Apaches*, Norman: University of Oklahoma Press, 1974, pp. 135–36. LR NMS Roll 8, P275, Pope to Parker, May

24, 1871; LR NMS, Roll 558, P536, Pope to commissioner, October 8, 1871; Piper to Pope, October 3, 1871; P319 Pope to Parker, June 28, 1871.

16. Thrapp, *Victorio and the Mimbres Apaches*, p. 136. Thrapp says $500. Other sources say $1,000 was offered and that Jeffords had a hard time collecting and may have gone with General Howard in hopes of doing so.

17. Old Camp Grant was near the mouth of Aravaipa Creek on the lower San Pedro River about seventy miles northeast of Tucson. It was officially closed March 29, 1873, but troops began the move to a new site in December 1872, near Mount Graham and Hooker's Sierra Bonita Ranch north of the Sulphur Springs Valley, and this was also called Camp Grant.

18. The first report from the Apache camp was by Whitman's surgeon, who reported having seen twenty-seven bodies and thinking there were more. Whitman reported sixty-three dead and amended that later to eighty. The burial detail told Whitman how many they'd buried. The Apache reported a higher figure. Some had run off to other bands and were thought dead. Children taken by the raiders may have been thought killed. In short, there was confusion. Later, higher figures have little basis in primary sources. The doctor's report and Whitman's are available in Tucson at AHS.

19. Through much of this period, military command structure and Indian Affairs organization are a study unto themselves. Arizona was part of the Department of the Pacific and reported to San Francisco. New Mexico was part of the Department of the Platte and reported to Fort Leavenworth, Kansas. This created difficulties in coordinating efforts with the Chiricahua Apache in both departments. Indian Affairs was under the Army with military officers as Indian agents and then under the Department of the Interior with agents sent by churches.

20. Sweeney, *Cochise*, p. 176. NA, RG393, LS, Fort McRae, Shorkley to Devin, January 8, 1872.

21. Many Spanish words are incorporated into their language. They also seem to use different nouns depending on the state of motion of an object. The language is tonal, like Chinese, and differing inflections result in differing meanings. There is a war language used only by men. There are many sounds unfamiliar to English speakers.

22. Lieutenant Moore hanged three of Cochise's relatives at Apache Pass in February 1861. One was Cochise's brother, Coyuntura. Apache familial relationships were often misunderstood partly because the kinship terms are not an exact match to English. Cousin may be misunderstood as brother and uncle as father. Cochise's father and two brothers were slain at councils with Mexicans in Sonora and Chihuahua, and this may be what the chief referred to. His people had been given poisoned food as well.

23. Sweeney, *Cochise*, p. 181. Henry Stuart Turrill, "A Vanished Race of Aboriginal Founders: An Address by Brig. General Henry Stuart Turrill, USA," February 14, 1907, AHS.

24. Sweeney, *Cochise, Firsthand Accounts*, p. 184.

25. Ibid., p. 180, n 4.

26. Hughes, Fred, *Arizona Daily Star*, January 20, 22, 27, 1886.

27. Howard, General Oliver Otis, *Famous Indian Chiefs I Have Known*, New York: The Century Co., 1908.

28. Sweeney, *Making Peace*, p. 30 and p. 133 n 18.

29. Howard, *Famous Indian Chiefs I Have Known*, pp. 115–16.

30. Sweeney, *Making Peace*, pp. 33–34.

31. Farish, Thomas F., *History of Arizona*, Volume 2, Chapter 10. Phoenix, AZ: Filmer Brothers, 1915, p. 231.

32. The Apache are matrilocal. Men go to live with the wife's family and band. She has the important inheritance, the places where her mother gathered wild foods.

33. The identification is not certain but William Gillespie, Forest Service archaeologist, who was familiar with the Dragoon Mountains, believed this was the place Sladen described (also see Sweeney, *Making Peace with Cochise*, p. 148 n83). This meadow is a stronghold in a way nothing in Stronghold Canyon can match. East Stronghold Canyon is associated with Cochise and his camp because it was there that he lived just before his death in June 1874. Near the mouth of West Stronghold Canyon is where peace talks took place.

34. We are told the Apache always referred to Cochise in the third person, never calling him by name. Apache superstition says that knowing a man's name gives you power over him. The war name, the name given in adulthood, is a family secret not shared with outsiders. Apaches went by their nicknames, one of the reasons we know so many of them by Spanish names. In Cochise's case, the name taboo seems to have extended even to his nickname.

35. Sweeney, *Making Peace*, p. 63.

36. Ibid., pp. 64–65.

37. In 1895, Jeffords took Alice Rollins Crane to the spot, and she photographed this distinctive boulder.

38. In 1913, Billy Fourr, whose ranch was nearby, and who had been shown the meadow by Jeffords, took Thomas Farish to the place. He photographed it. The oak tree in the photo has since fallen and lies on the ground.

39. Howard, p. 133.

40. United States Department of the Interior, *Annual Report of the Commissioner of Indian Affairs, 1873*, Washington, DC: Government Printing Office, 1873, p. 292.

Chapter 8: The Chiricahua Agency

1. This is new Camp Grant near Mount Graham north of the Sulphur Springs Valley and not the scene of the 1872 massacre.

2. Cramer, Captain Harry G., "Tom Jeffords—Indian Agent," *Journal of Arizona History* 17 (Autumn 1976), p. 267. Crook to Adjutant General, December 13, 1872, LR BIA.

3. Cramer, "Tom Jeffords," p. 270.

4. Grant, W.S. "Captain Jeffords," Oral History, Tucson AHS, 5 November 1926.

5. Kitt, Mrs. George F., "Reminiscences of William Ohnesorgen," Biographical File, AHS Tucson, October 22, 1929, pp. 5–6.

6. Cramer, "Tom Jeffords."

7. William Ohnesorgen, born Germany 1849, died May 1, 1933. Came to Texas in 1853 with his family. Settled in Tucson in 1868 and moved to Tres Alamos on the San Pedro River in 1871. He ran a stage station and a toll bridge across the San Pedro at San Pedro Crossing (now Benson). Bailey, Lynn R., and Don Chaput, *Cochise County Stalwarts: A Who's Who of the Territorial Years,* Tucson: Westernlore Press, 2000.

8. Cramer, "Tom Jeffords," p. 276. Jeffords to Commissioner, September 11, 1874, LR BIA.

9. "The Cachise Reserve," *Arizona Citizen,* July 12, 1873.

10. Sweeney, *Cochise: First Hand Accounts,* p. 267.

11. Zebina Nathaniel Streeter, aka Don Casimero, aka the White Apache, was born in New York, October 8, 1838. He was raised in California among the family of his father's Mexican wife. At age eleven he ran away to sea. In 1864, he was commissioned as an officer in the California Native Cavalry but was soon cashiered for drunkenness. He enlisted in the same unit, but apparently did not deploy to Arizona with his company. He played a role as a mercenary in the Mexican fight against the Emperor Maximillian. He worked for Jeffords on the reservation off and on, lived with an Apache woman, and seems to have fallen into disfavor. Jeffords said, "That little Mexican knows better than to come around the agency." In 1876, he rode with Geronimo and Juh. He was killed in Mexico in the 1880s by the brother of his current girlfriend. Bailey, Lynn R, *White Apache: The Life and Times of Zebina Nathaniel Streeter,* Tucson: Westernlore Press, 2010. Prezelski, Tom, *Californio Lancers: The First Battalion of Native Cavalry in the Far West, 1863 to 1866,* Norman: University of Oklahoma Press, 2015. Thrapp, Dan L., *Encyclopedia of Frontier Biography,* Lincoln: University of Nebraska Press, 1988.

12. Frederick George Hughes was born in England in 1837. Came to Arizona with the California Column in 1862. Was employed as a clerk by agent Piper at Canada Alamosa until hired by Jeffords. He stayed on until 1874 and returned in 1876. Later he was clerk of Pima County, president of the Arizona Pioneers Association, and president of the Arizona State House. In the 1890s, his wages were reduced by Pima County and he turned to gambling to make up the deficit. Naturally, this had the opposite effect. He prevailed upon the State House to vote $3,000 to fund the Pioneer Society (now the Arizona Historical Society). As president of the society, he signed for the money and then fled to Sonora. He returned, was convicted, and was sent to Yuma Territorial Prison. His friends prevailed on the governor to pardon him and he was released. He died September 16, 1911, when a lightning bolt struck him in the forehead as he sat on his front porch. Fred Hughes Bio Files, Tucson, AHS.

13. Cramer, "Tom Jeffords," p. 266.

14. No trace of the agency remains today. The Cienega, once swampy, has mostly dried up. The agency was about twenty-five miles south of today's San Simon on I-10 on the San Simon River. It was a stopping place on the southern emigrant trail and later attracted the Cow-Boys, Curly Bill Brocius and Ike Clanton, who had a ranch in the same area.

15. Southeast Arizona was once a malarial zone. Soldiers at Fort Buchanan, founded in 1856 on Sonoita Creek, suffered in the summer months. Even Captain Richard Ewell had the fever. The site of Fort Huachuca was selected in 1877 on a spot away from swamps. As late as the 1920s, the Army was blowing up beaver dams in the San Pedro Valley to reduce breeding grounds for mosquitos.

16. William Vandever, Indian Inspector, NA, RG75, M1070, R1, Vandever to Edward Smith, CIA, October 18, 1873. Sweeney, *Cochise: First Hand Accounts*, p. 271.

17. "Gen. Vandever on Indian Affairs," *Arizona Citizen*, February 7, 1874.

18. "On Both Sides of the Line," *Arizona Citizen*, November 29, 1873.

19. "Letter from Jeffords," *Arizona Citizen*, October 4, 1873.

20. Bailey, *Henry Clay Hooker*, p. 43.

21. *Arizona Citizen*, April 4, 1874.

22. Personal communication from Lynn R. Bailey, June 11, 2014: "The blanket story is the other way round [Hooker to Cochise]. Hooker purchased two blankets from the San Francisco woolen mill in 1873. One for Thomas Jeffords and one for Cochise. For a short while both were on display at the Yuma office of Willliam B. Hooper Company. You can read about it in the *Arizona Sentinel*, January 24, 1874, p. 2. I have more on the blankets in my files."

23. Cramer, "Tom Jeffords," p. 275. Jeffords to Commissioner, September 1, 1874, LR BIA.

24. In 1904, the agent for the Jicarilla Apache convinced President Teddy Roosevelt that the Jicarilla reservation did not include any arable land and was at best suited to grazing. President Roosevelt, who had been a cowboy, doubled the size of the reservation and the Apaches were permitted to begin raising sheep.

25. "Veil with Cachise," *Arizona Journal Miner*, January 9, 1874.

26. Viola, Herman J., ed., *The Memoirs of Charles Henry Veil: A Soldier's Recollections of the Civil War and the Arizona Territory*, New York: Orion Books, 1993, p. 139.

27. This argues for his sincerity in writing to Lieutenant Drew of the Canada Alamosa Reservation that he should not drink with old Chief Loco. He also wrote to his friend and sometime partner, Nicholas Rogers, not to give whiskey to the Apache at Sulphur Springs Ranch. Rogers was selling whiskey to the soldiers from Fort Bowie. While Jeffords was not afraid to drink with his friend Cochise, it appears he did not allow liquor on the reservation, other than the Apache brew, *tiswin*.

28. Thrapp, *Victorio*, p. 166.

29. Ibid., pp. 165–66.

30. Ibid.

31. Sweeney, *Cochise: First Hand Accounts*, p. 286.

32. Thrapp, *Victorio*, p. 167.

33. I think he referred to Jeffords's lack of education and difficulty in writing. Vandever proposes no other shortcomings, though he tried.

34. Oral history video tape on hand at the Chiricahua Regional Museum.

35. Farish, *History of Arizona*, pp. 236–37.

36. Other sources say this was a blanket given the chief by Hooker.

37. Sweeney, *Cochise: First Hand Accounts*, p. 287.

38. Growing up on the Jicarilla Apache Reservation I've seen it done.

39. After years away, I found it very difficult to learn the fate of missing friends because the Apache will not speak the name of the dead for fear of calling them back.

40. Cramer, "Tom Jeffords," p. 286.

41. The Brunckow was Arizona's murder house, with some sources claiming twenty-seven murders at Brunckow's cabin. Brunckow and two companions were slain on July 23, 1860. On June 5, 1874, Marshal Milton Duffield, the owner before Jeffords, was also murdered there. In 1879, J. W. Houten, owner of an adjoining claim, was also slain. Young, Roy B., "Graves Lie Thick: Murders at the Brunkow Mine," *Journal of Wild West History Association*, II/3, June 2009.

42. *Arizona Daily Star*, October 4, 1879. Cramer was mistaken. Tom didn't operate these mines until 1879.

43. Cramer, "Tom Jeffords," p. 286.

44. Ibid., p. 289. Jeffords to Commissioner, April 27, 1876, October 3, 1876, LR BIA.

45. *Weekly Citizen*, April 15, 1876. For assertion that Geronimo was with Eskinya and Pionsenay at the time Rogers and Spence were killed, see Fred Hughes, "Geronimo: Some Facts Concerning the Wily Old Apache Chief," *Arizona Daily Star*, March 8, 1890. Orisoba O. Spense was awarded the Medal of Honor in 1869 for the fight against Cochise in Chiricahua Pass. He is buried at Fort Bowie NHS.

46. *Weekly Citizen*, April 15, 1876.

47. C. B. McLellan to T. J. Jeffords, May 23, 1876, published in *Arizona Weekly Miner*, June 9, 1876.

48. Referred to as San Jose Mountains. Today, five miles south of the Mule Mountains, San Jose Peak stands just beyond the Mexican border. Names change, leading to confusion.

49. The Iron Monster was an outcropping of iron ore that stood above Tombstone Canyon. After 1877, Bisbee grew up in this place. The Iron Monster would have been in front of the Copper Queen Mine before the monster was removed to make way for Highway 80. Both Tom Jeffords and Lieutenant Henely say that they passed through the Mule Mountains and encountered the Apache at San Jose Peak. Today the peak we know as San Jose is in Sonora, but their accounts also say

they were fifteen miles north of the line, which argues that the Iron Monster is the correct site. "A Letter from Camp Bowie," *Citizen*, April 15, 1876.

50. *Weekly Journal-Miner*, April 14, 1876; Lieutenant Henely to editors, *Weekly Citizen*, September 30, 1876.

51. Wasson, John, "Jeffords a devil," *Citizen*, May 20, 1876.

52. Also called Jonathan and Casimiro, Zebina Streeter was named as the middle-man in these illegal transactions. He was born in New York and taken to California by his father while still very young. He learned to speak Spanish and many thought him a Mexican. He served as an officer with the Native California Lancers during the Civil War and fought in Mexico after the war. He seems to have been a friend of Jeffords, though Jeffords at one point said that Streeter knew better than to come around the Agency. He may have married an Apache woman. Bailey, *White Apache*.

53. "Jeffords defense," *Arizona Miner*, June 16, 1876.

54. The Dutch Reformed Church sent out Clum as Indian agent. Later he was editor of the *Tombstone Epitaph* and mayor of that town.

55. Bailey, *White Apache*, p. 81.

56. Ibid.

Chapter 9: Making a Fortune, 1877–1892

1. De Stefano, William, "Tom Jeffords, Capitalist," Arizona–New Mexico Histor-ical Convention, Tucson, April 1995. AHS, Tucson, p 1.

2. This property is also called the Bronco in newspapers and documents of the time. Frederick Brunckow was a mining engineer who came to Arizona to work for Charles Poston's Sonora Mining and Exploring Company. The Brunckow mine is located about a mile east of the San Pedro River at Charleston and about seven miles west of Tombstone.

3. Mine Claims, Cochise County Recorder, p. 4.

4. "Mining Affairs," *Arizona Citizen*, August 4, 1877.

5. Brunckow. It's also misspelled as Bronco and a nearby hill bears this corruption as its name.

6. "Another Important Mining Case," *Arizona Weekly Citizen*, August 4, 1881.

7. Parsons, George W., and Lynn R. Bailey, ed., *A Tenderfoot in Tombstone, the Private Journal of George Whitwell Parsons: The Turbulent Years, 1880–82*, Western-lore Publications, 1996, p 67. "Rusticating in the Huachucas," *Citizen*, August 14, 1881. Mine Claims, Cochise County Recorder, July 22, 1878.

8. The remains of Brunckow's cabin are still visible from Charleston Road.

9. "John Jeffords," Biofile, AHS Tucson, Box 66. "Lead for Dinner," *Tombstone Nugget*, September 8, 1881.

10. Mine Claims, Cochise County Recorder.

11. Quit claim deeds are contrasted with warranty deeds. In a warranty deed, the seller warrants that he owns the property and all the rights pertaining thereto

except as specified. In a quit claim, the seller acknowledges possible defects in the title and merely transfers anything he may own.

12. "Tom Jeffords, Tom Fitch, Copper Queen," *Tombstone Republican*, February 22, 1884.

13. Mine Claims, Cochise County Recorder, p. 634.

14. "Tom Jeffords in the Altar District," *Citizen*, July 31, 1880.

15. At this point in time, men who worked cattle were called drovers or stockmen. Cow boys refers to outlaws. Cow Boys, capitalized, was a loose confederation of Cochise County rustlers, outlaws, and stage robbers. Thus in the song when the dying cow boy sings: "I'm a young cow boy and I know I done wrong," he's telling us he's an outlaw. The Cow Boys of Charleston and Galeyville were the enemies of the Earps and Doc Holliday. The Clantons and McLaurys, who faced off against the Earps, were small-time ranchers who rustled and bought cattle from rustlers, thus making the cows "legal." We might call it cattle laundering.

16. Being a stockman, a cowboy, in the Wild West, was an inherently violent way of life. Cattle are highly mobile wealth and invite rustlers. So part of the stockman's job is to fend them off. The Homestead Acts allowed a man to claim 160 acres. This was fine for a farm, but not nearly enough for a ranch. Today, in Cochise County, Arizona, land that used to be Cochise's reservation, grazing runs as poor as four units, four cows and calves, per section, 640 acres. Cattlemen laid claim to thousands of acres and to watering places. Since the claim had little or no legal basis, they could only defend it against all comers with violence. Thus the stockman tended to violence and when he couldn't find work was apt to use his skills with weapons to make a living.

17. "Tombstone Water Venture," *Citizen*, May 30, 1879.

18. "Jeffords water venture," *Citizen*, April 18, 1879.

19. "Artesian Wells," *The Arizona Sentinel*, December 20, 1879.

20. "Water Company Forfeiture of Bond," *Citizen*, December 18, 1881.

21. "Water bond," *Citizen*, June 11, 1882.

22. Traywick, Ben, *Tyzaalton (Red Beard)*, Tombstone: Red Marie's Bookstore, 1987. Pima County docket, May 4, 1880. In February 1869, Tom's partner Dr. J. C. Handy had been the assistant surgeon along with Major Perry, Lieutenant Guthrie, and sixty-two soldiers when their peace mission made contact with Cochise near his stronghold in the Dragoon Mountains. It is recorded that Dr. Handy's wife was along with them. Nothing else is known of her and she disappears from history soon after.

23. "Mine Sale Head Center & Yellow Jacket." *Phoenix Herald*, August 16, 1879.

24. Jeffords, Thomas Jefferson. "Jeffords, Thomas Jefferson, 1832–1914, Papers 1883–1888," Legal File, AHS Tucson, 1883–1888, Box 1.

25. H. R. Jeffords was an attorney in Tucson at this time. I have been unable to find any familial connection to Tom.

26. Cammack, Sister Alberta, "A Faithful Account of the Life and Death of Doctor John Charles Handy," *The Smoke Signal* 52 (1989).

27. Jeffords, "Thomas Jefferson Jeffords."

28. Mary Page Scott was from one of Tucson's oldest Anglo families and well thought of. She was the daughter of Larcena Pennington Page who remarried after Apaches killed her husband in 1860. Larcena was taken by Apaches that year and nearly killed, spending fourteen days crawling back to civilization. See Roberts, Virginia Culin, *With Their Own Blood: A Saga of Southwestern Pioneers*, Fort Worth: Texas Christian University Press, 1992. In 1870, Handy killed a man in a duel. He was eventually shot down on the streets of Tucson and his murderer was not indicted, as Handy was recognized as a man of ill-temper given to quarrelsomeness.

29. Cammack, "A Faithful Account."

30. "Mining Notice—attempt to jump the Omega," *Citizen*, January 15, 1881.

31. "The Omega Mine," *Citizen*, December 3, 1882.

32. "The Omega Explosion," *Citizen*, April 8, 1883.

33. "Sheriff's Sale—Omega Mine," *Citizen*, October 10, 1885.

34. *Daily Star*, October 4, 1879.

35. Fort Huachuca was established in 1877 by the 6th Cavalry at the base of the Huachuca Mountains in the canyon of Huachuca Creek. It was picked as a site away from malarial influences, sitting astride smuggling routes from Sonora. It is about twenty miles southwest of Tombstone, eight miles west of the San Pedro River, and ninety miles southeast of Tucson.

36. Personal communication, Lynn Bailey, Fort Huachuca Sutlership, August 3, 2014.

37. De Stefano, William, "Tom Jeffords, Capitalist," Arizona–New Mexico Historical Convention. Tucson, April 1995. AHS, Tucson, p. 10.

38. Ibid., p. 5.

39. NARA RG 94, Records of the Adjutant General's Office, ACP File Pertaining to T. J. Jeffords as Post Trader at Fort Huachuca, Arizona Territory.

40. Adjutant is a military title for an administrative assistant, a secretary. An adjutant general is the secretary to a general. All correspondence between military headquarters is sent between adjutants. The Adjutant General is the adjutant to the Chief of Staff, the senior general running the army.

41. The store stood in Huachuca Canyon up-canyon from current-day sergeant majors' quarters at the base of Reservoir Hill. Steven Gregory of the Fort Huachuca Museum has located a photo from 1914 showing an adobe sutler's store in the correct location. It seems likely this fine-looking building was Jeffords's store.

42. De Stefano, "Tom Jeffords, Capitalist."

43. Dr. Bernard and Jeffords became friends.

44. Theobald, John O., and Lillian Theobald, *Arizona Territory: Post Offices and Postmasters*, Phoenix, AZ: Arizona Historical Foundation, 1961.

45. Dry washing is used when there isn't sufficient water to work a placer. Earth is placed in a blanket and tossed repeatedly into the air until all the lighter material is blown away by the wind and only gold remains.

46. *Arizona Daily Citizen*, August 6, 1891.

47. Paul was the Republican sheriff of Pima County and a friend and ally of Wyatt Earp.

48. Those passing through Tucson on I-10 may have noticed Silverlake Road near the junction with I-19. Silverlake is no longer there. It was a millpond on the Santa Cruz River that supplied flour to southern Arizona and New Mexico from the 1850s to the 1890s.

49. "A Candidate's Escape at Silverlake," *Citizen*, June 28, 1884.

50. "Jeffords for sheriff of Cochise County," *Tombstone Epitaph*, July 14, 1888.

51. *Arizona Star*, July 2, 1889.

52. *Arizona Citizen*, June 5, 1875.

53. Jeffords, Thomas Jefferson, January 30, 1884, Box 66, Biofile, AHS, Tucson.

54. Juh is pronounced "who" or "whoa." He was an important war leader of the Nednhi, but he stuttered. Geronimo was his voice. Having an open mouth and complaining loudly was Geronimo's principal accomplishment. Fred Hughes suspected that the Army made him out to be more than he was because he was a known troublemaker. He was not a chief, nor was he a medicine man. He didn't make herbal remedies or conduct sings to cure the sick. He did have a powerful, personal war medicine or power. He was said to be able to detect approaching foes.

55. Asa Daklugie, son of Juh, in Ball, Eve, *Indeh: An Apache Odyssey*, Provo, Utah: Brigham Young University, 1980.

56. *Arizona Star*, September 27, 1877.

57. *Arizona Miner*, September 21, 1877.

58. "Summoned to Camp Thomas," *Citizen*, September 11, 1881.

59. "Last of the Renegades," *Citizen*, October 2, 1881.

60. "Military Matters," *Citizen*, October 9, 1881.

61. "General Miles and Jeffords," *Arizona Silver Belt*, September 25, 1886.

Chapter 10: Owl Head Buttes, 1892–1914

1. The Owl Heads are visible from I-10 at Red Rock south of Picacho Butte about fifteen miles to the east.

2. "New Mining District—Owl Heads," *Citizen*, January 31, 1880.

3. In Tombstone, George Parsons frequently took jobs doing assessment work for others. Parsons, George W., and Lynn R. Bailey, ed., *A Tenderfoot in Tombstone: The Private Journal of George Whitwell Parsons: The Turbulent Years, 1880-1882*, Tucson: Westernlore Press, 1996.

4. *Arizona Weekly Enterprise*, July 29, 1882.

5. Letter, Department of Mineral Resources, State of Arizona, November 30, 1973, Subject: Field Visit. In Sonnichsen Papers, MS1475, Box 66, AHS, Tucson. The letter states that in 1894, Jeffords transferred the claims to Morajeski, who held them until 1912. This seems to be a misunderstanding since Jeffords didn't meet Morajeski until after 1904. I believe the transfer took place in 1912 and that

Morajeski then immediately transferred ownership to the Owl Heads Mining and Trust in which Morajeski owned a large interest.

6. Ascarza, William, "Mine Tales: Tortolitas attracted limited mining interest," *Arizona Daily Star*, June 14, 2015.

7. The quote from the *West Southern Arizona News Examiner* came with an internet link, which has since become defunct, and no proper date. The author of this biography has located several small mines on the Owl Head Buttes and a home site that match the description. The legal description given with the filing of the claims reads "three miles north of the smelter" and thus isn't very helpful. This quote is the best information available on the location of the house and some of the claims and so it is included. The mines are on Jeffords Mine Road which may be confirmation of a sort.

8. "Tom Jeffords's Mine & House," *The West Southern Arizona News Examiner*, http://soaznewsx.com/The-West/ID/493/Thomas-Jefferson-Jeffords-and-Southern -Arizona.

9. One source says 1856, another 1861. The census places her home at birth in Iowa, but her wedding license says Illinois.

10. So far I have found no record of military service for him, so I assume the title was honorific. I have discovered articles on engineering that he wrote and he worked as an engineer for the City of Los Angeles.

11. "Alice Rollins Crane," *The Oasis*, November 9, 1895.

12. "Arizona Indians," *Arizona Weekly Journal-Miner*, November 13, 1895.

13. Fred Higbee died and was buried in Los Angeles before Alice went to the Yukon. He was about eighteen.

14. "Alice Rollins-Crane," *Wikipedia*, http://en.wikipedia.org/wiki/Alice_Rollins -Crane.

15. "An American Woman with Active Career," *Arizona Republican*, June 3, 1912.

16. Ibid. "The Prehistoric Ruins of Casa Grande," *Overland Monthly and Out West Magazine*, Volume 36, Issue 214.

17. When it's raining, smoke does not rise in columns. It stays near the ground.

18. "In Cochise's Stronghold: An Adventure Which Befell Mrs. Alice Rollins Crane, Authoress," *Arizona Daily Star*, November 21, 1895.

19. Sweeney, *Making Peace*, pp. 19–21.

20. "An American Woman with Active Career," *Arizona Republican*, June 3, 1912.

21. Jaastad, Ben, "George Oakes, 1840–1917," Oral History Interview, Tucson, May 11, 1955, AHS.

22. "Col. L.P. Crane Receives a Divorce," *Los Angeles Herald*, November 1, 1900.

23. There are numerous spellings of this name. Alice did not want to be called Countess. Instead she insisted on Madam.

24. "To Kondike, a Los Angeles Woman On Her Way," *Los Angeles Herald*, January 16, 1898.

25. Michelson, Miriam, "The Conqueror of the Klondike," *San Francisco Call*, January 19, 1898.

26. "Feminine Personals," *Omaha Daily Bee*, September 4, 1898.

27. "Mrs. Crane Returns," *San Francisco Call*, August 28, 1899.

28. Ibid, Traywick, p. 18.

29. Transfer of Claims to Alice Rollins Crane, Pinal County Recorder, Florence, AZ Book 18, p. 438, October 16, 1900.

30. Crane, Alice Rollins. *Smiles and Tears from the Klondyke: A Collection of Stories and Sketches*. New York: Doxie's, 1901.

31. "Alice Gets the Bounce," *Yukon Sun*, September 3, 1903.

32. "An American Woman with Active Career," *Arizona Republican*, June 3, 1912.

33. "Final Separation of the Morajeskas," *Arizona Republican*, June 22, 1914.

34. "Completes Contract for Ray Company," *Arizona Republican*, March 24, 1910.

35. "Russian Count Held for Attacking Wife in Tucson," *El Paso Herald*, September 6, 1913.

36. "American Wife of Count asks Divorce," *El Paso Herald*, September 24, 1913.

37. Morajeska, Victor. Estate of Tom Jeffords, AHS, Tucson.

38. "Pioneers Hold Funeral for Captain Jeffords," *Citizen*, February 21, 1914.

39. I didn't feel right including the photos here. They are available at the Arizona Historical Society.

40. "Pioneers Hold Funeral for Captain Jeffords," *Citizen*.

41. "Jeffords, the Friend of Old Cochise, Dies," *Citizen*, February 20, 1914.

42. Morajeska, Victor. Estate of Tom Jeffords, AHS, Tucson.

43. It's not there. I've looked.

44. Jaastad, "George Oakes, 1840–1917," pp. 56–57.

45. "Madame Morajeska in Big Mining Deal," *Mojave County Miner*, January 23, 1915.

46. "Count Badly Beaten Up," *Arizona Republican*, January 15, 1916.

Bibliography

1. I created the Jeffords and Rollins family trees and have a high degree of confidence in their content.

Index